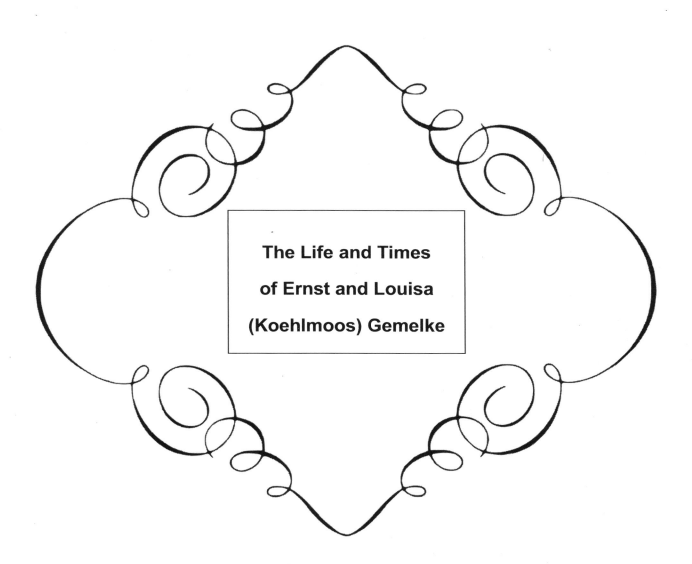

**The Life and Times
of Ernst and Louisa
(Koehlmoos) Gemelke**

LaRayne M. Topp

DEDICATION

In loving tribute to Ernst and Louisa (Koehlmoos) Gemelke
and to those whose lives they've touched.

CONTENTS

ACKNOWLEDGMENTS

My sincere appreciation to all who have contributed to this book, whether by relating stories they've heard or those they remember, to all who have contributed information, and to those who have loaned photographs from their private collections for the completion of this history. Special thanks to Donald Adams and Mark Bruggeman for the research they have completed for the family trees included. I have indicated within these pages those who have contributed memories. Those who have contributed photographs include the following: Judy Daum Allvin, Coreen Brueggeman Carnes, Patrick Demuth, Jo Janulewicz Freel, Sandy Fritz, Marlene Vollmer Hansen, Clara Heinemann, Sandra Peterson Kennedy, Kathy Podany Koehlmoos Lynn Heinold Koehlmoos, Lyla Koehlmoos, Betty Koehlmoos, Mildred Tesch Krambeck, Stacey Puett Nelson, Lillian Koehlmoos Penn, Ellen Peterman, Stacey Nelson Puett, Kathy Penn Quinn, Nancy Petersen Rauss, David Reimnitz, Celia Siecke, Sheila Race Stuthman, Sally Roenfeldt Stuthman, David Tobias and Shirley Gemelke Willers and any others I have inadvertently neglected to mention. Also, thanks to First Trinity Lutheran Church at Altona and St. John's Lutheran Church at Pilger for assistance in the way of church records and photographs, and Barbara Stuthman Greunke for work in editing.

All because two people fell in love

Mr. and Mrs. Henry Koehlmoos

Requests the honor of

your presence

at

the marriage of their daughter

Louise

to

Ernst Gemelke

Thursday afternoon, March 9, 1911

at the German Lutheran Church

at one thirty

Altona, Nebraska

Reception at the home of the bride's parents

Ernst Gemelke

Louisa Koehlmoos

First Altona Church - Built in 1887

FIRST TRINITY LUTHERAN CHURCH
ALTONA, NEBRRASKA.
This first building, constructed in 1887,
was replaced with a second church building in 1911.
Louisa and Ernst were married in March of 1911
and the new building was dedicated in December of the same year.
This first church may be the one
in which they were married

Mr. and Mrs. Ernst Gemelke
March 9, 1911

Ernst and Louisa were both 23 when they got married.

Front row: Louisa (Koehlmoos) and Ernst Gemelke;
back row, left to right: Gustav Gemelke, Herman Koehlmoos, Ella Gemelke
and Sophie Koehlmoos

Memory

Millie (Gemelke) Janulewicz remembered her mother, Louisa, telling about a barn dance or a party she went to after Ernst was no longer working for her father as a hired man. She had come to the party with another man in a horse and buggy. Somehow the other man's horse got loose. "Dad takes Mom home, and they started going together and lived happily ever after," Millie said.

Viola (Gemelke) Brueggeman remembered hearing, however, that Ernst kicked the horse so he would run away. "He took my mother home," Viola said.

"I thought that was the joke part of it. I didn't know any of that was true," Millie said.

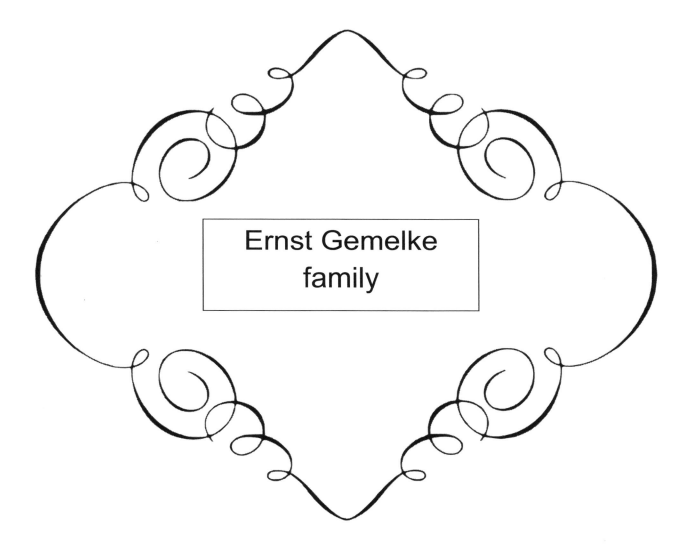

Ernst Gemelke
family

Henry Gemelke

Gustav's Grandpa
(Gus Reseburg)

(Gus Lienburg)
Gustav's Grandma

Sophie Jaeneke
Janecke
Janicke

Henry and Sophie Gemelke by Viola and Mark Brueggeman

This is a short history and family journal of Henry and Sophie Gemelke, as we know it. It is not known where Henry grew up, only that his mother's maiden name was Lindwedel. She had three children: Herman, Maria and Henry. Herman and Maria came to America first, sometime before 1895 (exact date not known). Maria married William Blume and Herman married Dorathea Blume, William's sister. Both couples settled in South Dakota.

Henry's wife Sophie Jaeneke (Janeck) was raised in Hainhaus, near the Bissendorf Church in Hanover Province, Germany. Hainhaus was a small village, consisting of about three adjoining farms. The people lived in the village and their farms were around it. Sophie's father was a land owner and Henry was a tenant on their land.

Sophie and Henry were married in 1877. They had six children: Alwine (Alvina), Herman, Friedrich, Ernst, Gustav and Ella. Herman (Henry's son) came to the United States in 1895. His uncle Herman sent money for him to come. At this time they lived in Elgin, Illinois. In 1902, Herman (Henry's son) went back to Germany to visit his family. His parents celebrated their 25th wedding anniversary that year.

Returning to the United States with Herman was his sister Alvina and her husband Gustav Leseberg and daughter Erna. The Lesebergs settled in Altona, Nebraska, north of the town of Wisner, Nebraska. Herman and his uncle Herman later joined them there.

Ernst Gemelke, son of Henry and Sophie Gemelke, was born on January 18, 1888, at Hainhaus near Bissendorf, in Hanover, Germany. Ernst worked as a waiter at a train depot café in Germany to earn his ticket to America. He came to the United States in 1905 at the age of 17 and took a train to Wisner, Nebraska. He stayed with his sister Alvina and her husband until moving to Pilger, Nebraska. He was employed by Heinrich Koehlmoos as a farm hand.

Ernst married Louisa Koehlmoos on March 9, 1911, at the Lutheran Church in Altona, Nebraska. They lived on their farm northwest of Pilger until Ernst's death in June of 1944. Louisa then moved to the town of Pilger. Later she moved to the Stanton Nursing Home where she died on November 13, 1979.

Henry and Sophie, and children Gustav and Ella, came to the United States in 1906. It took one week to get to New York from Bremerhaven, Germany, sailing on the ship, *The Kaiser Wilhelm de Grossen.* They stayed in New York until the emigrant train carried them to Wisner, Nebraska.

In 1913, Herman (Henry's son) became ill with a throat problem and went back to Germany for treatment. He died in Germany on May 6, 1913, and was buried there. He was married to Emma Etta Dohren, and the couple had one daughter.

Frederick (Fritz) never came to America but remained in Germany. He was married and had one daughter named Wilhelma.

Alvina and her family later moved to Canyon, Texas. Ernst, Gustav and Ella made their homes at Pilger as farmers. Ella was the second wife of Henry Siemsglusz.

Note: Naturalization papers for Sophie were taken out on July 8, 1918 (LaRayne {Gemelke} Topp)

Family history by Patrick Demuth, Worthington, Minnesota

Friedrich Gemelke

All we know about Friedrich is that his wife's maiden name was Lindwedel. I don't know her first name. I know he had at least two sons and possibly a daughter. His sons were 1. Henry, 2. Herman, and his daughter was Maria. She married William C. Blume.

Henry and Sophie Gemelke

Henry was born in 1851 somewhere in Germany. It is not known where Henry grew up. Henry (Heinrick) is the son of Friedrich Gemelke. His mother's maiden name was Lindwedel. Her first name is not known. Henry became a tenant farmer at Hainhous near the Bissendorf Church in Hanover Province, Germany. This is where he met Sophie.

Sophie Jaeneke was born at Hainhous on January 20, 1854. Her parents owned the land that Henry was farming. Henry and Sophie were married in 1877.

They had six children. The first one of them to come to the United States was Herman. Herman came over in 1895 on money sent to him by his uncle Herman who was already there. Herman settled by Elgin, Illinois, with his uncle. The next to come over was Alvina. Alvina's brother-in-law visited Germany and talked Alvina and her husband into coming back with him in 1902. Alvina and her husband, Gus Leseburg, settled north of Wisner, Nebraska. In 1903 both Hermans moved to Wisner also. Ernst came over next in 1905 and settled in Nebraska too.

Henry and Sophie came over in 1906. They brought Gustav and Ella with them. They sailed from Bremerhaven, Germany, on the ship, *Kaiser Wilhelm de Grossen*. It took one week to get to New York. They then took the train to Wisner, Nebraska. Their other son, Fritz, never came to the United States.

Sophie passed away on July 25, 1921. Henry died on October 19, 1928. Both are buried at Pilger, Nebraska.

Gustav and Marie Gemelke

Gustav was born in Germany on November 15, 1889. He is the son of Henry and Sophie (Jaeneke) Gemelke. In 1906 he came to the United States with his parents. They sailed from Bermerhaven, Germany, on the ship *Kaiser Wilhelm de Grossen*. It took one week to get to New York. There they went by train to Wisner, Nebraska, where his sister Alvina already lived.

Marie was born in Elgin, Illinois, on August 15, 1891, to Adolf and Dorathea (Dannenbrink) Blume. She started school there. At the age of nine years she moved with her family to a farm near Armour, South Dakota. She finished school which was near their home in Valley Township. She stayed at home, helping out until 1925. She met Gustav Gemelke in 1912 at the age of 18 years at both their Uncle Bill and Aunt Marie (Gemelke) Blumes' home. They mostly corresponded at this time as they decided not to get married yet. They saw each other again about ten years later when they decided to get married. They had a family wedding. They made their home on a farm north of Pilger, Nebraska. Their home was blessed with three children: Oscar, Shirley and Marvin.

They moved into the town of Pilger in the fall of 1955. In 1956 they moved back out to their farm again and lived there for another year. They moved back to their home in town where they stayed the rest of their lives.

Gustav died on September 15, 1968, with a kidney complication. Marie lived until June, 1984.

Gemelke family, taken in Germany. From the left: front row: Ella, Sophie, Henry, Gustav; back row: Friedrich and Ernst. It may have been taken sometime after 1902, as the two oldest, Alwine (Alvina) and Herman, are not pictured; they may have already emigrated to America by that time.

Ernst Friedrich Wilhelm Gemelke

Note: Doris Ritze said that her father and Ernst received two years of English instruction and either graduated or were confirmed on the same day. This may have been completed through Catechism classes at First Trinity Lutheran Church at Altona or through regular classes at the First Trinity Parochial School or country school near Altona. Wilhelm Gemelke is listed among the First Trinity confirmands in 1906, although Ernst was confirmed in Germany. Ernst's two middle names are Friedrich and Wilhelm, so the listing could refer to him. Or, Doris's father attended District 37 and the Altona Trinity Lutheran Parochial School, both in Wayne County (*Pilger, Nebraska, Century Edition 1887-1987*), so Ernst could have attended either of those schools. (LaRayne {Gemelke} Topp)

The site of the Jaeneke farm is now an exclusive golf park near Hainhaus, as inscribed on the large stone near the entrance. A number of houses remain in the village itself which would have stood when Henry and Sophie lived there. The Jaeneke home has been torn down and the doorway was incorporated into the front door of the clubhouse.

Those who owned the farmland lived in the village and went out to the surrounding farms to work. Three farms made up what is now the golf park. They raised potatoes, sugar beets and corn.

Note: Dale and I visited Hainhaus and in this part of Germany families often lived in a building in which the family lived in one half (or the upstairs) and the livestock lived in pens on the other half. In the house/barn we visited, the fire to keep the family warm was in the center of the building; it also warmed the livestock. There were no chimneys in these homes so the heat and smoke filled the building. Hams were sometimes hung overhead to cure, and often people living in these house/barns smelled of smoke. A kitchen and bedrooms were on one side of the house and animals on the other. If a family was wealthy, they had fancy windows on the kitchen side. Families slept in large boxes, all together, with curtains across the front to keep out the drafts (LaRayne {Gemelke} Topp)

The family home at Hainhaus. Homes were built with living quarters on one end and space for livestock, feed and bedding on the other. The home (above) has since been torn down and the door was incorporated into a fine clubhouse situated on the Hainhaus golf course which once comprised the family farm.

The top and bottom photographs may or may not be the same fence in Hainhaus
yesterday (above) and today (below)

This may be the school Ernst attended in Hainhaus

A typical barn/home today in Hainhaus

The Lutheran Church at Bissendorf, a larger town approximately ten miles from Hainhaus, attended by Henry and Sophie Gemelke and family while they made their home at Hainhaus.

Views from the balcony of the Lutheran Church at Bissendorf.

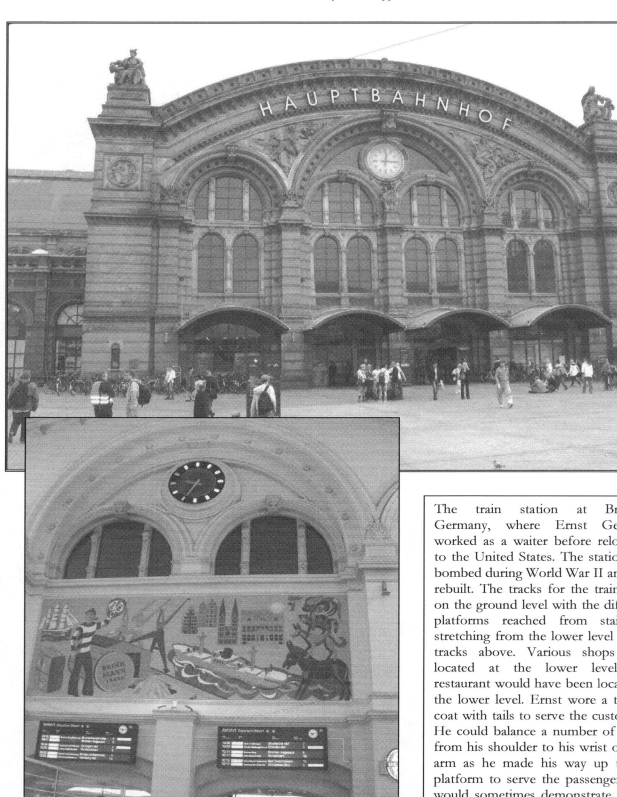

The train station at Bremen, Germany, where Ernst Gemelke worked as a waiter before relocating to the United States. The station was bombed during World War II and was rebuilt. The tracks for the train were on the ground level with the different platforms reached from staircases stretching from the lower level to the tracks above. Various shops were located at the lower level; the restaurant would have been located at the lower level. Ernst wore a tuxedo coat with tails to serve the customers. He could balance a number of plates from his shoulder to his wrist on one arm as he made his way up to the platform to serve the passengers. He would sometimes demonstrate to the Gemelke children how this was done. If the passengers weren't through eating, he would ride with the train to the next stop to retrieve the plates and silverware and bring them back.

Windmill at Bremen, Germany.

Views of Olde Town Bremen

Wording on the back of this postcard, written in German: Soltau, November 14, 1911. Dear Brother, For your birthday yesterday we send our heartfelt congratulations and best greetings. The card will arrive too late, nevertheless it is meant earnestly. Didn't you get our picture of our business-house? The picture on the back is our house next to the business so the business is on the right of the house and on the left side our garden into the back-house. The 1. April we will move into the apartment with the three windows. Now you have our entire housing in pictures. Greetings, your Fritz (Fred) and Lisabeth (Elizabeth) Note: Dad (Emil) said they ran a delicatessen, a candy shop, with "delicate tastings." (LaRayne {Gemelke} Topp)

Ella Gemelke, seated; back, from the left: Ernst Gemelke and Gustav Gemelke.

Note: This photograph could have been taken in Germany or the United States. It may be Henry Gemelke standing, far left, and the woman near him may be either his wife Sophie or daughter Ella. (LaRayne {Gemelke} Topp)

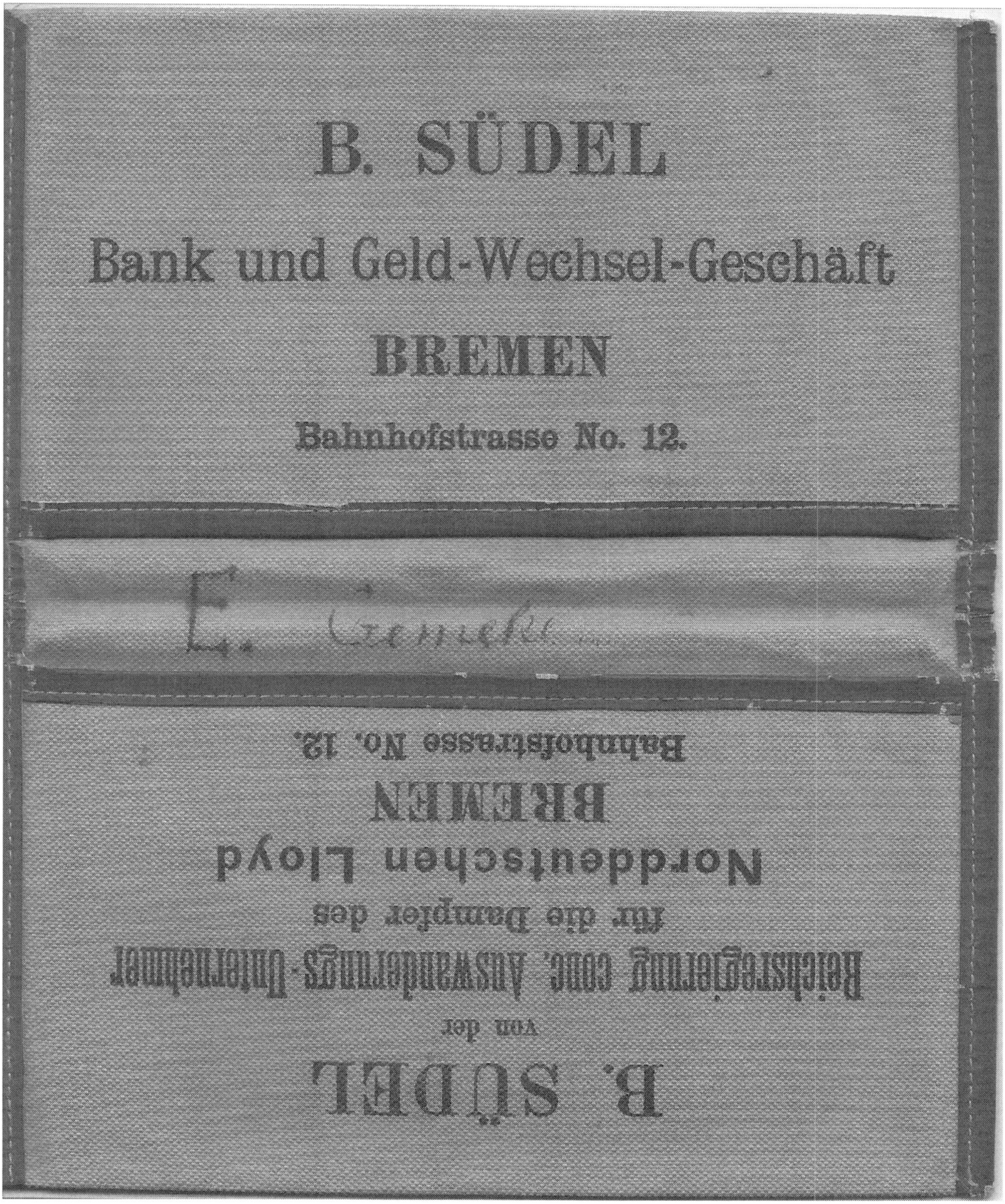

B. SÜDEL

Bank und Geld-Wechsel-Geschäft

BREMEN

Bahnhofstrasse No. 12.

E. Gemelke

Bahnhofstrasse No. 12.

BREMEN

Norddeutschen Lloyd

für die Dampfer des

Reichsregierung conc. Auswanderungs-Unternehmer

von der

B. SÜDEL

These are the front and back of a postcard sent to Ernst Gemelke while he was living in Hanover and working at this spa. It is addressed simply to *Herr* E. Gemelke, Bartender, in Bremen at the Central Hotel. The message is a request for information.

Ernst's passage record from Bremerhaven, line four

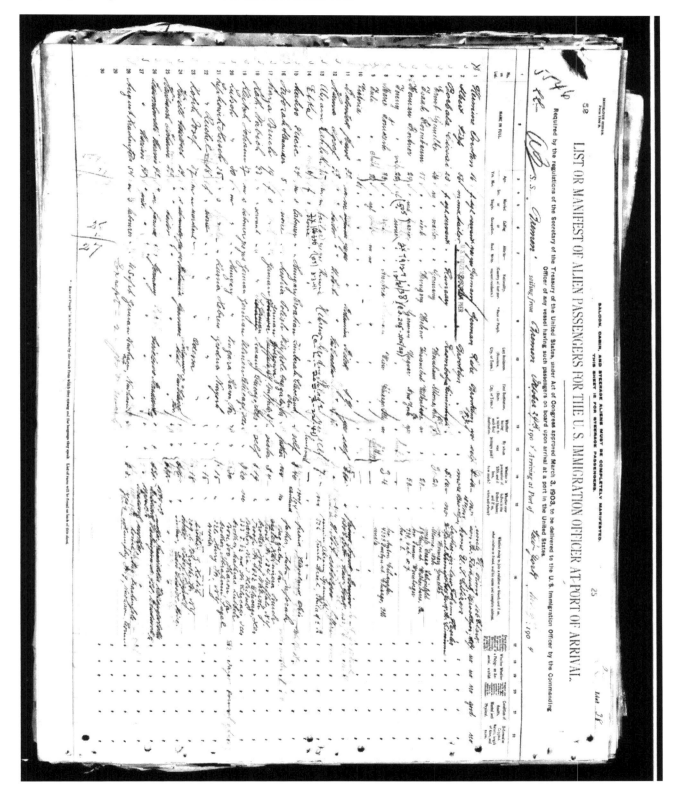

Henry, Sophie, Gustav and Ella's passage record on the *Kaiser Wilhelm de Grossen*, lines eight through eleven

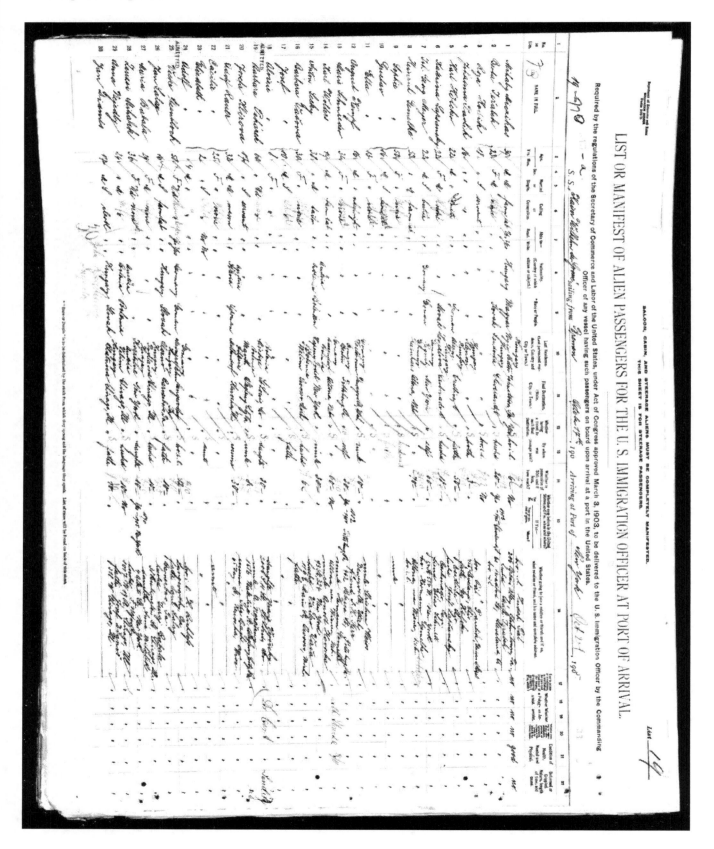

No. 92

NATURALIZATION SERVICE

[To be given to the person making the Declaration]

UNITED STATES OF AMERICA

DECLARATION OF INTENTION

(Invalid for all purposes seven years after the date hereof)

The State of Nebraska } ss: In the District Court

Stanton County of Stanton County, Nebraska

I, Ernst Frederick Wilhelm Gemelke, aged 23 years, occupation Farmer, do declare on oath that my personal description is: Color White, complexion Dark, height 5 feet 9¼ inches, weight 150 pounds, color of hair Black, color of eyes Brown other visible distinctive marks Scar at the outer corner of right eye I was born in Hainhaus, Germany on the 18th day of January, anno Domini 1888; I now reside at Pilger, Nebraska

(Give number, street, city or town, and State.)

I emigrated to the United States of America from Bremen, Germany on the vessel Bremen; my last

(If the alien arrived otherwise than by vessel, the character of conveyance or name of transportation company should be given.)

foreign residence was Bremen, Germany

It is my bona fide intention to renounce forever all allegiance and fidelity to any foreign prince, potentate, state, or sovereignty, and particularly to William II German Emperor, of whom I am now a subject; I arrived at the port of New York, in the State of New York, on or about the 8th day of November, anno Domini 1904; I am not an anarchist; I am not a polygamist nor a believer in the practice of polygamy; and it is my intention in good faith to become a citizen of the United States of America and to permanently reside therein: SO HELP ME GOD.

Ernst Friedrich Wilhelm Gemelke

(Original signature of declarant.)

Subscribed and sworn to before me this 2nd

[SEAL]

day of January, anno Domini 1912

W. J. McFarland

Clerk of the District Court

No. 47

ORIGINAL

UNITED STATES OF AMERICA

Department of Commerce and Labor
BUREAU OF IMMIGRATION AND NATURALIZATION
DIVISION OF NATURALIZATION

PETITION FOR NATURALIZATION

District court of Stanton County, Nebraska

In the matter of the petition of Ernst Fredrick Wilhelm Gemelke to be admitted a citizen of the United States of America.

To the District court of Stanton County, Nebraska.

The petition of Ernst Fredrick Wilhelm Gemelke respectfully shows:

First. My full name is Ernst Fredrick Wilhelm Gemelke

Second. My place of residence is number _____ street, Town of Pilger

State of Nebraska

Third. My occupation is Farmer

Fourth. I was born on the 18th day of January, anno Domini 1888, at Kirchaw, Germany

Fifth. I emigrated to the United States from Bremen, Germany on or about the 29th day of October anno Domini 1904, and arrived at the port of New York, in the United States, on the vessel Bremen.

Sixth. I declared my intention to become a citizen of the United States on the 2d day of January, anno Domini 1912 at Stanton, Nebraska in the District Court of Stanton County, Nebraska

Seventh. I am married. My wife's name is Louisa Gemelke She was born in Stanton county Nebraska and now resides at Pilger, Nebraska I have 2 children, and the name, date and place of birth, and place of residence of each of said children is as follows: Herbert, Henry Gemelke, Born April 29th 1914, Gertrude Sophia Maria, Born June 18th 1915; Both in Stanton county Nebraska where they now reside

Eighth. I am not a disbeliever in or opposed to organized government or a member of or affiliated with any organization or body of persons teaching disbelief in organized government. I am not a polygamist nor a believer in the practice of polygamy. I am attached to the principles of the Constitution of the United States, and it is my intention to become a citizen of the United States and to renounce absolutely and forever all allegiance and fidelity to any foreign prince, potentate, state, or sovereignty, and particularly to William II German Emperor of which at this time I am a subject; and it is my intention to reside permanently in the United States.

Ninth. I am able to speak the English language.

Tenth. I have resided continuously in the United States of America for a term of five years at least immediately preceding the date of this petition, to wit, since the 8th day of November, anno Domini 1904, and in the State of Nebraska for one year at least next preceding the date of this petition, to wit, since the 13th day of November, anno Domini 1904.

Eleventh. I have not heretofore made petition for citizenship to any court. I made petition for citizenship to the _____ Court of _____ at _____ on the _____ day of _____, anno Domini 1 _____, and the said petition was denied by the said Court for the following reasons and causes, to wit, _____, and the cause of such denial has since been cured or removed.)

Attached hereto and made a part of this petition are my declaration of intention to become a citizen of the United States and the certificate from the Department of Commerce and Labor required by law. Wherefore your petitioner prays that he may be admitted a citizen of the United States of America.

Dated May 29" 1916

Ernst Fridrich Wilhelm Gemelke
(Signature of petitioner.)

The State of Nebraska }
Stanton county }

Ernst Fredrick Wilhelm Gemelke, being duly sworn, deposes and says that he is the petitioner in the above-entitled proceeding; that he has read the foregoing petition and knows the contents thereof; that the same is true of his own knowledge, except as to matters therein stated to be alleged upon information and belief, and that as to those matters he believes it to be true.

Ernst Fridrich Wilhelm Gemelke

Subscribed and sworn to before me this 29th day of May, anno Domini 1916

[SEAL]

W. J. McFarland Clerk,
_____ Clerk.

* If the alien arrived otherwise than by vessel, the character of conveyance or name of transportation company should be given.

Declaration of Intention and Certificate of Landing from Department of Commerce and Labor filed this 29th day of May 1916

_____ Clerk.
_____ Clerk.

AFFIDAVIT OF WITNESSES

District court of Stanton county, Nebraska

In the matter of the petition of Ernst Fredrick Wilhelm Gemelke to be admitted a citizen of the United States of America.

The State of Nebraska }
Stanton County } ss:

William Page occupation Farmer residing at Pilger, Nebraska and August Melcher occupation Farmer residing at Pilger, Nebraska each being severally, duly, and respectively sworn, deposes and says that he is a citizen of the United States of America; that he has personally known Ernst Fredrick Wilhelm Gemelke, the petitioner above mentioned, to be a resident of the United States for a period of at least five years continuously immediately preceding the date of filing his petition, and of the State in which the above-entitled application is made for a period of more than five years immediately preceding the date of filing his petition; and that he has personal knowledge that the said petitioner is a person of good moral character, attached to the principles of the Constitution of the United States, and that he is in every way qualified, in his opinion, to be admitted a citizen of the United States.

William Page

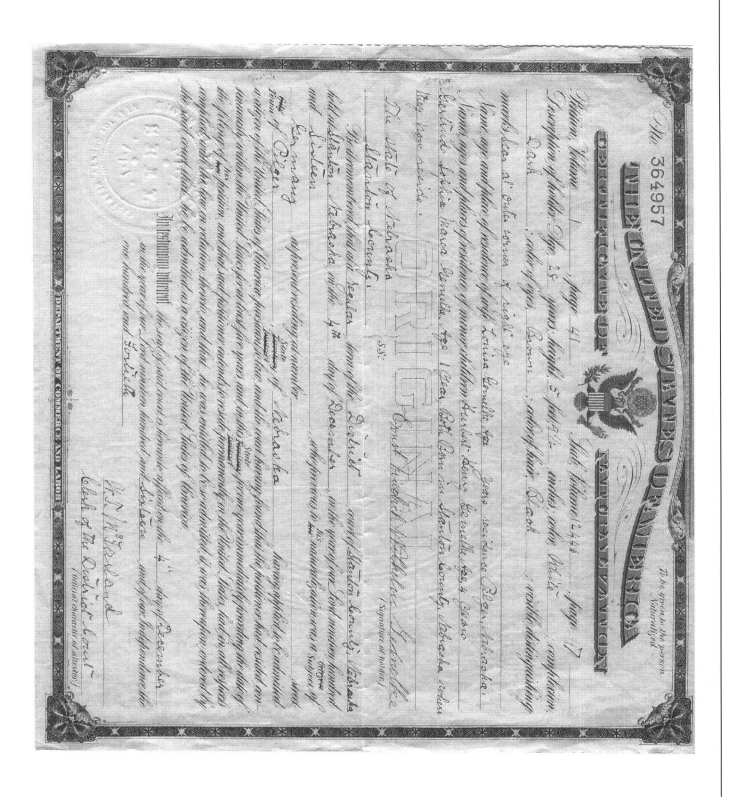

Ernst Gemelke Siblings

Alwine (Alvina) Gemelke, oldest daughter of Henry and Sophie Gemelke

Born in Germany, July 4, 1878

Died, July 17, 1962, in Canyon Texas, at the age of 84 years

Emigrated to America in 1902

Married Gustave Leseburg

The couple had three children

Erna Sophie was born in Germany, June 9, 1899. Erna died March 21, 1992, in Gravette, Arkansas, at 92 years of age. She married Carl (Charly) Bauer on August 30, 1917. Carl was born April 30, 1891. Carl died November 22, 1971, at 80 years of age.

Gustave was born in Altona, Nebraska, July 10, 1903. Gustave died April 25, 1992, in Monett, Missouri, at 88 years of age. He married Ella Tusek, June 1, 1933.

Irene Augusta was born in Canyon, Texas, January 14, 1910. Irene died December 8, 1993, in Canyon Texas, at 88 years of age. She married Raymond Ray Tusek in Texas, July 28, 1932. Raymond was born in South Dakota on March 6, 1911. Raymond died May 12, 1990, in Amarillo, Texas, at 79 years of age.

Note: Erna told me the family story was that Erna was born in Germany, Gustave in the United States, and Irene in Texas. (LaRayne {Gemelke} Topp)

Erna (Leseburg) Bauer, oldest daughter of Alvina (Gemelke) and Gustave Leseburg

Note: The last time Emil and Bernitha Gemelke visited Erna she was in her 80s, I believe, and was out scooping feed to 80 head of cattle by hand. (LaRayne {Gemelke} Topp)

Front, from the left: Elsie, Leona, Leonard, Charly; and back: Erna

Irene and Ray Tusek in approximately 1949. Front row, from the left: Loretta, Melvin, Linda, Robert, behind him is David, behind him is Glenn, Waldon (far right), behind him is Norman; parents are holding Clinton. Not yet born are Diane, Pamela and Rhonda.

Gustave and Ella (Tusek) Leseburg
and daughter Gladys

Sisters, above: Alvina Gemelke, left, and
Ella Gemelke.

Right: Ella Gemelke, left, and Alvina Gemelke

June 15, 1998 – Contributed by Mark Brueggeman

Alvina Gemelke Family Journal

This is the family journal of Alvina Gemelke, daughter of Henry Gemelke. She had three children, Erna, Gustave, and Irene.

First Generation

1. **ALWINE (ALVINA)[1] GEMELKE**, daughter of Henry Gemelke and Sophie Jaeneke was born in Germany July 4, 1878. Alwine died July 17, 1962 in Canyon, Texas, at 84 years of age.

She married **GUSTAVE LESEBERG**. Gustave was born February 24, 1873. Gustave died February 17,1939 in Canyon, Texas, at 65 years of age.

She emigrated, 1902. Point of origin: pt of origin unknown.

Alwine (Alvina) Gemelke and Gustave Leseberg had the following children:

2	i.	ERNA SOPHIE[2] was born June 9, 1899.
3	ii.	GUSTAVE was born July 10, 1903.
4	iii.	IRENE AUGUSTA was born January 14, 1910.

Second Generation

2. **ERNA SOPHIE[2] LESEBERG** (*Alwine (Alvina)[1] Gemelke*) was born in Germany June 9, 1899. Erna died March 21, 1992 in Gravette, Arkansas, at 92 years of age.

She married **CARL (CHARLY) BAUER** August 30, 1917. Carl was born April 30, 1891. Carl died November 22, 1971 at 80 years of age.

Erna Sophie Leseberg and Carl (Charly) Bauer had the following children:

5	i.	ELSIE ALVINA[3] was born July 9, 1918.
6	ii.	LEONARD CARL was born July 24, 1920.
7	iii.	LEONA IRENE was born July 2, 1927.

3. **GUSTAVE[2] LESEBERG** (*Alwine (Alvina)[1] Gemelke*) was born in Altona Nebraska July 10, 1903. Gustave died April 25, 1992 in Monett, Mc   , at 88 years of age.

He married **ELLA TUCEK** June 1, 1933.

Gustave Leseberg and Ella Tucek had the following child:

8	i.	GLADYS[3] was born on (birth date unknown).

4. **IRENE AUGUSTA[2] LESEBERG** (*Alwine (Alvina)[1] Gemelke*) was born in Canyon Texas January 14, 1910. Irene died December 8, 1993 in Canyon Texas, at 83 years of age.

She married **RAYMOND RAY TUCEK** in Texas, July 28, 1932. Raymond was born in South Dakota March 6, 1911. Raymond died May 12, 1990 in Amarillo Texas, at 79 years of age.

Irene Augusta Leseberg and Raymond Ray Tucek had the following children:

    i. NORMAN RAY[3] was born March 31, 1936. He married WANDA MONTELLA LOVE January 26, 1957.

    ii. GLENN EUGENE was born May 6, 1939. He married WALTINE CASSANDRA BEAVERS August 25, 1961.

iii. WELDON CHARLES was born August 27, 1940. Weldon died April 13, 1983 at 42 years of Truck Accident He married GWYNNITH DELAINE NEELEY.

iv. MELVIN LEWIS was born February 15, 1942. He married BARBARA DEE BANKS.

v. DAVID LEE was born July 15, 1943. He married RITA FREEMAN.

vi. LORRETTA IRENE was born October 24, 1944. She married WILLIAM EDWARD COX June 26, 1963.

vii. LINDA JOAN was born May 1, 1946. She married HOWARD RAY MOGG.

viii. ROBERT DEAN was born July 13, 1947. He married MARTHA LOUISE MANLEY.

ix. CLINTON TRAVIS was born January 13, 1949.

x. DIANE LORRAINE was born November 7, 1950. She married HARVEY TURNER.

xi. PAMELA KAY was born May 2, 1955. She married PHILLIP STEVENS April 13, 1974.

xii. RHONDA LOU was born March 2, 1957. She married WILKES ARMSTRONG STEVENS February 8, 1975.

Third Generation (following page)

5. ELSIE ALVINA³ BAUER (*Erna Sophie² Leseberg, Alwine (Alvina)¹ Gemelke*) was born in Texas July 9, 1918.

She married **PHILIP RICKWARTZ** August 28, 1940. Philip died April 22, 1978.

Elsie Alvina Bauer and Philip Rickwartz had the following children:

9	i.	CHARLENE MARY⁴ was born May 31, 1941.
10	ii.	CLEMENTINE ALVINA was born May 31, 1942.
11	iii.	BERNETT LOUISE was born July 15, 1943.
12	iv.	LEON BERNARD was born August 26, 1944.
13	v.	STANLEY JOSEPH was born August 18, 1946.
14	vi.	CARLDEAN WILLIAM was born July 9, 1950.

6. LEONARD CARL³ BAUER (*Erna Sophie² Leseberg, Alwine (Alvina)¹ Gemelke*) was born in Texas July 24, 1920.

He married twice. He married **BERTHA SCHOENBERGER** August 6, 1947. Bertha died January 15, 1971. Bertha was divorced from Leonard Carl Bauer 1960. He married **ANNA LEE WHORTON JOHNSON** April 8, 1967. Had a child by previous marriage - Earlene Johnson Brown May 1, 1947

Leonard was divorced from Bertha Schoenberger 1960.

Leonard Carl Bauer and Bertha Schoenberger had the following children:

15	i.	JUDY CAROL⁴ was born March 29, 1949.
16	ii.	LEONARD (LENNY) was born July 12, 1952.

7. LEONA IRENE³ BAUER (*Erna Sophie² Leseberg, Alwine (Alvina)¹ Gemelke*) was born in Texas July 2, 1927. Leona died October 1, 1997 at 70 years of age.

She married **CHARLIE KNOX** August 20, 1947. Charlie died July 30, 1974.

Leona Irene Bauer and Charlie Knox had the following children:

17	i.	ERNETTA IRENE⁴ was born July 10, 1948.
18	ii.	BRENDA JOYCE was born December 1, 1951.
19	iii.	PATSY LYNN was born July 18, 1953.
20	iv.	KARIN SUE was born January 10, 1956.
21	v.	TIMMIE LOU was born February 19, 1959.
22	vi.	PEGGY ANN was born December 11, 1960.
23	vii.	CHARLEY GILMORE (JUNIOR) was born June 20, 1962.
24	viii.	TRUITT GARY was born September 4, 1963.

8. GLADYS³ LESEBERG (*Gustave², Alwine (Alvina)¹ Gemelke*) was born in Texas on (birth date unknown). She married **LEE ROY BAUER**.

Gladys Leseberg and Lee Roy Bauer had the following children:

- i. RICH⁴ was born on (birth date unknown).
- ii. CHERYL was born on (birth date unknown).
- iii. LEAH was born on (birth date unknown).

Fourth Generation

9. **CHARLENE MARY[4] RICKWARTZ** (*Elsie Alvina[3] Bauer, Erna Sophie[2] Leseberg, Alwine (Alvina)[1] Gemelke*) was born May 31, 1941.

She married **RONALD BRIGHTWELL** October 4, 1958.

Charlene Mary Rickwartz and Ronald Brightwell had the following children:

    i. RONALD LINDEN[5] was born May 4, 1959.
    ii. PATRICIA ANN was born October 1, 1960.
    iii. RENEA LYNN was born November 20, 1963.

10. **CLEMENTINE ALVINA[4] RICKWARTZ** (*Elsie Alvina[3] Bauer, Erna Sophie[2] Leseberg, Alwine (Alvina)[1] Gemelke*) was born May 31, 1942.

She married **DAVID TINNES** November 24, 1962.

Clementine Alvina Rickwartz and David Tinnes had the following children:

    i. MICHAEL TIMATHY[5] was born September 10, 1963.
    ii. PATRICK PHILIP was born April 4, 1966.

11. **BERNETT LOUISE[4] RICKWARTZ** (*Elsie Alvina[3] Bauer, Erna Sophie[2] Leseberg, Alwine (Alvina)[1] Gemelke*) was born July 15, 1943.

She married twice. She married **JOHN SPIER** June 15, 1962. John was divorced from Bernett Louise Rickwartz 1975. She married **JEFF JARVIS** November 17, 1978.

Bernett was divorced from John Spier 1975.

Bernett Louise Rickwartz and John Spier had the following children:

    i. SUZANNE MARIE[5] was born February 24, 1963.
    ii. STEPHANIE ANN was born January 16, 1967.
    iii. STEPHAN JOHN was born February 25, 1969.

12. **LEON BERNARD**[4] **RICKWARTZ** (*Elsie Alvina*[3] *Bauer, Erna Sophie*[2] *Leseberg, Alwine (Alvina)*[1] *Gemelke*) was born August 26, 1944.

He married twice. He married **SHARON GOWAN** January 20, 1966. Sharon was divorced from Leon Bernard Rickwartz October 1972. He married **SABRA ASBURN** November 4, 1977.

Leon was divorced from Sharon Gowan October 1972.

Leon Bernard Rickwartz and Sabra Asburn had the following child:

      i.   JON CHRISTOPHER[5] was born July 1,1974. Jon was adopted December 1982. Biological mother is Sabra Asburn

13. **STANLEY JOSEPH**[4] **RICKWARTZ** (*Elsie Alvina*[3] *Bauer, Erna Sophie*[2] *Leseberg, Alwine (Alvina)*[1] *Gemelke*) was born August 18, 1946.

He married **VICKIE KILGORE** November 13, 1964.

Stanley Joseph Rickwartz and Vickie Kilgore had the following children:

      i.   STANLEY JOSEPH[5] was born August 15, 1965.
     ii. SHANNON DIANE was born December 28, 1966.
    iii. CARL LYNN was born April 18, 1969.

14. **CARLDEAN WILLIAM**[4] **RICKWARTZ** (*Elsie Alvina*[3] *Bauer, Erna Sophie*[2] *Leseberg, Alwine (Alvina)*[1] *Gemelke*) was born July 9, 1950.

He married **TEDDY SHIPP** October 20, 1972.

Carldean William Rickwartz and Teddy Shipp had the following children:

      i.   AMELIA ANN[5] was born May 19, 1974.
     ii. JESSIE WILLIAM was born June 8, 1975.

15. **JUDY CAROL**[4] **BAUER** (*Leonard Carl*[3], *Erna Sophie*[2] *Leseberg, Alwine (Alvina)*[1] *Gemelke*) was born March 29, 1949.

She married **WILLIAM PORTER** June 15, 1968.

Judy Carol Bauer and William Porter had the following children:

      i.   WADE HORTAN[5] was born March 18, 1968. *ADOPTED*
     ii. CARLA LEANNE was born December 22, 1973. Carla was adopted.

16. **LEONARD (LENNY)**[4] **BAUER** (*Leonard Carl*[3], *Erna Sophie*[2] *Leseberg, Alwine (Alvina)*[1] *Gemelke*) was born July 12, 1952.

He married **BARBARA WETZEL** Dec 31, 1971. Barbara was divorced from Leonard (Lenny) Bauer

October 1981.

Leonard was divorced from Barbara Wetzel October 1981.

Leonard (Lenny) Bauer and Barbara Wetzel had the following children:

    i. MICHEAL LEN[5] was born July 5, 1975.
    ii. JOSHUA CARL was born january 26, 1980.
    iii. CECELIA MARIE was born April 8, 1981.

17. **ERNETTA IRENE[4] KNOX** (*Leona Irene[3] Bauer, Erna Sophie[2] Leseberg, Alwine (Alvina)[1] Gemelke*) was born July 10, 1948.

She married **JIMMY BEHRENDS** December 26, 1965. Jimmy was born September 16, 1946.

Ernetta Irene Knox and Jimmy Behrends had the following children:

    i. SHEILA DAWN[5] was born January 3, 1967.
    ii. RICHARD EUGENE was born September 24, 1968.

18. **BRENDA JOYCE[4] KNOX** (*Leona Irene[3] Bauer, Erna Sophie[2] Leseberg, Alwine (Alvina)[1] Gemelke*) was born December 1, 1951.

She married **JACKIE SPRINKLES** June 29, 1969. Jackie was born November 12, 1947.

Brenda Joyce Knox and Jackie Sprinkles had the following children:

    i. JOYCE LYNN[5] was born January 22, 1972.
    ii. CANDICE RENEA was born March 23, 1974.
    iii. JASON WARREN was born March 12, 1977.

19. **PATSY LYNN[4] KNOX** (*Leona Irene[3] Bauer, Erna Sophie[2] Leseberg, Alwine (Alvina)[1] Gemelke*) was born July 18, 1953.

She married **DONALD COOK** August 22, 1971. Donald was born September 14, 1953.

Patsy Lynn Knox and Donald Cook had the following children:

    i. DONALD BRENT[5] was born March 4, 1975.
    ii. KACI LYNN was born december 26, 1978.
    iii. CYNTHIA GAIL was born january 8, 1981.
    iv. DUSTIN WARREN was born April 28, 1983.

20. **KARIN SUE[4] KNOX** (*Leona Irene[3] Bauer, Erna Sophie[2] Leseberg, Alwine (Alvina)[1] Gemelke*) was born January 10, 1956.

She married **LLOYD LANG** July 28, 1981. Lloyd was born April 19, 1956.

Karin Sue Knox and Lloyd Lang had the following children:

    i. LLOYD DEAN[5] was born january 31, 1983.
    ii. MISTY DAWN was born September 22, 1985.

21. **TIMMIE LOU**[4] **KNOX** (*Leona Irene*[3] *Bauer, Erna Sophie*[2] *Leseberg, Alwine (Alvina)*[1] *Gemelke*) was born February 19, 1959.

He married **IKIE LEE OWENS** September 2, 1978. Ikie was born October 15, 1958.

Timmie Lou Knox and Ikie Lee Owens had the following children:

    i. ALICIA MARIE[5] was born March 19, 1982.
    ii. KEVIN ALLEN was born October 12, 1984.

22. **PEGGY ANN**[4] **KNOX** (*Leona Irene*[3] *Bauer, Erna Sophie*[2] *Leseberg, Alwine (Alvina)*[1] *Gemelke*) was born December 11, 1960.

She married **BOBBY BEAL**.

Peggy Ann Knox and Bobby Beal had the following children:

    i. SHASTA ROANN[5] was born August 9, 1981.
    ii. COLBY LAMB was born May 12, 1984.

23. **CHARLEY GILMORE (JUNIOR)**[4] **KNOX** (*Leona Irene*[3] *Bauer, Erna Sophie*[2] *Leseberg, Alwine (Alvina)*[1] *Gemelke*) was born June 20, 1962.

He married twice. He married **TERESA HAWKINS** June 17, 1982. Teresa was divorced from Charley Gilmore (Junior) Knox Jun 15, 1985. He married **TERRY ANN HICKSON** June 27, 1986. Terry Ann had a daughter from a previous marriage Kimberly 10-10-1985

Terry was born September 21, 1965.

Charley was divorced from Teresa Hawkins Jun 15, 1985.

Charley Gilmore (Junior) Knox and Teresa Hawkins had the following child:

    i. CHERRIE MICHELLE[5] was born December 28, 1982.

Charley Gilmore (Junior) Knox and Terry Ann Hickson had the following child:

    ii. CHARLEY GILMORE (III) was born December 30, 1987.

24. **TRUITT GARY**[4] **KNOX** (*Leona Irene*[3] *Bauer, Erna Sophie*[2] *Leseberg, Alwine (Alvina)*[1] *Gemelke*) was born September 4, 1963.

He married **JENNIFER PHILPOT** September 20, 1985. Jennifer was born August 21, 1968.

Truitt Gary Knox and Jennifer Philpot had the following child:

    i. RICHARD JOHN[5] was born May 4, 1986.

Herman, oldest son and second child of Henry and Sophie Gemelke

Born in Germany

Died, May 6, 1913, in Germany

Emigrated to America in 1895

Married Emma Etta Dohren

The couple had one daughter

Note: I am unsure as to the origin of this photograph or location. Herman Gemelke inscribed on the tomb could be either Herman or his Uncle Herman Gemelke.

I am unable to make out anything other than the name and R.I.P. at the top.

A note taped to the back of the photograph says, *Heir Ruht Trennung! O wie Schwer bist du!* Oh, how difficult are you. (LaRayne {Gemelke} Topp)

Ellen Glover was born to Herman F. and Emma Etta Dohren Gemelke January 20, 1913, three miles north of the Highway 275 and 15 intersection at Pilger. She was assisted into the world by Dr. Reid as were all of her children.

A month after her birth, her father with a Mr. Walters left for Germany. Mr. Gemelke had a medical problem with his throat, and his family thought their old family doctor could help. However, this was not to be. He died May 6, 1913, and was buried in Germany. During the war, the cemetery was bombed and there is no sign of the grave left.

Ellen's mother then moved a mile farther north to the Nick Dohren farm. She was given 80 acres of a quarter section by her father and had to pay for the other half.

Another tragic happening befell the family when her grandmother Dohren who had diabetes had to have her leg amputated. A team of nurses and a doctor from Norfolk converted the dining room table into an operating table. During the surgery, grandpa Dohren walked the floor and soon eight-year-old Ellen walked behind him. She has never forgotten the sound of that surgery. *Pilger, Nebraska, Century Edition, 1887-1987*

Emma (Herman) Gemelke

Funeral Services for Mrs. Emma Etta Gemelke, 80, of Pilger were held on January 29, 1971, at St. John's Lutheran Church in Pilger with the Rev. Eugene W. Juergensen officiating. Burial was in the Pilger Cemetery.

Organist was Mrs. John Goeller Jr., who accompanied Mrs. Bill Jacobs and Mrs. Eugene W. Juergensen. Pallbearers were Norbert Husmann, Orville Tobias, Russell Tiedtke, Emil Gemelke, Marvin Gemelke and Sanford Glover.

Mrs. Gemelke was born near Pilger on January 23, 1891, to Nicholas Dohren and Sophia nee Bohlmann. She was baptized and confirmed on March 14, 1914, and was one of the first members of St. John's Lutheran Church at Pilger, which was organized in 1915.

She attended grade school north of Pilger in District 18. She was a member of the St. John's Ladies Aid from 1931 to 1934. She passed away at the Wayne Hospital.

Survivors are her daughter, Ellen Glover of Pilger; two brothers, William Dohren of Pilger and Henry Dohren of Denver, Colorado; one sister, Mrs. Herman Husmann; five grandsons—Verlyn Glover of Pilger; Elwyn Glover, Lincoln; Robert Glover, North Hollywood, California; Nordell Glover, Pilger; Darwyn Glover, Dakota City; one granddaughter Mrs. E. P. Willis, Sargeant Bluffs, Iowa.

Following the death of her husband Herman F. Gemelke, she has made her home with her daughter, Mrs. Ellen Glover at Pilger.

June 15, 1998 – Contributed by Mark Brueggeman

Herman Gemelke Family Journal

This is the family journal of Herman Gemelke, son of Henry Gemelke. He had one daughter, Ellen.

First Generation

1. **HERMAN[1] GEMELKE**, son of Henry Gemelke and Sophie Jaeneke was born in Hanover Germany before 1895, the first event for which there is a recorded date. Herman died May 6, 1913 in Germany. One month after Ellens birth, Herman went back to Germany. He had a throat problem and went for medical help. He died May 6, 1913 and was buried in Germany.

He married **EMMA DOHREN**.

He emigrated, 1895. Point of origin: pt of origin unknown.

Herman Gemelke and Emma Dohren had the following child:

    2   i.   ELLEN[2] was born January 20, 1913.

Second Generation

2. **ELLEN[2] GEMELKE** (*Herman[1]*) was born in Pilger Nebraska January 20, 1913.

She married **FRANK GLOVER**. Frank died April 29, 1953.

Ellen Gemelke and Frank Glover had the following children:

    i.   MARLEE[3] was born on (birth date unknown). Lives in Fort Ma Jave Arizona
    ii.   ROBERT was born on (birth date unknown). Lives in Milwaukee Oregon
    iii. NORDELL was born on (birth date unknown). Lives in Randolph Kansas
    iv. ELWYN was born on (birth date unknown). Lives in Lincoln Nebraska
    v.   DARWYN was born on (birth date unknown). Lives in Dakota City Nebraska
    vi. VERLYN was born before June 12, 1978, the first event for which there is a recorded date. Verlyn died June 12, 1978.

Friedrich (Fritz), second son and third child of Henry and Sophie Gemelke

Born in Germany

Died in Germany

Did not emigrate to America

Married Elisabeth Denecke

The couple had one daughter, Wilhelma

Taken from German Newspaper, October 11, 1960. Translation below.

Ihre Goldene Hochzeit

frierten am 11. Oktober in Soltau, Wilhelmstr. 26, der Kaufmann Friedrich Gemelke u. Frau Elisabeth geb. Denecke. Herr Gemelke stammt aus Hannover, seine 'Frau aus Burgdorf. In Burgdorf wurde das Parr vor 50 Jahren von Pastor Brandes getraut. Herr Gemelke lernte in Hannover und kam 1905 als Gehilfe zu Kaufmann Springhorn nach Sultau. 1910 eröffnete er sein Geschäft in der WilhelmstraBe, das er bis 1956 führte und dann verpachtete. Er wurde 1923 Mitbegründer der EDEKA in Sultau. October 11, 1960.

Golden Anniversary

On October 11 in Soltau, businessman Friedrich Gemelke and his wife Elisabeth nee Denecke. Mr. Gemelke is from Hannover and Mrs. Gemelke is from Burgdorf. They were wed 50 years ago in Burgdorf by Pastor Brandes. Mr. Gemelke was educated in Hannover and in 1905 became an apprentice to businessman Springhorn at Soltau. In 1910, he purchased a business in Wilhelmastrasse and rented it out in 1956. In 1923, he was one of the founders of EDEKA (a supermarket corporation) in Soltau.

Elisabeth, Wilhelma and Fritz Gemelke

Wilhelma, daughter of Fritz and Elisabeth, and husband

Note: I remember Dad (Emil) saying that Wilhelma's husband disappeared during the beginning of World War II, that he was a teacher and some of them were taken first. My notes following a visit with Aunt Ella Siemsglusz, who kept in contact with Fred's family, say that Wilhelma's second husband was a Grohehoz. This is a photograph of either Wilhelma's first or second husband. (LaRayne {Gemelke} Topp)

Hitler's view on education was that it served a sole purpose—to ensure that a child was loyal to the Nazi state to ensure that the Third Reich lasted for 1000 years. A lot of the Nazi education system also reflected Hitler's educational experiences. After his failure to get into the Academy of Fine Arts in Vienna Hitler developed a loathing of intellectuals who in his opinion based their teaching on what could be learned behind desks or in lecture halls. C. N. Trueman, *Adolf Hitler and Education*

Ernst, third son and fourth child of Henry and Sophie Gemelke

Born in Germany January 18, 1888

Died, June 28, 1944, in Pilger, Nebraska.

Emigrated to America in 1905

Farmer

Married Louisa Koehlmoos

The couple had seven children

Below, front row, from the left: Viola, Ernst, Louisa, Mildred; back row: Anita, Gertrude, Herbert, Emil and Wilhelma

Ernst Gemelke

Ernst Gemelke was given Christian burial on Wednesday, June 28, 1944, in St. John's Lutheran Church of Pilger, with the former pastor, Walter H. Koenig in charge. The funeral address was based in Matthew 25: 19-21.

Ernst Friedrich Wilhelm Gemelke was the son of Heinrich Gemelke and his wife Sophie (nee Jaeneke). He was born on January 18, 1888, at Hainhaus, near Bissendorf, Province Hanover, Germany. As an infant, he was dedicated to the Lord through holy baptism in the German Lutheran Church at Bissendorf. Here, too, he was confirmed in 1902. For two years after, he continued to receive religious instruction.

He began training as an apprentice in the hotel business in Germany, but in 1904 he came to America to join his sister, Mrs. Alwine Leseberg, who lived near Altona, Nebraska, having also come from Germany two years earlier. He now worked on various farms, first near Altona and then near Pilger, for Henry Koehlmoos Sr. All this time, he was affiliated with the Trinity Lutheran Church of Altona.

In 1911, he was joined in holy wedlock with Miss Louisa Koehlmoos by Pastor Frederick Schaller of Trinity Lutheran Church of Altona. He now made his home with his bride on a farm 2 ½ miles north of Pilger. Soon after he acquired the quarter section directly west of here, where he built the home which the family used until the time of his death.

The Lord blessed their home with seven children, all of whom survive their father.

Mr. Gemelke was very active in organizing a church of the pure word of God in Pilger. His efforts and persistence, joined with that of some of his relatives and friends, begun in 1911, finally in 1915 led to the organizing of St. John's Evangelical Church (U.A.C.) of Pilger, Nebraska. He was the first one to sign the constitution among the nine charter members. He was also chosen as the first secretary of the congregation. In this capacity he served the congregation until 1931, when he was elected as an elder of the congregation. This important office he held until the time of his death. He was also the able chairman of the meetings of the congregation for the last twelve years of his life.

In 1928 he was chosen as one of the members of a building committee, who were to see about the building of a church building for the small congregation, of which at that time he was one of the leading members. Nothing came of those plans. In 1933, he served on a similar committee, and again in 1935, when his dream of St. John's having a church of its own came true.

In 1933, he also served on a committee to obtain a resident pastor for his beloved St. John's Church. In 1936, as first delegate to a Synodical Convention from St. John's of Pilger, he signed the constitution of Synod in the name of the congregation. In recent years, he was especially active in wiping out the church debt and procuring a new parsonage. St. John's of Pilger will certainly miss his unflagging interest in and consecrated work for its welfare. In all things, he showed himself an earnest, zealous Christian. He was also interested in civic and agricultural projects.

The last two years Mr. Gemelke had not been feeling well at all. Still it was a great shock to his family, his church and friends, when last Saturday morning, June, 24, 1944, he was stricken in Pilger, while he was fixing his tire at the filling station, with a severe heart attack, and passed to his reward in heaven. The Lord wished thus to take His servant home.

He attained the age of 56 years, five months and six days and is mourned by his devoted wife, Mrs. Louisa Gemelke of Pilger, his two sons, Herbert, a Pfc. in the military police of the U.S. Army stationed in Washington, D.C. and Emil at home; his five daughters, Gertrude (Mrs. Floyd Vollmer of Wisner, Nebraska), Wilhelma (Mrs. Ivan Kemper of Norfolk, Nebraska), Anita, Viola and Mildred, all still at home; also two brothers, Friedrich, still living, when last heard of, in Germany, and Gustav of Pilger; also two sisters, Alwine, (Mrs. Leseberg of Canyon, Texas) and Ella (Mrs. Siemsglusz of Norfolk, Nebraska); also one granddaughter, Gloria Vollmer. His parents and one brother Herman preceded him into death.

Interment was in the Pilger cemetery. Pallbearers were: W. T. Burris, Paul Schneider, Ed Hasenkamp, Herman Ritze, Harvey Petersen, John Dohren and Herman Husmann.

Blessed are the dead, which die in the Lord, from henceforth; yea.

Louisa Gemelke

Funeral services for Mrs. Ernst (Louisa) Gemelke were held Saturday morning, November 17, at St. John's Lutheran Church in Pilger. The Rev. Willard Kassulke officiated with burial in the Pilger Cemetery.

Mrs. Louisa Gemelke was born on February 20, 1888, to Henry and Maria (nee Mindemann) Koehlmoos in rural Pilger in Stanton County, Nebraska. She was baptized and confirmed at Trinity Lutheran Church in Altona, Nebraska.

On March 9, 1911, she was given in marriage to Ernst Gemelke. To this union two sons and five daughters were born. Mrs. Gemelke and her husband were instrumental in the founding of St. John's Lutheran Church in Pilger which organized officially as a congregation in 1935 (of which she was a charter member.)

Mrs. Gemelke passed away suddenly on November 13, 1979, at the Stanton Nursing Home at the age of 91.

She was preceded in death by her parents, her husband, one daughter, two grandchildren, three brothers and three sisters.

Survivors include her two sons, Emil of Pilger and Herbert of Byron, Minnesota; four daughters, Mrs. Viola Brueggeman of Norfolk, Nebraska, Mrs. Wilhelma Kemper of San Antonio, Texas, Mrs. Anita Reimnitz of Corsica, South Dakota, and Mrs. Mildred Janulewicz of North Platte; 19 grandchildren and 26 great-grandchildren.

. . . . . and through the years . . . . . .

From the left,
Louisa Koehlmoos
Gemelke,
Ella Gemelke
Siemsglusz
and Ernst's
cousin Frieda
Gemelke Hallstein

June 15, 1998 Contributed by Mark Brueggeman

First Generation

8. **ERNST FRIEDRICH WILHELM**[3] **GEMELKE** (*Henry*[2], *(Father)*[1]) was born in Hainhaus Bisendorf Hanover Germany January 18, 1888. Ernst died June 28, 1944 in Pilger Nebraska, at 56 years of age. His body was interred in Pilger Cemetery.

He married **LOUISA KOEHLMOOS** in Lutheran Church in Alton Nebraska, March 9, 1911. Louisa was born in Altona, Nebraska February 20, 1888. She was the daughter of Heinrich Koehlmoos and Maria Mindemann. Louisa died November 13, 1979 in Stanton, Nebraska, at 91 years of age.

He emigrated, 1905. Point of origin: pt of origin unknown.

Ernst Friedrich Wilhelm Gemelke and Louisa Koehlmoos had the following children:

    i.   HERBERT HENRY[4] was born in Pilger Nebraska April 29, 1912. Herbert died December 19, 1984 at 72 years of age. He married MARGARET PRICE in Washington D.C., May 12, 1944. Margaret was born in Swea City, Iowa March 27, 1912.

    ii. GERTRUDE ELLA was born in Pilger Nebraska June 18, 1915. Gertrude died June 12, 1973 in California, at 57 years of age. She married FLOYD VOLLMER in Pilger Nebraska, April 3, 1938. Floyd was born May 23, 1914.

    iii. WILHELMA DORTHEA was born in Pilger Nebraska May 21, 1917. She married IVAN KEMPER in Pilger Nebraska, March 9, 1937. Ivan was born December 25, 1910.

    iv. EMIL GUSTAVE was born in Pilger Nebraska June 12, 1919. He married BERNITHA HASENKAMP in Pilger Nebraska, August 30, 1944. Bernitha was born in Pilger Nebraska March 23, 1923.

    v.   ANITA ALVINA was born in Pilger Nebraska December 6, 1923. She married GEORGE REIMNITZ in Pilger Nebraska, June 20, 1948. George was born in South Dakota February 22, 1924.

    vi. VIOLA MARIE was born in Pilger Nebraska February 13, 1926. She married ROBERT ALEXANDER BRUEGGEMAN in Norfolk, Nebraska, September 8, 1957. Robert was born in Norfolk, Nebraska April 3, 1920.

    vii. MILDRED IRENE was born in Pilger Nebraska July 11, 1930. She married LEO JANULEWICZ

in Omaha, Nebraska. October 14, 1961. Leo was born in Loop City, Nebraska, September 27, 1924.

Second Generation

2. HERBERT HENRY² GEMELKE (*Ernst Friedrich Wilhelm¹*) was born in Pilger Nebraska April 29, 1912. Herbert died December 19, 1984 at 72 years of age.

He married **MARGARET PRICE** in Washington D.C., May 12, 1944. Margaret was born in Swea City, Iowa March 27, 1912.

Herbert Henry Gemelke and Margaret Price had the following children:

8	i.	ROBERT ERNEST³ was born February 26, 1945.
9	ii.	MARY CINDA was born March 8, 1949.
	iii.	RICHARD CARL was born January 22, 1951. Richard died July 10, 1954 at 3 years of age.

3. GERTRUDE ELLA² GEMELKE (*Ernst Friedrich Wilhelm¹*) was born in Pilger Nebraska June 18, 1915. Gertrude died June 12, 1973 in California, at 57 years of age.

She married **FLOYD VOLLMER** in Pilger Nebraska, April 3, 1938. Floyd was born May 23, 1914.

Gertrude Ella Gemelke and Floyd Vollmer had the following child:

| 10 | i. | GLORIA³ was born September 28, 1941. |

4. EMIL GUSTAVE² GEMELKE (*Ernst Friedrich Wilhelm¹*) was born in Pilger Nebraska June 12, 1919.

He married **BERNITHA HASENKAMP** in Pilger Nebraska, August 30, 1944. Bernitha was born in Pilger Nebraska March 23, 1923.

Emil Gustave Gemelke and Bernitha Hasenkamp had the following children:

11	i.	DUANE EDWARD³ was born August 4, 1945.
	ii.	RONNIE LEROY was born in Norfolk, Nebraska June 3, 1947.
12	iii.	LARAYNE was born September 23, 1951.

5. ANITA ALVINA² GEMELKE (*Ernst Friedrich Wilhelm¹*) was born in Pilger Nebraska December 6, 1923.

She married **GEORGE REIMNITZ** in Pilger Nebraska, June 20, 1948. George was born in South Dakota February 22, 1924.

Anita Alvina Gemelke and George Reimnitz had the following children:

13	i.	RUSSELL GEORGE[3] was born May 8, 1949.
14	ii.	KARIN LOUISE was born May 13, 1950.
15	iii.	MARJEAN MARIE was born July 30, 1951.
16	iv.	DOUGLAS PAUL was born October 23, 1952.
17	v.	JOYCE ELAINE was born July 1, 1955.
18	vi.	DAVID ERNEST was born April 21, 1957.
19	vii.	JAMES ROBERT was born August 6, 1958.
	viii.	SHEILA KAYE was born March 1, 1969.

6. **VIOLA MARIE[2] GEMELKE** (*Ernst Friedrich Wilhelm[1]*) was born in Pilger Nebraska February 13, 1926.

She married **ROBERT ALEXANDER BRUEGGEMAN** in Norfolk, Nebraska, September 8, 1957. Robert was born in Norfolk, Nebraska April 3, 1920.

Viola Marie Gemelke and Robert Alexander Brueggeman had the following children:

20	i.	MARK DAVID[3] was born April 28, 1959.
21	ii.	COREEN ELIZABETH was born July 22, 1960.
	iii.	BARBARA LOUISE was born in Norfolk, Nebraska January 5, 1965. She married RICHARD NAVE in Kansas City, Missouri, March 20, 1993. Richard was born November 2, 1965.

7. **MILDRED IRENE[2] GEMELKE** (*Ernst Friedrich Wilhelm[1]*) was born in Pilger Nebraska July 11, 1930.

She married **LEO JANULEWICZ** in Omaha Nebraska, October 14, 1961. Leo was born in Loop City, Nebraska September 27, 1924.

Mildred Irene Gemelke and Leo Janulewicz had the following children:

i. RENAE JEANINE[3] was born in Omaha Nebraska April 10, 1963.
ii. JOLENE MARIE was born in Omaha Nebraska June 19, 1968. She married MICHAEL FREEL in Omaha Nebraska, October 12, 1996. Michael was born May 16, 1968.

Third Generation

8. **ROBERT ERNEST³ GEMELKE** (*Herbert Henry²*, *Ernst Friedrich Wilhelm¹*) was born in Swea City, Iowa February 26, 1945. Robert died August 15, 1995 at 50 years of age.

He married **LOUISE IDA ENGLER** in Minnesota, July 15, 1967. Louise was born in Iowa March 11, 1946.

Robert Ernest Gemelke and Louise Ida Engler had the following children:

22   i.   TRINA ELIZABETH⁴ was born March 28, 1970.
         ii. ROBERT ERNEST JR. was born February 7, 1972. He married REBECCA RAE October 7, 1997. Rebecca was born April 4, 1969.
        iii. MARK ROBERT was born July 18, 1979.

9. **MARY CINDA³ GEMELKE** (*Herbert Henry²*, *Ernst Friedrich Wilhelm¹*) was born in Norfolk, Nebraska March 8, 1949.

She married **CHARLES SCHNEITER** in Byron, Minnesota, December 30, 1967. Charles was born December 4, 1946.

Mary Cinda Gemelke and Charles Schneiter had the following children:

23   i.   LISA MARIE⁴ was born July 21, 1968.
         ii. PATRICIA ANN was born July 22, 1969.
24   iii. RICHARD CHARLES was born July 26, 1970.
        iv. JEFFREY ALLEN was born June 6, 1972. He married CAROLE LEE in Rocester, Minnesota, October 4, 1996. Carole had two children by previous marriage, Collen and Samantha

            Carole was born June 17, 1967.

10. **GLORIA³ VOLLMER** (*Gertrude Ella² Gemelke*, *Ernst Friedrich Wilhelm¹*) was born in Pilger, Nebraska September 28, 1941.

She married **CLIFFORD DU PRAS** July 15, 1962. Clifford was born March 1935. Clifford died 1997.

Gloria Vollmer and Clifford Du Pras had the following children:

  i. ROGER LEE[4] was born February 3, 1964. Roger died February 3, 1964 at less than one year of age.

  ii. MICHELLE NICOLE was born June 28, 1965. Michelle died June 28, 1965 at less than one year of age.

25   iii. MICHAEL ANTONY was born April 25, 1966.

  iv. BRIAN DAVID was born in Sacramento, California June 15, 1967.

11. **DUANE EDWARD**[3] **GEMELKE** (*Emil Gustave*[2], *Ernst Friedrich Wilhelm*[1]) was born in Norfolk, Nebraska August 4, 1945.

He married **LINDA STEWART** in Pilger, Nebraska, January 22, 1967. Linda was born in Nebraska March 22, 1948.

Duane Edward Gemelke and Linda Stewart had the following children:

26   i. KRISTINE[4] was born November 14, 1968.

  ii. MICHAEL was born in Hennepin County, Minnesota March 5, 1972. He married JENNIFER MARKKANEN in Brooklyn Park, Minnesota, November 25, 1995. Jennifer was born in Hennepin County, Minnesota October 16, 1972.

  iii. NATHAN was born in Hennepin County, Minnesota December 30, 1976.

12. **LARAYNE**[3] **GEMELKE** (*Emil Gustave*[2], *Ernst Friedrich Wilhelm*[1]) was born in Norfolk, Nebraska September 23, 1951.

She married **KEVIN KARL MEYER** in Pilger Nebraska, January 2, 1969. Kevin was born in West Point, Nebraska April 6, 1951.

LaRayne Gemelke and Kevin Karl Meyer had the following children:

27   i. TRISHA JO[4] was born August 8, 1969.

  ii. BRENDA MARIE was born in West Point Nebraska November 3, 1971. She married HAROLD BREITKREUTZ in Wisner, Nebraska, June 19, 1993.

  iii. CLINTON KEVIN was born October 21, 1975.

13. **RUSSELL GEORGE**[3] **REIMNITZ** (*Anita Alvina*[2] *Gemelke*, *Ernst Friedrich Wilhelm*[1]) was born in Parkston, South Dakota May 8, 1949.

He married twice. He married **JUDY HERMAN** May 3, 1974. Judy was divorced from Russell George Reimnitz. He married **GLADYS PERMANN MENZEL** September 18, 1993.

Russell was divorced from Judy Herman.

Russell George Reimnitz and Judy Herman had the following children:

  i. JAYCENT RUSSELL[4] was born April 15, 1976.

  ii. TAWYA ELLEN was born May 27, 1978.

  iii. KATRINA KAY was born September 18, 1979.

14. **KARIN LOUISE**[3] **REIMNITZ** (*Anita Alvina*[2] *Gemelke, Ernst Friedrich Wilhelm*[1]) was born in Parkston, South Dakota May 13, 1950.

She married **HOWARD MUELLER** December 19, 1970.

Karin Louise Reimnitz and Howard Mueller had the following children:

    i.   JEFFREY PAUL[4] was born October 24, 1974.
    ii. GREGG HOWARD was born March 23, 1977.
    iii. KERRY LOUISE was born February 27, 1979.
    iv. MELLISSA KAYE was born October 4, 1980.
    v. SCOTT PHILLIP was born September 23, 1983.
    vi. NICOLE ELAINE was born November 30, 1987.

15. **MARJEAN MARIE**[3] **REIMNITZ** (*Anita Alvina*[2] *Gemelke, Ernst Friedrich Wilhelm*[1]) was born in Parkston South Dakota July 30, 1951.

She married **VERN MATHIS** June 29, 1973. Vern was divorced from Marjean Marie Reimnitz.

Marjean was divorced from Vern Mathis.

Marjean Marie Reimnitz and Vern Mathis had the following children:

    i.   ANGELA JEAN[4] was born December 23, 1975. She married JERAMY PETERS July 26, 1997.
    ii. SHAWN ALVIN was born December 2, 1977.
    iii. MARIE KATHLEEN was born December 28, 1979.
    iv. APRIL LOUISE was born August 29, 1984.

16. **DOUGLAS PAUL**[3] **REIMNITZ** (*Anita Alvina*[2] *Gemelke, Ernst Friedrich Wilhelm*[1]) was born in Parkston South Dakota October 23, 1952.

He married **BONNIE JEAN KLUMB** October 10, 1975.

Douglas Paul Reimnitz and Bonnie Jean Klumb had the following children:

    i.   JOSEPH PAUL[4] was born October 12, 1979.
    ii. LEAH LOUISE was born May 18, 1982.
    iii. HANNAH JOY was born June 5, 1985.
    iv. JEDIDIA PAUL was born November 28, 1988.

17. **JOYCE ELAINE**[3] **REIMNITZ** (*Anita Alvina*[2] *Gemelke, Ernst Friedrich Wilhelm*[1]) was born in Parkston South Dakota July 1, 1955.

She married **IRA CURTIS VAN DRONGELAN** July 23, 1976.

Joyce Elaine Reimnitz and Ira Curtis Van Drongelan had the following children:

    i.   KRISTIE JOY[4] was born January 22, 1977.
    ii. STACIE LYNN was born September 13, 1978.

    iii. SPENCER PAUL was born August 18, 1980.
    iv. VICKIE LOUISE was born July 9, 1982.
    v. RACHEL EILEEN was born February 3, 1984.
    vi. CARLYLE LEE was born May 13, 1985.

18. DAVID ERNEST[3] REIMNITZ (*Anita Alvina[2] Gemelke, Ernst Friedrich Wilhelm[1]*) was born in Parkstor South Dakota April 21, 1957.

He married **JANE HOPPER** May 9, 1981.

David Ernest Reimnitz and Jane Hopper had the following children:

    i. AMBER DAWN[4] was born May 28, 1984.
    ii. ADAM was born November 8, 1987.

19. JAMES ROBERT[3] REIMNITZ (*Anita Alvina[2] Gemelke, Ernst Friedrich Wilhelm[1]*) was born in Parksto: South Dakota August 6, 1958.

He married twice. He married **KRISTY LOU ASTROM** September 4, 1982. Kristy was divorced from James Robert Reimnitz. He married **TAMERA KAY CALLIES** October 6, 1990.

James was divorced from Kristy Lou Astrom.

James Robert Reimnitz and Tamera Kay Callies had the following children:

    i. AHNNA[4] was born on (birth date unknown).

James Robert Reimnitz and Kristy Lou Astrom had the following children:

    ii. JUSTINE LOUISE was born January 28, 1983.
    iii. JOSLYN ROANA was born January 28, 1983.

James Robert Reimnitz and Tamera Kay Callies had the following children:

    iv. MEGAN DENISE was born January 16, 1992.

20. MARK DAVID[3] BRUEGGEMAN (*Viola Marie[2] Gemelke, Ernst Friedrich Wilhelm[1]*) was born in Norfolk, Nebraska April 28, 1959.

He married **SADIE LUCILLE YOUNG** in McAlester Oklahoma, January 14, 1989. Sadie's son by previous marriage (James Cioni)

Sadie was born in Antlers Oklahoma May 4, 1963.

Mark David Brueggeman and Sadie Lucille Young had the following children:

    i. SARAH MARIE[4] was born in McAlester, Oklahoma February 27, 1990.
    ii. LISA LYNN was born in Mcalester, Oklahoma April 24, 1991.

21. **COREEN ELIZABETH[3] BRUEGGEMAN** (*Viola Marie[2] Gemelke, Ernst Friedrich Wilhelm[1]*) was born in Norfolk, Nebraska July 22, 1960.

She married **JEFFERY CARNES** in Lincoln, Nebraska, May 4, 1985. Jeffery was born May 22, 1951. Jeffery was divorced from Coreen Elizabeth Brueggeman in Lincoln, Nebraska, 1996.

Coreen was divorced from Jeffery Carnes in Lincoln, Nebraska, 1996.

Coreen Elizabeth Brueggeman and Jeffery Carnes had the following child:

    i. EMILY MICHELLE[4] was born in Lincoln, Nebraska August 9, 1990.

Fourth Generation

22. **TRINA ELIZABETH⁴ GEMELKE** (*Robert Ernest³, Herbert Henry², Ernst Friedrich Wilhelm¹*) was born March 28, 1970.

She married **JAMES VINCENT SCHRADER** May 22, 1993.

Trina Elizabeth Gemelke and James Vincent Schrader had the following child:

     i. ELIZABETH RAE⁵ was born January 30, 1996.

23. **LISA MARIE⁴ SCHNEITER** (*Mary Cinda³ Gemelke, Herbert Henry², Ernst Friedrich Wilhelm¹*) was born July 21, 1968.

She married **TYE KLEEBERGER** in Rochester, Minnesota, April 6, 1991. Tye was born October 8, 1970.

Lisa Marie Schneiter and Tye Kleeberger had the following children:

     i. BRIANA LEE⁵ was born December 14, 1989.
    ii. CORY WILLIAMS was born October 21, 1991.

24. **RICHARD CHARLES⁴ SCHNEITER** (*Mary Cinda³ Gemelke, Herbert Henry², Ernst Friedrich Wilhelm¹*) was born July 26, 1970.

He married **DORATHEA COLSCH** in Rochester Minnesota, December 7, 1996. Dorathea was born February 19, 1973.

Richard Charles Schneiter and Dorathea Colsch had the following children:

     i. JESSICA ANN⁵ was born May 19, 1994.
    ii. CHARLES HERBERT was born September 19, 1997.
   iii. JAMES WILLIAM was born September 19, 1997. James died September 19, 1997 at less than one year of age.

25. **MICHAEL ANTONY[4] DU PRAS** (*Gloria[3] Vollmer, Gertrude Ella[2] Gemelke, Ernst Friedrich Wilhelm[1]*) was born in Sacramento, California April 25, 1966.

He married **CHRISTINA SCHESSLER** August 9, 1986.

Michael Antony Du Pras and Christina Schessler had the following children:

      i. MICHELLE[5] was born October 7, 1987.
     ii. DANIEL JOSEPH was born April 21, 1989.

26. **KRISTINE[4] GEMELKE** (*Duane Edward[3], Emil Gustave[2], Ernst Friedrich Wilhelm[1]*) was born in Hennepin County, Minnesota November 14, 1968.

She married **STEPHAN HANSON** in Brooklyn Park Minnesota, August 3, 1991. Stephan was born in Madison Wisconsin December 25, 1965.

Kristine Gemelke and Stephan Hanson had the following child:

      i. RYAN STEWART[5] was born in Madison Wisconsin June 30, 1995.

27. **TRISHA JO[4] MEYER** (*LaRayne[3] Gemelke, Emil Gustave[2], Ernst Friedrich Wilhelm[1]*) was born in West Point Nebraska August 8, 1969.

She married **WILLIAM LOMBARD** in Wayne, Nebraska, October 24, 1992.

Trisha Jo Meyer and William Lombard had the following child:

      i. TARA JO[5] was born May 25, 1994.

Gustav, fourth son and fifth child of Henry
and Sophie Gemelke

Born November 15, 1889, in Germany

Died, September 15, 1968,
at Pilger, Nebraska.

Emigrated to America in 1906

Married Marie Blume

The couple had three children

From left: Marvin, Oscar, Gustav, Marie and Shirley Gemelke

Gustav and sisters, Alvina Gemelke Leseburg, left, and Ella Gemelke Siemsglusz

Gustav H. Gemelke

Funeral services for Gustav H. Gemelke, 78, of Pilger, Nebraska, who died Sunday morning at a Norfolk hospital, were conducted Tuesday afternoon, September 17, 1968, at St. John's Lutheran Church in Pilger. The Rev. H. M. Roth officiated and burial was in the Pilger cemetery.

Anthems were sung by Wilfred Hasenkamp and Pastor Roth. Mrs. John Goeller was organist. Pallbearers were Merlin Hasenkamp, Norbert Husmann, Adolph Koehlmoos, William Koehlmoos, Henry Stuthman and Orville Tobias, all of Pilger.

Gustav H. Gemelke, son of Henry Gemelke and Sophie Jaeneke, was born November 15, 1889, in Hainhaus, Province Hanover, Germany, and died at a Norfolk hospital Sunday morning, September 15, 1968, having attained an age of 78 years and 10 months.

Mr. Gemelke was baptized and confirmed in the Lutheran Church in the town of his birth and adhered to the profession of this church throughout his life, being a faithful and charter member of St. John's Lutheran Church, Pilger, at the time of his death.

He was educated and grew to manhood in the town of his birth. In October of 1905, at the age of 16, he immigrated to America and located on a farm in Stanton County north of Pilger in March of 1906.

While living here he was united in marriage with Miss Marie Blume on June 25, 1925, the ceremony being performed in Armour, South Dakota. This union was blessed with two sons, Oscar and Marvin, and one daughter, Shirley. After their marriage they lived on a farm until June of 1957 when they retired to Pilger which has been their home ever since.

For the past five weeks, Mr. Gemelke had been confined in a Norfolk hospital after having been in failing health for the past several months. This illness proved to be his last.

Among those mourning his death are his wife, Marie Gemelke of Pilger; two sons, Oscar Gemelke and Marvin Gemelke, both of rural Wayne; one daughter, Shirley (Mrs. Wendell Willers) of Omaha; one sister, Ella (Mrs. Henry) Siemsglusz of Stanton.

Marie Gemelke

Funeral services for Marie Gemelke, 92, of Wisner and formerly of Pilger, were held Wednesday, June 6, 1984, at St. John's Lutheran Church in Pilger. The Rev. Michael Gruhn officiated with burial in the Pilger Cemetery.

Casketbearers were Terry Gemelke, Robert Nelson, Tim Schutz, James Willers, Steve Gemelke, Roger Willers, Dave Scott and Brian Willers.

Marie Dorathea Gemelke was born August 15, 1891, at Elgin, Illinois, to Adolph and Dorathea Dannenbrink Blume and died Sunday, June 3, 1984, at the Wayne hospital.

She married Gustave H. Gemelke on June 25, 1925, at Armour, South Dakota. The couple farmed north of Pilger until moving into town in the fall of 1957. Mr. Gemelke died in 1968. Mrs. Gemelke has resided at the Wisner Manor the past three years.

She is survived by two sons, Oscar and Marvin, both of Wayne, Nebraska; one daughter, Mrs. Wendell (Shirley) Willers of Omaha; ten grandchildren, 11 great-grandchildren; three sisters, Mrs. Dorothy Hawley and Mrs. Ervin (Regina) Grosz of Armour and Mrs. Louise Stredrusky of Lake Andes, South Dakota.

She was preceded in death by her husband, parents, seven brothers and four sisters.

Memories of Gustav and Marie

Marie was born in Elgin, Illinois. She started school there. At the age of nine years she moved with her family to a farm near Armour, South Dakota. She finished school which was near their home in Valley Township. She stayed at home, helping out till 1925. She met Gustav Gemelke in 1912 at the age of 18 years at both their Uncle Bill and Aunt Marie Blumes' home. They mostly corresponded at this time as they decided not to get married yet. They saw each other again about ten years later when they decided to get married. They had a family wedding. They made their home on a farm north of Pilger, Nebraska.

Their home was blessed with three children: Oscar Adolf Henry Gemelke, Marvin Herbert Gemelke and Shirley Marie Gemelke.

They moved into the town of Pilger in the fall of 1955. In 1956 they moved back out to their farm again and lived there for another year. They moved back to their home in town and Marie still is living there. At the age of 84 years she still does her own housekeeping. She attends regularly the Blume Family Reunion each year at the 4-H Building. This reunion is the first Sunday in August.

Her hobbies are handiwork. She likes to work in her garden. They both enjoyed playing cards and watching TV. They have ten grandchildren and two great-grandchildren.

Postscript: She surprised everyone when she had her two granddaughters drive her out to attend the silver anniversary of Ivan and Lena Bialas at the Pineview Hall on April 26, 1976. She looked magnificent. She enjoyed dancing with her brother Fredrick and others. She has a productive garden and does her own yard work and housekeeping. (*Blume family history book*)

Dad (Gustav) was only 16 when they came over and they left one brother behind. I know they lived in a house in Germany with livestock (Shirley {Gemelke} Willers)

Marie was born in Elgin, Illinois, and moved to South Dakota at the age of nine. She attended school in Valley township. She met Gustav H. Gemelke in 1912 at her Uncle Bill's house (Uncle Bill Blume was married to Gustav's aunt Marie (Gemelke) Blume. Marie decided to not marry Gustav in 1912 because he was hard of hearing and she was worried the loss of hearing would be passed on to their children. They saw each other again ten years later and they decided to marry. (Marvin Gemelke, written by his granddaughter Stacey {Nelson} Puett)

Gustav and Marie moved to a small farm north of Pilger, Nebraska. They had three children: two boys and one girl. In June of 1954, a tornado struck the Gemelkes' farm and destroyed a portion of the house including the pantry. They lived and worked on their farm from 1925 until 1955, when they moved into the town of Pilger. They continued to move between the farm and town for a few years. Gustav died in 1968 from kidney complication, so Marie made her home in Pilger. She continued to live on her own, doing her own housework, handiwork, and gardening for many years. Marie enjoyed attending the annual family reunion. She died at the ripe age of 92 years in 1984. (Marvin Gemelke, written by his granddaughter Stacey {Nelson} Puett)

One of the last times I saw Marie, she was headed to the home of Henry and Rosie Willers who lived across the street from the Methodist Church in Pilger. They were the parents of Wendell Willers. One of the grandsons had picked her up from her house across town on his motorcycle and she was riding on the back. I was a little afraid of Uncle Gustav as his voice sounded so gruff. Looking back, I'm sure it's was his German accent which I now love and wish I could hear from him once again. (LaRayne {Gemelke} Topp)

My aunt (Luetta Reuter) enjoyed dancing with Gustav. He would dance in circles, and then he would say, "Now we'll unwind." (LaRayne {Gemelke} Topp)

Contributed by Mark Brueggeman, June 15, 1998

9. **GUSTAVE HENRY[3] GEMELKE** (*Henry[2], (Father)[1]*) was born in Hanover Germany November 15, 1889. Gustave died September 15, 1968 at 78 years of age.

He married **MARIE BLUME** in Armour, South Dakota, June 25, 1925. Marie was born in Elgin, Illinois August 15, 1891. Marie died June 3, 1984 at 92 years of age.

He emigrated, 1906. Point of origin: pt of origin unknown.

Gustave Henry Gemelke and Marie Blume had the following children:

    i. OSCAR[4] was born in Pilger Nebraska August 5, 1926. He married JEANETTE KUMM March 21, 1945. Jeanette was born December 25, 1927.

    ii. MARVIN was born in Pilger Nebraska February 18, 1928. He married DARLENE ANN MEWIS January 17, 1954. Darlene was born March 11, 1929.

    iii. SHIRLEY was born in Pilger Nebraska January 26, 1933. She married WENDELL ARLEN WILLERS in Pilger Nebraska, August 27, 1950. Wendell was born in Pilger Nebraska April 17, 1927.

Second Generation

2. **OSCAR[2] GEMELKE** (*Gustave Henry[1]*) was born in Pilger Nebraska August 5, 1926. He married **JEANETTE KUMM** March 21, 1945. Jeanette was born December 25, 1927.

Oscar Gemelke and Jeanette Kumm had the following child:

    5   i. BEVERLY KAY[3] was born October 27, 1947.

3. **MARVIN[2] GEMELKE** (*Gustave Henry[1]*) was born in Pilger Nebraska February 18, 1928. He married **DARLENE ANN MEWIS** January 17, 1954. Darlene was born March 11, 1929.

Marvin Gemelke and Darlene Ann Mewis had the following children:

           i. TERRY LEE[3] was born November 27, 1954.
    6   ii. CONNIE SUE was born August 26, 1956.
    7   iii. BRENDA FAYE was born September 27, 1958.
    8   iv. STEVEN RAY was born October 18, 1961.

4. **SHIRLEY[2] GEMELKE** (*Gustave Henry[1]*) was born in Pilger Nebraska January 26, 1933. She married **WENDELL ARLEN WILLERS** in Pilger Nebraska, August 27, 1950. Wendell was born in Pilger Nebraska April 17, 1927.

Shirley Gemelke and Wendell Arlen Willers had the following children:

    9   i. LINDA SUE[3] was born June 23, 1951.
   10   ii. JAMES ARLEN was born October 4, 1952.
   11 iii. ROGER WENDELL was born October 25, 1953.
   12 iv. JAN MARIE was born September 27, 1956.
   13   v. BRIAN LEE was born April 4, 1958.

Third Generation

5. **BEVERLY KAY[3] GEMELKE** (*Oscar[2], Gustave Henry[1]*) was born October 27, 1947. She married **MACK (II) WAINWRIGHT** September 27, 1968.

Beverly Kay Gemelke and Mack (II) Wainwright had the following child:

    i. MACK (III)[4] was born October 6, 1969.

6. **CONNIE SUE[3] GEMELKE** (*Marvin[2], Gustave Henry[1]*) was born August 26, 1956.

She married **LAUREN JAY JOHNSON** May 2, 1987. Lauren had a son by previous marriage (Jeramiah Jay) 2-3-1980

Lauren was born March 28, 1959.

Connie Sue Gemelke and Lauren Jay Johnson had the following children:

    i. ASHLEY ANN[4] was born May 25, 1988.
    ii. TIFFANY RAE was born June 20, 1990.

7. **BRENDA FAYE[3] GEMELKE** (*Marvin[2], Gustave Henry[1]*) was born September 27, 1958. She married **BOB NELSON** October 27, 1979. Bob was born November 25, 1953.

Brenda Faye Gemelke and Bob Nelson had the following children:

    i. JENNIFER[4] was born December 24, 1980.
    ii. STACY was born April 1984.

8. **STEVEN RAY[3] GEMELKE** (*Marvin[2], Gustave Henry[1]*) was born October 18, 1961. He married **PAULA CLAUSSEN** August 31, 1991. Paula was born December 29, 1970.

Steven Ray Gemelke and Paula Claussen had the following child:

i. ZACHERY[4] was born August 22, 1995.

9. **LINDA SUE**[3] **WILLERS** (*Shirley*[2] *Gemelke*, *Gustave Henry*[1]) was born in Pilger Nebraska June 23, 1951.

She married **DAVID B. SCOTT** September 1, 1973. David was divorced from an unknown person January 1997. David was divorced from Linda Sue Willers January 1997.

Linda was divorced from David B. Scott January 1997.

Linda Sue Willers and David B. Scott had the following child:

i. WENDY RAE[4] was born July 17, 1976.

10. **JAMES ARLEN**[3] **WILLERS** (*Shirley*[2] *Gemelke*, *Gustave Henry*[1]) was born in Pilger Nebraska October 4 1952.

He married **ROBYN KUEHL** in Houston Texas, February 26,1983.

James Arlen Willers and Robyn Kuehl had the following children:

i. LOWELL[4] was born March 19, 1985.
ii. JARED was born November 15, 1986.

11. **ROGER WENDELL**[3] **WILLERS** (*Shirley*[2] *Gemelke*, *Gustave Henry*[1]) was born in Pilger Nebraska October 25, 1953.

He married **INDRA HAKK** in Moorhead Minn, July 15, 1978. Indra was divorced from Roger Wendell Willers 1988.

Roger was divorced from Indra Hakk 1988.

Roger Wendell Willers and Indra Hakk had the following children:

i. MICHAEL W[4] was born August 21, 1980.
ii. MATTHEW was born April 19, 1982.
iii. DANIEL was born April 23, 1984.

12. **JAN MARIE**[3] **WILLERS** (*Shirley*[2] *Gemelke*, *Gustave Henry*[1]) was born in Omaha, Nebraska September 27, 1956.

She married **TIMOTHY SCHUTZ** in Ralston, Nebraska, May 3, 1980.

Jan Marie Willers and Timothy Schutz had the following children:

i. ANDREW[4] was born October 16, 1982.
ii. SHEILA MARIE was born September 4, 1985.

13. **BRIAN LEE[3] WILLERS** (*Shirley[2] Gemelke, Gustave Henry[1]*) was born in Omaha Nebraska April 4, 1958.

He married **JANN SJOBERG** in Ralston, Nebraska, March 29, 1980.

Brian Lee Willers and Jann Sjoberg had the following children:

    i.   JUSTIN[4] was born September 30, 1980.
   ii.   SHANE was born June 4, 1982.
  iii.   JOSHUA was born xxxx 21,1984.
  iv.   MIRANDA was born May 7, 1990.

Ella Gemelke, second daughter and youngest child of Henry and Sophie Gemelke

Born July 11, 1893, in Hanover, Germany

Died November 26, 1981, at Stanton, Nebraska

Services at St. John's Evangelical Lutheran Church, Stanton, Saturday, November 28, 1981

Interment: Pilger Cemetery, Pilger, Nebraska

Emigrated to America in 1906

Married Henry Siemsglusz

The couple had one son

No photograph of Ella's family available

Sisters-in-law Louisa Koehlmoos Gemelke, left, and Ella Gemelke Siemsglusz

Ella Siemsglusz

Services for Ella Siemsglusz, 87, Stanton, will be at 2 p.m. Saturday, November 28, 1981, at St. John's Evangelical Lutheran Church. The Rev. William Bader will officiate with burial in the Pilger cemetery.

The daughter of Mr. and Mrs. Henry Gemelke was born July 11, 1893, at Germany and died Thursday at the Stanton Nursing Home.

Surviving are one son, Walter of Harrisburg, Illinois; two daughters, Mrs. Elsie Meyer of Eugene, Oregon, and Mrs. Mabel Conrad of Stanton; 14 grandchildren and several great-grandchildren.

She was preceded in death by her husband, two sons, four brothers and one sister.

Henry Siemsglusz

Henry August Siemsglusz, the son of Mr. and Mrs. Henry Siemsglusz, was born August 17, 1885, at Oerpe, Province Hanover, Germany, and departed this life Tuesday night, June 25, 1935, at the age of 49 years, ten months and eight days.

When but three years old he was brought to this country by his parents where they settled in their new home near Paulina, Iowa.

On April 3, 1908, he was confirmed in the Lutheran faith in the Zion Lutheran Church of Paulina, Iowa, later transferring his membership to St. John's Church at Pilger.

On December 12, 1909, he entered the estate of holy wedlock with Miss Frieda Gemelke. This union was blessed with five children, one of whom preceded him in death in infancy. On November 17, 1920, his wife passed away. He was married to Miss Ella Gemelke on May 18, 1922. One son was born to this union.

The deceased moved from Iowa to Pilger in April 1923 where he was in business until about two years ago. His health started to fail about the first of this year and he gradually got worse until a few days ago when he was taken to a Norfolk hospital for a major operation which he underwent successfully. Soon after, his condition became worse and he passed quietly away Tuesday evening, surrounded by his family.

He leaves to mourn his passing his loving wife, three sons, Alvin of Norfolk and Walter and Werner of Pilger; two daughters, Mrs. Elsie Meyer and Mrs. Mabel Rabbass of Wisner; his aged father-in-law Herman Gemelke; one sister, Mrs. Sophie Proehl of Paulina, Iowa; one brother, Otto Siemsglusz of Bingham Lake, Minnesota; besides a host of other relatives and friends.

Funeral services were held from St. John's Lutheran Church, preceded by a short service at the family home, with the Rev. Walter H. Koenig in charge. Burial was made in the Pilger cemetery.

Pallbearers were Earl Schlecht, Paul Siecke Jr., Ed Hasenkamp, Herman Ritze, Otto Thies and Jess Waite.

Sincere sympathy is extended the relatives in their bereavement.

Those from out-of-town attending the funeral were Mrs. Emma Gemelke of Bushnell, Mrs. Sophie Proehl, Mrs. Emma Imwicke, Wm. Proehl, Henry Proehl, Mrs. Rosa Hager and Albert and Edwin Hager of Paulina, Iowa, Mr. and Mrs. Henry Westphal of Primghar, Iowa, Mr. and Mrs. August Jolas of Sutherland, Iowa, Mrs. Mary Krumm of Lake Park, Minnesota, Mr. and Mrs. Otto Siemsglusz and son, Edward, and Mrs. Reinhardt Schuknecht of Bingham Lake, Minnesota, Mrs. Wm. Blume, Mrs. Louie Blume and Adolph Blume of Armour, South Dakota, Mr. and Mrs. Henry Prien and Wm. A. Blume of Parkston, South Dakota.

In 1922 Henry Siemsglusz opened a pool hall in a former doctor's building. He later moved to a block building, purchasing it in 1927. *Pilger, Nebraska, Centennial Edition, 1887-1987*

June 15, 1998 – Contributed by Mark Brueggeman

Second Generation

2. **WERNER² SIEMSGLUSZ** (*Ella¹ Gemelke*) was born in Pilger Nebraska January 31, 1924. Werner died February 3, 1977 at 53 years of age.

He married **NAOMI BROOKS** in Stanton Nebraska, June 18, 1945. Naomi was born June 30, 1925.

Werner Siemsglusz and Naomi Brooks had the following children:

    i.   MICHAEL³ was born June 23, 1946. He married KATHY FARNER.
   ii.   DIANE was born December 22, 1951. She married ROBERT WOLF.
  iii.   KIM was born June 14, 1954. He married JOLENE BROWN.

Martin Lehman

Services for Martin Lehman, 85, of Stanton, will be at 2 p.m. Friday at St. John's Evangelical Lutheran Church. The Rev. P. William Bader will officiate. Burial will be in the Stanton Cemetery. He died Tuesday at a Norfolk hospital (1986).

He was born December 4, 1900, in Stanton County, the son of Frederick and Martha (Biehle) Lehman. He attended District 21 School. In 1914 he was confirmed at St. John's Lutheran Church. He and Inez Napier were married June 2, 1929, at Firth. She died May 23, 1979.

Survivors include three daughters, Mrs. Milburn (Leona) Schurtleff of Fairbury, Mrs. Lawrence (Helen) Johnsen of Elmwood and Mrs. Larry (Marlene) Waller of Ewing, 10 grandchildren and 13 great-grandchildren.

Besides his wife, he was preceded in death by his parents, four brothers and three sisters.

> Note: I think this is how the story goes: Martin's wife went to the hospital for an extended stay and Ella Siemsglusz took care of his daughters and house. I believe she was widowed at that time. Once the daughters grew up and moved away, Aunt Ella stayed. Whenever Aunt Ella came to any family gatherings, Martin brought her. I never saw one without the other. I asked my dad once (Emil Gemelke) if she was his housekeeper or his girlfriend. He said he wondered the same thing himself. (LaRayne {Gemelke} Topp)

Note: Aunt Ella was my favorite aunt. She was the only one we really knew. She would have us over to Martin Lehmans. (Millie {Gemelke} Janulewicz)

Note: This may be the home Henry and Sophie Gemelke lived in when they came to America. I believe they lived and farmed on land immediately north of the Pilger Cemetery. It came to be known as the Stuthman farm. The house was later moved and turned to face the opposite direction on the farm directly south of the Cemetery. (LaRayne {Gemelke} Topp) Notice the little girl with the dog and another sitting in a stroller.

Below, seated from the left: Irene Leseburg on lap of Sophie Gemelke, Gus Leseburg on ground, Herb Gemelke on lap of Henry Gemelke, unidentified but possibly Gustav Gemelke, Ella Gemelke, Erna Leseburg; back row from the left: Ernst and Louisa Gemelke, Alvina and Gustave Leseburg.

Sophie Gemelke with grandchildren, from the left: Erna Leseburg, Herbert Gemelke on her lap, Gustave and Irene Leseburg

Death in my memory is of my Grandfather Gemelke's last days. We were all gathered together and the doctor was going to give Grandpa a hypo to ease the pain. (This was at the Ella Siemsglusz home in Pilger.) He got scared and went to the neighbor screaming for help. His screaming and begging for help I'll never forget. (Emil Gemelke)

Pilger Cemetery, north section, bottom third

Taking another step back.....

Looking at Ernst Gemelke's ancestry

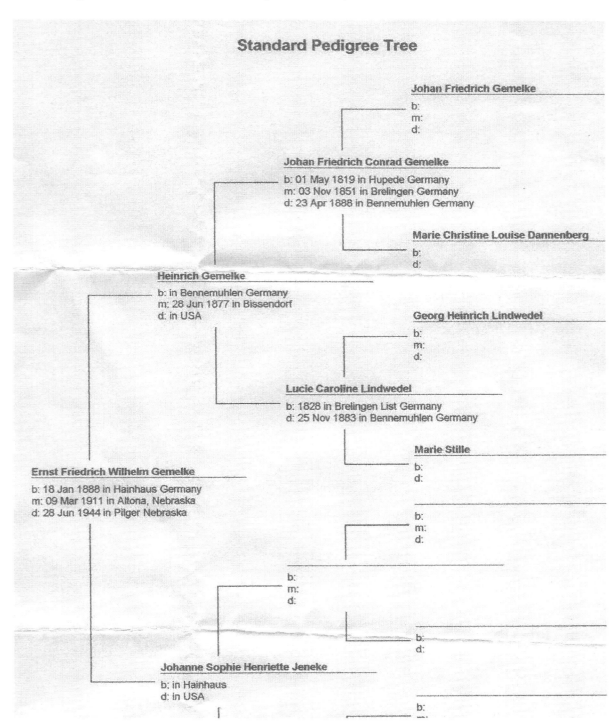

Standard Pedigree Tree

Johan Friedrich Gemelke
b:
m:
d:

Johan Friedrich Conrad Gemelke
b: 01 May 1819 in Hupede Germany
m: 03 Nov 1851 in Brelingen Germany
d: 23 Apr 1888 in Bennemuhlen Germany

Marie Christine Louise Dannenberg
b:
d:

Heinrich Gemelke
b: in Bennemuhlen Germany
m: 28 Jun 1877 in Bissendorf
d: in USA

Georg Heinrich Lindwedel
b:
m:
d:

Lucie Caroline Lindwedel
b: 1828 in Brelingen List Germany
d: 25 Nov 1883 in Bennemuhlen Germany

Marie Stille
b:
d:

Ernst Friedrich Wilhelm Gemelke
b: 18 Jan 1888 in Hainhaus Germany
m: 09 Mar 1911 in Altona, Nebraska
d: 28 Jun 1944 in Pilger Nebraska

b:
m:
d:

b:
m:
d:

b:
d:

Johanne Sophie Henriette Jeneke
b: in Hainhaus
d: in USA

b:

Henry Gemelke had two siblings: Herman and Maria. Herman and Maria came to America first, sometime before 1895 (exact date not known). Maria married William Blume and Herman married Dorathea Blume, William's sister. According to the Viola and Mark Brueggeman history, both couples settled in South Dakota.

Henry Gemelke Dies Saturday from *The Stanton Register*, Stanton Nebraska

Henry Gemelke was born December 16, 1851, at Brelingen Province Hanover, Germany. He was baptized and confirmed in the Lutheran faith. On June 29th, 1877, he was united in marriage to Miss Sophia Jaeneke. To this union six children were born, four sons and two daughters: Alvine, Herman, Frederick, Ernest, Gustav and Ella.

On October 27th, 1905, he, with his wife and two youngest children came to America, and on March 1, 1906, started farming on a farm near Pilger, where he lived until death claimed him on Saturday, October 19th, at the age of 77 years, ten months and three days.

He retired from active farming in 1922 and since that time has made his home with his son, Gustav.

He was preceded in death by his wife in July 1921 and his son Herman in 1913.

Mr. Gemelke has been afflicted with heart trouble for the past several years.

He was a firm believer in the Lutheran faith, being one of the founders of the St. John's Lutheran congregation that is now established in Pilger.

He leaves to mourn his death, three sons and two daughters: Ernst and Gustav of Pilger, Frederick of Solton, Germany, Mrs. Ella Siemsglusz of Pilger, and Mrs. Alvine Leseberg of Canyon, Texas; four daughters-in-law, two sons-in-law, 14 grandchildren, three great-grandchildren, one brother, Herman Gemelke of Paullina, Iowa, and a sister, Mrs. Marie Blume of Armour, South Dakota, and a number of other relatives.

The Rev. J. H. Tegler conducted the funeral services Tuesday afternoon at 1:00 o'clock at the farm home and at 2:00 o'clock in the church.

Burial took place in the Pilger cemetery.

Herman and Dorathea Gemelke Henry's brother and wife (Contributed, writer unknown)

Herman was born on February 3, 1863, at Brelingen in Hanover Province, Germany. Herman is the son of Friederick Gemelke. His mother's first name is not known. Her last name was Lindwedel. In March of 1863 he was baptized and later instructed in the Lutheran Faith.

In May of 1886 at the age of 23, he came to the United States and made his home in Elgin, Illinois. I think he farmed at this time. Herman was the first Gemelke to come over. He *may* have come over after his wife-to-be.

In 1887 he married Dorathea (Dreta) Blume. She was born Maria Dorathea Wilhelmine Blume on September 30, 1860, at Nopke; that is a village near Hanover, Germany. Dorathea is the daughter of Deitrich Blume and Louise Heine. She came to the United States in 1885 with her whole family.

They had two sons and two daughters. One daughter died in infancy. 1. Louis Friederick Deitrich (after his two grandfathers) 2. Frieda and 3. Herman Mickel.

In 1895 Herman (Henry's brother) sent money to his nephew Herman (Ernst's brother) in Germany to come to the United States. Later the rest of his brother's family and his brother Henry came over.

Dorathea died September 6, 1897; she was almost 37 years old. After she died he moved to Nebraska in 1903 with his nephew and his son Louis. Herman's niece and her husband had moved to Wisner, Nebraska, the year before.

In 1914 Herman moved to Paullina, Iowa, where his daughter Frieda lived with her husband. He stayed there until Frieda died in 192. He then moved back to Pilger in 1930 where he made his home with his son-in-law, Henry Siemsglusz. When Henry died in 1935, Herman lived with his granddaughter until his death in 1938.

> Note: Dad (Emil) said his parents spoke often of a Herman Mickel; he didn't know why he was called that. Cousins Herman (Henry's son), Herman Mickel (Henry's brother Herman's son) and Pete Andersen (father of Lester {Dane} Andersen) ran steam engines pulling plows that broke sod around the area. (LaRayne {Gemelke} Topp)

Louis and Ruby Gemelke Henry's nephew and wife

Louis Fredrick Dedrick Gemelke was born on September 16, 1888, (or 9-16-1887), in Elgin, Illinois (or North Platte, Illinois). He is the son of Herman Gemelke and Dorathea Blume. His middle names are from his two grandfathers' first names. Sometime after his mother died, Louis moved to Nebraska, 1903, with his father. There they farmed and owned and ran a threshing machine and steam engine. They had a big crew and thrashed around Pilger, Nebraska.

On November 2, 1910, in Stanton, Louis married Ruby Wood. Ruby is the daughter of Andrew Jackson Wood and Ida Mae Kratz. She was born on August 2, 1890, in Idaho.

They had ten children and lived on different farms around Pilger. On February 1, 1932, Louis had a heart attack and died at the age of 44.

Ruby stayed in Nebraska after Louis died. She worked for sick people keeping house. In 1939, she moved to Minnesota. The rest of her family lived by Russell. This is where she lived the rest of her life. Ruby died on May 29, 1945, in the University Hospital in Minneapolis.

Francis and Dorothy Demuth

Francis was born on a farm north of Russell, Minnesota, on January 25, 1921, to Paul and Louise Demuth. He started farming on the family farm and continued to after his father retired to Marshall, Minnesota.

On May 28, 1941, Francis was married to Dorothy Gemelke, a daughter of Louis and Ruby (Wood) Gemelke of Stanton, Nebraska. Dorothy was born on September 24, 1920.

They had seven children: Mary (Krull) is a teacher in St. Louis, Missouri; Larry is farming north of Russell; Shirley (Sienko) does office work in Minneapolis; Mick lives in Gary, South Dakota, and drives truck; Randy lives by Lynd and works for Minnesota Electric; Ronald farms by Russell; and Patrick is an electrical lineman in Worthington, Minnesota.

Francis passed away on August 11, 1986, at the age of 65. He is buried in the Calvary Cemetery in Marshall. Dorothy now lives in the village of Russell.

Frieda and Henry Siemsglusz Henry's niece and her husband and also (later) his son-in-law

Frieda was born December 24, 1890, in Plato Center, Illinois. She was the daughter of Herman and Dorathea Gemelke. She was seven years old when her mother died. She spent the following years with her relatives in South Dakota.

When Frieda was 19 she married Henry Siemsglusz in a country church in O'Brien County, Iowa, on December 12, 1909. Her brother Louis Gemelke was a witness for her.

Henry Siemsglusz was born in Hanover Germany on August 17, 1885, to Henry and Kathryn Siemsglusz. He was 23 when he married Frieda. Henry and Frieda farmed in O'Brien County, Iowa. Henry had a sister and her family living in that area. They had four children: Alvin, Elsie, Walter and Mabel.

When Frieda was 30 years old she became ill. On November 11, 1920, she died at her home of pneumonia. She is buried at the Paullina, Iowa, cemetery. There is no stone for her that I can find.

Henry remarried a cousin of Frieda's. On May 18, 1922, Henry married Ella Gemelke in Pilger, Nebraska. He had one child, Werner, with Ella. At this time he sold farm implements in Pilger. On June 25, 1935, Henry passed away. He is buried in Pilger.

Herman Gemelke (brother of Henry)

Funeral services were held Saturday afternoon at 1:30 from St. John's Lutheran Church, Pilger, for Herman Gemelke, who passed away Wednesday evening. The Rev. W. H. Koenig was in charge of the services. Burial was made in the Pilger cemetery.

Herman Gemelke, the youngest son of Mr. and Mrs. Friedrich Gemelke, was born February 6, 1963, at Brelingen, Province Hanover, Germany. In March of the same year he was baptized and in due course, was instructed and confirmed in the Lutheran faith.

In May 1886 he came to this country and made his home at Elgin, Illinois. In 1887 he was united in marriage to Dorathea Blume. To this union were born four children, two sons Louis and Herman and two daughters, Elsie and Frieda. His wife and children all preceded him in death, his wife in 1893.

He came to Nebraska in 1903, and since 1911 made his home with his daughter, Frieda. In 1914 he moved to Paullina, Iowa, and in 1930 returned to Pilger where he made his home with a son-in-law, Henry Siemsglusz, and after the death of the latter, with his granddaughter, Mrs. Elsie Meyer.

Mr. Gemelke had been in failing health for the past five years, although was able to be up and around. His last illness came upon him Tuesday, June 21, 1938, and Wednesday evening he entered his eternal home. He attained the age of 75 years, four months and 20 days.

He leaves to mourn his passing 19 grandchildren, four great-grandchildren, two daughters-in-law, one sister, Mrs. Marie Blume of Armour, South Dakota, and a host of other relatives and friends.

Pallbearers were Wm. and John Dohren, Otto Thies, Herman Frevert, Henry Koehlmoos and E.C. Krueger.

Louisa Koehlmoos
family

Front row, from the left: Heinrich Koehlmoos, Henry, Louisa, Maria; back row: Wilhelmina (Minnie), Herman, Frederick, Dorothea (Dora). Not pictured: Carolina (Lena), Maria and Sophia who died as infants, and youngest daughter Sophie. Perhaps this was taken after the death of Carolina which took place in 1901.

*Heinrich Koehlmoos, born June 10, 1849, in Hanover Germany. Died February 18, 1919, age 69 years, eight months, eight days

*Maria Mindemann, born March 1, 1849, in Mecklenburg, Germany. Died December 11, 1917, age 68 years, nine months, ten days

*Married in Cook County, Illinois, at Coopers Grove

* According to Louisa (Koehlmoos) Gemelke information to follow

The chart on following page was written by Louisa (Koehlmoos) Gemelke. Various websites such as Ancestry.com show varying information, some of it inaccurate. I believe this is the only accurate record, written by Louisa Koehlmoos who knew firsthand the family members involved. Louisa does not list Sophie, possibly because she was the daughter of Minnie, raised by Heinrich and Sophia. Grandma (Louisa) said it was confusing to her when she was young because her father would say, "Louisa is the youngest," but then there was Sophie. (LaRayne {Gemelke} Topp)

your
Grand father

Heinrich Koehlmoos
Born June 10, 1849
in Hanover
Germany
Died Feb 18, 1919
age 69 yrs 8 mos 8 days
your Grandmother

Maria Mindeman
Koehlmoos
Born Mar 1, 1849
in Mecklenburg
Germany
Died Dec 11, 1917
age 68 yrs 9 mos 10 days

They were married
in
Cook Co Ill
at Corpus Grove.

Fred Koehlmoos was born Nov 11, 1871, married Apr 3, 1902
born at Corpus Kris Kll
died Apr 6 1945

Herman Koehlmoos was born May 19, 1873 at Corpus
Grove, Cook Co. Ill, Died Jan 12, 1931

Carolina Koehlmoos Vosforman Died in 1901

Maria Koehlmoos died in infancy about 1 week

Sophia Koehlmoos died in infancy about 2 weeks

Maria Koehlmoos died in infancy about 1 week

Wilhelmina Koehlmoos Lewis born Mar 17
1881 married Feb 27, 1908, Died Dec 16, 1966

Dorothea Koehlmoos Stuhlman born May 10, 1883
married Feb 14, 1902

Henry Koehlmoos born Mar 7 1886
married Sept 8 1910

Louisa Koehlmoos Gemelke born Feb 20 1888
married March 9 1911

Marie Auguste Sophie Friederike Mindemann

Information from Ancestry.com, listed by Sheila (Race) Stuthman

Marie was born on March 1, 1849, in Schulenberg, Großherzogtum Mecklenburg Schwerin, Germany.

She was baptized on March 4, 1849, at Marlow, Mecklenburg, Deutschland.

Her parents are Johann Joachim Christian Mindemann, 1805 to 1885, and Wilhelmina Sophia Friederike Buckholdt, born in 1807. Death date unknown.

She arrived in America at age 19 in 1868, and was married in 1870 at age 21 to Johann Heinrich "Henry" Koehlmoos, 1849 to 1918.

At age 21 she resided at Coopers Grove in Cook County, Illinois. Her oldest children were born in Coopers Grove. In March of 1886, when Maria was 37, her youngest son Henry was born near Pilger, Nebraska, so the family had moved by that time.

All about Louisa Gemelke's parents by Louisa Gemelke

(The following article was written by Louisa Gemelke about her parents, Heinrich and Maria (Mindemann) Koehlmoos. Seven of their children were born at Cooper's Grove, Illinois. The five living when they moved to Pilger were Lena Woockman, Fred Koehlmoos, Sr., Herman Koehlmoos, Dora Stuthman and Minnie Daum.

Two more were born after moving to Pilger. They were Henry Koehlmoos Sr. and Louis Gemelke. Arrival in Pilger—approximately 1884 or 1884. My parents both came from Germany and settled in Cook County, Illinois, where they met and married. They had seven children and worked on many different farms. They wanted to start on their own so they homesteaded near Boone, Iowa. Somebody stole his stake, so having no proof that the stake was stolen, they went on to my father's cousin at Wisner, Nebraska. They had five children then, two had passed away. We all first lived in a granary while he was building a one-room house on a place he bought for a very low price. That place is now the Adolph Koehlmoos farm.

I remember one time Mother ran out of flour so Father went into the store for flour. Flour had gone up a dime that week, and Father did not have that extra dime. So he went on back home. My mother insisted that she needed the flour so he went to his cousin's and borrowed a dime, then back to the store, which had just closed. The storekeeper, recognizing him from being there before, opened up and gave him the flour so he did not have to go empty handed again. So you can see people in those days had very little money and had to get by on what they had.

My mother was a very determined woman—after the house was completed, we still did not have a well close to the house. She had to go quite a ways to the creek to get water which was a quarter of a mile away. Every evening she would take her pails and walk to the spring. She always heard dogs barking in the distance but when she found out they were wolves or coyotes, she made up her mind to have a well close to the house. She put on a pair of Father's overalls and started digging. After she came to water, Father took over and they had their first well. They had two wooden buckets with an arch over the top of the well with a wheel; when you could draw up the first bucket the empty one went down. Worked real well.

After they got on their feet they had cattle, hogs, chickens and also corn, wheat and oats. We always had a huge, big garden and canned lots of vegetables for the winter. Father always took enough wheat over to West Point to have it milled; that would last six months. Mother also made molasses, put cabbage into sauerkraut, also did beans the same way, in a salt brine. Beets, carrots, turnips and parsnips were put in a deep box in the cellar and covered with dry dirt or sand for the winter. Mother would dry apples and then use them in the wintertime in sauce with raisins, or put a handful in our school lunches or put into coffee cake.

We always butchered the middle of January. They would do two hogs one day and a beef the next. The women would always have to clean the casings yet that same day for sausage. Father would cut up the beef that was to be used for dried beef otherwise Mother would get the hams and bacon ready. They would be put down in a heavy salt brine and left for six weeks, then put in the smokehouse where they were smoked until they were nice and brown. Then they would be put in cloth sacks and wrapped in paper and stored in the oats bin. The sausage would be filled and also hung in the smokehouse, then packed in lard in stone jars and kept in the cellar. All the rest of the meat was canned and would usually last a year.

* * *

Following are Heinrich's naturalization papers. Note: Heinrich spells his last name Kohlmoos without the "e," and that he is 57 at the date of his naturalization. Early records at First Trinity Lutheran Church at Altona list family members' surnames as Kohlmoos. Heinrich states that he is a native of Prussia and renounces the King of Prussia. Prussia was a German state originated in 1525 with a duchy, a territory ruled by a duke or a duchess. The Duchy of Prussia was elevated to the Kingdom of Prussia in 1701. It is not to be confused with Russia.

FINAL NATURALIZATION RECORD,

Perkins Bros. Co., Printers and Binders, Sioux City, Iowa.

THE UNITED STATES OF AMERICA.

THE STATE OF NEBRASKA, } ss. **STANTON COUNTY,** . EIGHTH JUDICIAL DISTRICT OF NEBRASKA.

In the Matter of the Application of _Heinrich Kohlmoos_ _a native of_ _Prussia_ *to become a Citizen of THE UNITED STATES OF AMERICA.*

Be it Remembered, That on this _10th_ day of _September_, A. D. 1906, the same being the _1st_ judicial day of the regular _September_ A. D. 1906, term of the District Court of the State of Nebraska, within and for the County of _Stanton_ the Honorable _Guy T. Graves_, Judge, presiding, the following proceedings were had, to-wit:

There personally appears one _Heinrich Kohlmoos_ a native of _Prussia_, and now a resident of _Stanton_ County, in the State of Nebraska, and makes his application in open court to be naturalized and made a citizen and subject of THE UNITED STATES OF AMERICA. And, in support of such application for admission to citizenship, he presents and files herein the affidavits of himself, and of _Albert Pilger_ and _Adam Pilger_ his witnesses, duly made and executed in manner and form as required by law, and which affidavits are at this time duly and properly recorded and made a part of the record in this proceedings, the following being the full, complete, and correct record thereof, viz.:

AFFIDAVIT AND OATH OF APPLICANT.

THE STATE OF NEBRASKA, Stanton County, ss.

I, _Heinrich Kohlmoos_, heretofore a subject of _The King_ of _Prussia_, being duly sworn, do on my oath depose and say that I was born in _Molthof Amt Hoya Hanover_, in _Germany_ on or about the _8_ day of _June_, A. D. 1848, and came to the United States on or about the _1st_ day of _May_, A. D. 1868; that I do now, and have continuously, resided within the limits and under the jurisdiction of THE UNITED STATES OF AMERICA, since the _1st_ day of _May_, A. D. 1868, and within the State of Nebraska for more than one year last past, and that I now reside in_____, in the County of _Stanton_, and am by occupation a _Farmer_.

That heretofore, on the _8th_ day of _April_, A. D. 1899, I made my declaration under oath, in manner and form as provided by Section 2165 of the Revised Statutes of the United States, before _Louis Smithberger_, Clerk of the District Court of _Stanton County, Neb._ the same being a Court of Record having common law jurisdiction, and a seal and Clerk, that it was bona fide my intention to become a Citizen of THE UNITED STATES OF AMERICA, and to renounce forever all allegiance and fidelity to every foreign power, prince, potentate, state or sovereignty whatsoever, and particularly to _The King_ of _Prussia_, of _whom_ I was then a subject, the record of which declaration is herewith presented and submitted to the Court.

And I do further, on my oath, depose and say, that during the entire period of my residence within the United States as aforesaid I have behaved and deported myself as a man of good moral character, and that I am attached to the principles of the Constitution of the United States, and well-disposed to the good order, happiness, and prosperity of the same; that I do not disbelieve in, and am not opposed to, all organized government; that I am not, and have not been, a member of, or affiliated or otherwise connected with, any society or other organization entertaining and teaching such disbelief in or opposition to all organized government; that I do not believe in, advocate, or teach the duty, necessity, or propriety of the unlawful assaulting or killing of any officer or officers, either of specific individuals or of officers generally, of the Government of THE UNITED STATES OF AMERICA, or of any other organized government, because of his or their official character; that I have not violated any of the provisions of the Act of the Congress of THE UNITED STATES OF AMERICA, entitled "An Act to Regulate the Immigration of Aliens Into the United States," approved March 3rd, A. D. 1903, and that I have in all respects complied with the terms and provisions of the Statutes of the United States on the subject of naturalization.

And I do further solemnly swear and declare on oath that I will support the Constitution of THE UNITED STATES OF AMERICA and that I absolutely and entirely renounce and abjure forever all allegiance and fidelity to every foreign power, prince, potentate, state or sovereignty whatsoever, and particularly to _the King_ of _Prussia_ of _whom_ I was a subject; and that I have not borne any hereditary title or been of any order of nobility in the _Kingdom_ from which I came.

Heinrich Kohlmoos

Sworn to before me and in my presence subscribed by the said _Heinrich Kohlmoos_ this _10th_ day of _September_ A. D. 1906.

W. J. McFarland
Clerk of the District Court.

JUDGMENT AND ORDER OF NATURALIZATION.

THE UNITED STATES OF AMERICA.

THE STATE OF NEBRASKA, } ss. **EIGHTH JUDICIAL DISTRICT OF NEBRASKA.**
STANTON COUNTY.

In the Matter of the Application of _Heinrich Kohlmoos_ _____ a native of
Prussia _____ to become a Citizen of THE UNITED STATES OF AMERICA.

Now, on this _11th_ day of _September_ A. D. 1906, it being the _2d_ day of the regular _September_ A. D. 1906, term of the District Court of the State of Nebraska within and for _Stanton_ County, the same being a court of record, having common law jurisdiction and a seal and clerk, the application of _____ _Heinrich Kohlmoos_, a native of _Prussia_ _____, to be naturalized and made a citizen of THE UNITED STATES OF AMERICA, came on for hearing in open court before the Honorable _Guy T. Graves_, Judge, presiding, the applicant appearing in person with his witnesses, _Albert Pilger_ and _Adam Pilger_ _____.

And thereupon evidence in support of said application is introduced, and the affidavits of the applicant and his witnesses, _Albert Pilger_ and _Adam Pilger_, reciting and affirming the truth of every material fact requisite for naturalization, are duly made and recorded and presented in evidence herein, and the oral testimony of said applicant and witnesses is also taken and heard in open court.

And thereupon the Court, after considering the evidence, and inspecting the affidavits and the record herein, and being fully advised in the premises, finds that the said _Heinrich Kohlmoos_ _____, being a native of _Prussia_, and now of the age of _57_ years, has continuously resided within the limits and under the jurisdiction of THE UNITED STATES OF AMERICA for more than five years next preceding this date, and that he is now and has been for more than one year last past a resident of the State of Nebraska; that the said _Heinrich Kohlmoos_ _____ does not disbelieve in and is not opposed to, all organized government; that he is not and has not been a member of or affiliated or connected with any society, or organization entertaining and teaching such disbelief in, or opposition to all organized government; that he does not believe in, advocate, or teach the duty, necessity, or the propriety of the unlawful assaulting or killing of any officer or officers, either of specific individuals or officers generally, of the Government of the United States, or of any other organized government, because of his or their official character; and that he has not violated any of the provisions of the Act of the Congress of THE UNITED STATES OF AMERICA, approved March 3rd, 1903, entitled, "An Act to Regulate the Immigration of Aliens Into the United States."

And the Court further finds from the evidence herein that during the entire period of his residence within the United States as aforesaid the said _Heinrich Kohlmoos_ _____ has behaved and deported himself as a man of good moral character, and that he is attached to the principles of the Constitution of THE UNITED STATES OF AMERICA, and well disposed to the good order, happiness, and prosperity of the same; that heretofore, on the _8th_ day of _April_ _____, A. D. 1891, he made and filed his declaration under oath, before the clerk of a court of record having common law jurisdiction and a seal and clerk, that it was bona fide his intention to become a citizen of THE UNITED STATES OF AMERICA and to renounce forever all allegiance and fidelity to every foreign power, prince, potentate, state, or sovereignty whatsoever, and particularly to _The King_ _____, of _Prussia_ _____, of _whom_ _____, he was then a subject, in manner and form as required by Section 2165 of the Revised Statutes of the United States; that all the provisions of the Statutes of the United States with relation to the naturalization of aliens have been fully and in every respect complied with; that each and every material fact necessary or requisite for naturalization has been fully established and proven to the satisfaction of the Court, and that said applicant is entitled to be naturalized and admitted and made a citizen and subject of THE UNITED STATES OF AMERICA, upon taking the required oath of allegiance. _Heinrich Kohlmoos_ _____ being duly sworn, at this time declares on oath in open court that he will support the Constitution of THE UNITED STATES OF AMERICA, and that he absolutely and entirely renounces and abjures all allegiance and fidelity to every foreign power, prince, potentate, state, or sovereignty whatsoever, and particularly to _The King_ _____, of _Prussia_ _____, of _whom_ _____ he was heretofore a subject.

IT IS, THEREFORE, Ordered and adjudged by the Court that the said _Heinrich Kohlmoos_ _____ be, and he is hereby, naturalized and made and constituted a citizen and subject of

THE UNITED STATES OF AMERICA,

with all the rights, privileges, and immunities of such citizenship, as guaranteed by the Constitution and Laws of THE UNITED STATES OF AMERICA, and charged with all the duties and obligations imposed thereby. And the Clerk is hereby directed to issue to said _Heinrich Kohlmoos_ _____, under the seal of this court, a proper certificate of naturalization, in accordance with this judgment and order.

By the Court: _Guy T. Graves_ _____, Judge.

Attest: _H. F. McFarLand_ _____, Clerk.

Heinrich Koehlmoos (at this time he spells his name with the "e") purchased a farm from Hans Ronck and Maggie Ronck, husband and wife for $13,760, by assuming a mortgage from the Northwestern Mutual Life Insurance Company of Milwaukee, Wisconsin. The 160-acre farm is located in the South West Quarter of Section 15, Township 24, Range 3, East of the Sixth Principal Meridian. The deed was transferred from Hans Bonck and wife to Heinrich Koehlmoos only (it does not include Maria), filed February 22, 1910.

Note: Louisa wrote about the family first living in the granary before the house was built. The house is the building surrounded by trees and a white houseyard fence pictured a little right of center (follow the sidewalk up from the vehicle); the granary is the building just to the left of center, on the left or west side of the driveway. This granary may be the building in which the family lived when initially moving to Nebraska. (LaRayne {Gemelke} Topp)

Note: From what I remember my mom saying, our kitchen and the room above are the original home place, and the rest of the house was added on (bathroom, bedrooms, dining/living room, porch. (Franki {Koehlmoos} Parde)

**Heinrich and Maria Koehlmoos home in winter
at the time it was lived in by the Adolph and Lorraine Koehlmoos family**

Note: Kevin Meyer found information in a research of courthouse records of the following farms being "sold" to Heinrich and Maria's children "in consideration of one dollar" by Heinrich Koehlmoos, widower, all on April 23, 1918. My dad (Emil) always said the payment was one dollar plus love and affection. This list may not be all inclusive. (LaRayne {Gemelke} Topp)

332 - Henry Koehlmoos Jr.: 160 acres, more or less, North half of the South West Quarter of Section 10, township 24, North of Range Three, East of the 6th P.M.

333 - Herman Koehlmoos: 160 acres, North West Quarter of Section 12, township 24, North of Range Three, East of the 6th P. M.

334 - Louisa Gemelke: 160 acres, South West Quarter of Section 15, Township 24, North of Range Three, East of the 6th P. M.

335 - Fred Koehlmoos: 80 acres, more or less, North half of the North East Quarter of Section 23, Township 24, North of Range Three, East of the 6th P.M.

336 - Minnie Daum: 160 acres, more or less, North West Quarter of Section 24, township 24, North of Range Three, East of the 6th P. M.

337 - Sophia Koehlmoos: 80 acres, North half of the South East Quarter of Section 27, Township 24, North of Range three, East of the 6th P. M.

338 - Dora Stuthman: 160 acres, North East Quarter of Section 27, Township 24, North of Range three, East of the 6th P.M.

Note: A number of these farm have large, four-square houses on them. I was told that some of the children received a house and a barn along with the farm from their father Heinrich. My grandma Louisa wanted a furnace so she paid to have that installed herself. Her father thought it was unnecessary, but when he was older and stayed with each of his kids, in the winter he stayed with Louisa because she had a furnace. (LaRayne {Gemelke} Topp)

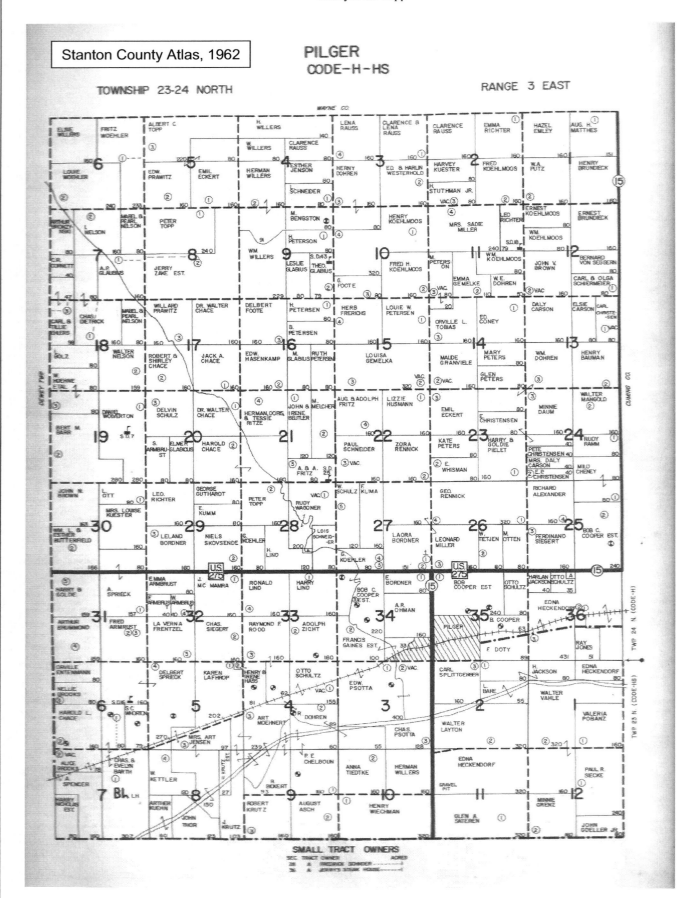

Stanton County Atlas, 1962

PILGER
CODE-H-HS

TOWNSHIP 23-24 NORTH

RANGE 3 EAST

SMALL TRACT OWNERS

Burial expenses for Heinrich Koehlmoos

In Account with *Ernest Gemelke* Dr.

Mar	2	Paid to Axen & Orris	$		
		in payment of burial			
		expense as per Stmt	245	75	

STATEMENT OF ACCOUNT OF

M *John H. Koehlmoos.*

Funeral Charges

WITH

THE PILGER FURNITURE STORE

Carl Axen, Proprietor.

PILGER, NEBRASKA, *3/2* 1918

Jan 21	1 Casket	160	00	
	Burial Robe	25	00	
	Embalming Body	25	00	
	Carriage (1 Auto Trip)	5	00	
	Hearse	15	00	$
	Flowers	15	00	
	Telephone Charges		25	
	Express on Flowers		50	
	total	245	75	

*Received Payment in full
from Ernst Gemelke
March 2nd 1918.*

*Axen & Orris
(by C Axen)*

st duly sworn, on oath

...ehlmoos

& $\frac{75}{100}$ Dollars,

...rial Exp

says th...

decease...

is just...

on the...

Sw...

e; and the amount of

...eon and unpaid.

Subscribed in my presence and sworn to before me this _17_ day of _Apr_ A. D. 1918

Notary Public.

MY COMMISSION EXPIRES OCT. 4m, 1923.

93

Burial of Heinrich and Maria (Mindemann) Koehlmoos at
First Trinity Lutheran Church Cemetery, Altona, Nebraska

Louisa (Koehlmoos) Gemelke's written account states that Heinrich Koehlmoos was born June 10, 1849, and died February 18, 1919, and that Sophia was born March 1, 1849, and died December 11, 1917. Records of First Trinity Lutheran Church, Altona, show that Maria's death was in 1916, and Henry's was in 1918. Courthouse records show that in April 1918, Henry was a widower when he transferred land to his children.

Louisa Koehlmoos Siblings

Frederick Carl Koehlmoos

Born November 11, 1871
at Coopers Grove, Illinois

Farmer

Married Louise Sophia Luehrman
April 3, 1902
First Trinity Lutheran Church,
Altona, Nebraska

The couple had six children

Died, June 4, 1945
at Pilger, Nebraska

Children:
Anna Marie Katharine
Bertha Emma
Emma
William (died as infant)
Lena
Norma (died as infant)
Hulda Dorothea
Fred Jr.

Fred and Louise Koehlmoos by Fred and Verona Koehlmoos, 1987, *Pilger, Nebraska, Century Edition, 1887-1987*

The Koehlmoos family came to America from Vechold, Germany. They settled in Cook County, Illinois (what is now Chicago). This is where Fred Sr. was born November 11, 1871. His parents were Henry and Maria (Mindemann) Koehlmoos. His education was only in the winter time, therefore, he only finished the third grade.

They moved to a farm north of Pilger in 1884. This is the farm where LeRoy Koehlmoos' family is now living. They were members of First Trinity Lutheran Church of Altona.

They were married on April 3, 1902, at First Trinity. They started their married life on the farm where William Koehlmoos now lives. They purchased a farm one mile north of there in July of 1913 and moved there. They built a new home and moved into it in late 1916. This is where they raised their six children (five daughters and one son).

They moved the old house to their other farm. It has been added to and remodeled, but it is still in use.

In 1936, Cooper and Chase took the International dealership in Pilger. They received a train-car load of tractors that they planned to auction off at their grand opening. Fred bought the first tractor they sold in Pilger that day for $500.

A hair-raising experienced took place in 1936, also. It was a hot, late August afternoon. Fred was filling the gas tank of his Buick in the home garage. At the same time he attempted to light his ever-present pipe; needless to say, it was a disaster. The Buick and the garage went up in flames. The Chevy sedan was miraculously saved and there were no bodily injuries.

Fred operated one of the first steam engine threshing machines in this area. He was a lover of horses and bought and raised quite a few. Most of the farming, at that time, was done with horse power so he used them all.

Louise was an efficient gardener and raised all their vegetables and fruits and preserved them for the family's use. She also raised many chickens, ducks and geese in addition to her other household duties.

Louise died December 1934. Fred died June 4, 1945.

Children, from the left: Fred Jr., Anna and Bertha. Not pictured: Emma, Lena and Hulda.

Descendants of Herman Koehlmoos (father of Heinrich) by Donald W. Adams

.... 3 Frederick Carl Koehlmoos b: November 11, 1871 in Cook County, Illinois d: June 4, 1945 in Wayne, Nebraska Number of children: 8
.... +Louisa Luehrman b: July 5, 1874 m: April 3, 1902 in Wayne County, Nebraska d: December 19, 1934 in Pilger, Nebraska Number of children: 8
.... 4 Anna Koehlmoos b: February 13, 1903 in Stanton County, Nebraska d: July 21, 1983 Number of children: 3
.... +Otto Mohfeld b: October 14, 1899 in Hanover, Germany m: March 1, 1933 in Wayne County, Nebraska d: April 10, 1899 in Omaha, Nebraska Number of children: 3
.... 5 Betty Ann Mohfeld b: March 22, 1934 in Stanton County, Nebraska Number of children: 2
.... +Carl Henshaw m: August 16, 1962 in Stanton County, Nebraska Number of children: 2
.... 6 Carol Ann Henshaw b: October 12, 1964
.... 6 Beth Laura Henshaw b: December 27, 1969
.... 5 Alvin Mohfeld b: April 30, 1937 in Stanton County, Nebraska Number of children: 4
.... +Eileen Wilhelm b: December 17, 1936 in Cuming County, Nebraska m: July 8, 1961 in Cuming County, Nebraska Number of children: 4
.... 6 Clark Otto Mohfeld b: May 7, 1962 Number of children: 1
.... +Connie Kratky Number of children: 1
.... 7 Brandon Clark Mohfeld b: October 2, 1990
.... 6 Scott Alvin Mohfeld b: September 26, 1963
.... 6 Judith Faye Mohfeld b: October 16, 1965
.... +Lyle Wayne Whitworth m: October 3, 1987
.... 6 Keith George Mohfeld b: June 21, 1968
.... 5 Harvey Mohfeld b: January 27, 1940 in Stanton County, Nebraska Number of children: 2
.... +Bonnie Fields m: August 25, 1963 in Wayne, Nebraska Number of children: 2
.... 6 Michael Gene Mohfeld b: August 16, 1965
.... 6 Kathy Irene Mohfeld b: May 31, 1968
.... 4 Bertha Emma Koehlmoos b: November 5, 1904 in Stanton County, Nebraska d: January 1959 in Wayne, Nebraska Number of children: 3
.... +Emil Schultz m: February 16, 1931 d: May 7, 1969 in Wayne, Nebraska Number of children: 3
.... 5 LeRoy Emil Schultz b: April 5, 1933 d: November 9, 1953
.... 5 Evelyn Maria Schultz b: November 1934 in November 1934
.... 5 Ellen Janelle Schultz b: January 28, 1938 Number of children: 2
.... +Larry Hofeldt m: March 29, 1959 in Wayne, Nebraska Number of children: 2
.... 6 Renae Hofeldt b: January 29, 1960
.... 6 David Larry Hofeldt b: August 26, 1961
.... 4 Emma Koehlmoos b: January 26, 1908 in Stanton County, Nebraska d: August 13, 1982 in Norfolk, Nebraska Number of children: 4
.... +Leo Richter b: September 6, 1904 in New Wells, Missouri m: February 7, 1937 in Stanton County, Nebraska d: December 26, 1977 in Norfolk, Nebraska Number of children: 4
.... 5 Marilyn Joanne Richter b: March 8, 1938 Number of children: 6
.... +Robert H. Claus b: July 22, 1931 m: June 30, 1957 in Wayne County, Nebraska Number of children: 6
.... 6 David Claus b: July 3, 1958
.... 6 Douglas Lee Claus b: June 20, 1959
.... 6 Darrel Dean Claus b: June 18, 1961
.... 6 Diane MariLynn Claus b: June 22, 1963
.... +Bruce D. Jacobson m: April 20, 1991
.... 6 Daniel Wayne Claus b: July 3, 1971
.... 6 Debra Sue Claus b: February 4, 1977
.... 5 Lois Elaine Richter b: July 23, 1939 Number of children: 4
.... +Grant Kalbfleisch m: June 6, 1959 in Wayne County, Nebraska Number of children: 4
.... 6 James Grant Kalbfleisch b: July 15, 1961
.... 6 John Irl Kalbfleisch b: March 6, 1965
.... +Linda Ann Skogen m: May 19, 1989
.... 6 July Marie Kalbfleisch b: November 26, 1972 d: December 14, 1972
.... 6 Jason Paul Kalbfleisch b: January 30, 1974
.... 5 Geraldine Richter b: May 26, 1942 Number of children: 2
.... +DALE YOUNG m: June 20, 1960 d: September 12, 1980 Number of children: 2
.... 6 Dale Allen Young b: April 15, 1961
.... 6 Jeffrey Boyd Young b: June 1, 1962 Number of children: 1
.... +Kim Rule m: August 20, 1983 Number of children: 1
.... 7 Nicholas Dale Young b: February 22, 1988
.... 5 Shirley Faye Richter b: December 7, 1944 Number of children: 2
.... +GARY McGILL b: February 2, 1943 m: March 23, 1964 Number of children: 2
.... 6 Robin Dee McGill b: November 10, 1964
.... 6 Troy Dale McGill b: April 25, 1968
.... 4 William Koehlmoos b: April 28, 1910 d: June 8, 1910
.... 4 Lena Koehlmoos b: May 9, 1911 in Stanton County, Nebraska Number of children: 2
.... +Clarence Rauss b: July 30, 1910 in Farrar, Missouri m: February 7, 1937 in Stanton County, Nebraska Number of children: 2
.... 5 Merlyn D. Rauss b: June 2, 1944 Number of children: 7
.... +Linda Zobel Bwens m: April 13, 1968 in Council Bluffs, Iowa
.... *2nd Wife of Merlyn D. Rauss:
.... +Barbara Long m: May 21, 1972 Number of children: 6

.... 6 Carrie Long
.... 6 Kevin Long
.... 6 Sandra Long
.... 6 Joy Long
.... 6 Holly Long
.... 6 Bernadette Rauss b: June 11, 1973 d: June 13, 1973
.... *3rd Wife of Merlyn D. Rauss:
.... +Nancy (Peterson) Von Seggern m: April 30, 1982 in Yankton, South Dakota Number of children: 1
.... 6 Natalie Blaine Rauss b: January 18, 1984
.... 5 Lynell Darlene Rauss b: June 24, 1946 d: May 26, 1963
. 4 Norma Koehlmoos b: June 17, 1913 d: September 13, 1913
. 4 Hulda Dorothea Koehlmoos b: July 29, 1914 in Stanton County, Nebraska Number of children: 5
..... +Raymond Elmer Kumm b: September 6, 1913 in Cuming County, Nebraska m: June 20, 1938 Number of children: 5
.... 5 Lorene Louise Kumm b: January 19, 1939 Number of children: 4
.... +Marvin Lee Belgum b: March 3, 1933 in Scottsbluff, Nebraska m: June 6, 1957 Number of children: 4
.... 6 Micke Belgum b: March 19, 1960 Number of children: 1
.... +Sherry Wylie m: June 7, 1979 Number of children: 1
.... 7 Sherrie Wylie Belgum b: June 7, 1980
.... 6 Mark Belgum b: December 21, 1963
.... 6 Matthew Belgum b: February 27, 1964
.... 6 Lisa Belgum b: December 20, 1969
.... 5 Joyce Jean Kumm b: December 7, 1940 Number of children: 2
.... +Frederick Charles Ash b: February 9, 1935 m: December 29, 1957 Number of children: 2
.... 6 James Matthew Ash b: August 25, 1958
.... +Betty Jean Brooke m: 1977
.... 6 Joen Elizabeth Ash b: June 29, 1960
.... +Brooke
.... 5 Janice May Kumm b: January 10, 1943 Number of children: 3
.... +Charles Jess Collins b: August 7, 1942 m: June 1, 1962 Number of children: 3
.... 6 Steven Charles Collins b: December 7, 1963
.... +Jackie Waline m: 1982
.... 6 Ronnie Ray Collins b: January 29, 1966
.... 6 Jeana Collins b: November 22, 1968
.... 5 Melvin Ray Kumm b: June 21, 1946 Number of children: 2
.... +Patricia Dedlow Number of children: 2
.... 6 Amy Kumm b: August 23, 1972
.... 6 Ryan Ray Kumm b: February 14, 1976
.... 5 Marlin Vernell Kumm b: July 1, 1948 Number of children: 3
.... +JoAnne Sessler m: October 25, 1976 in Gering, Nebraska Number of children: 1
.... 6 Timothy David Kumm b: April 1, 1977
.... *2nd Wife of Marlin Vernell Kumm:
.... +Karen Kilpatrick m: November 14, 1980 Number of children: 1
.... 6 Justin Jay Kumm b: June 9, 1981
.... *3rd Wife of Marlin Vernell Kumm:
.... +Karen Kilpatrick m: November 14, 1980 Number of children: 1
.... 6 Justin Jay Kumm b: June 9, 1981
. 4 Fred Koehlmoos b: January 28, 1917 in Stanton County, Nebraska d: December 5, 1988 Number of children: 4
..... +Verona Kumm b: December 4, 1920 in Cuming County, Nebraska m: February 20, 1938 in Wayne County, Nebraska Number of children: 4
....: 5 Kenneth Frederick Koehlmoos b: July 7, 1941 Number of children: 2
.... +Barbara Stuthman b: September 18, 1940 m: May 28, 1961 in Wayne County, Nebraska Number of children: 2
.... 6 Dawn Marie Koehlmoos b: December 11, 1963
.... 6 Beth Ann Koehlmoos b: February 5, 1965 Number of children: 1 — 2
.... +Jeffrey Alan Young m: November 2, 1984 Number of children: 1 2
.... 7 Zachary Alan Young b: February 20, 1988
.... 5 Larry LeRoy Koehlmoos b: April 21, 1944 Number of children: 2
.... +Karen Lee Ann Oetken b: November 28, 1944 m: February 23, 1964 in Emerson, Nebraska Number of children: 2
.... 6 Randall LeRoy Koehlmoos b: June 2, 1965
.... 6 Steve William Koehlmoos b: April 20, 1968 Number of children: 1
.... +Shelly Pety m: March 11, 1989 Number of children: 1
.... 7 Jonathan Steven Koehlmoos b: June 26, 1989
.... 5 Mary Ann Koehlmoos b: September 21, 1946 Number of children: 3
.... +Ronald Wemhoff b: May 5, 1942 m: August 2, 1969 Number of children: 3
.... 6 Anthony Robert Wemhoff b: July 20, 1970
.... 6 Lori Marie Wemhoff b: November 9, 1971
.... 6 Kevin LeRoy Wemhoff b: November 30, 1973
.... 5 Mardell Jolene Koehlmoos b: June 9, 1950 Number of children: 2
.... +Robert Hendren m: October 15, 1969
.... *2nd Husband of Mardell Jolene Koehlmoos:
.... +James L. Kropp b: December 11, 1946 m: October 3, 1970 in Norfolk, Nebraska Number of children: 2
.... 6 Renae Lynn Kropp b: May 1, 1971
.... 6 Brian James Kropp b: March 4, 1972

Herman Phillip Carl August Koehlmoos

Born May 10, 1873
at Coopers Grove, Illinois

Farmer

Married Annie Marie (Mary)
Duesterbach

The couple had five children

Died, January 12, 1931,
at Norfolk, Nebraska

Buried at Wayne, Nebraska

Wedding of Herman Koehlmoos
and Annie Marie (Mary)
Duesterbach

May 7, 1914

Obituary Mary (Herman) Koehlmoos

Funeral services were conducted August 14, 1966, at St. John's Lutheran Church in Pilger for Mrs. Mary Koehlmoos, 81.

Pastor H. M. Roth was in charge. Burial was in the Trinity Lutheran Cemetery at Altona, south of Wayne. Pallbearers were Fred Koehlmoos, Adolph Koehlmoos, Henry Stuthman Jr., Otto Daum, Emil Gemelke and Emil Rieck.

Annie Marie Koehlmoos, daughter of Mr. and Mrs. Carl Duesterbach, was born in Kingsbury County, South Dakota, February 23, 1885. She died August 11, 1966, at the Pierce Manor Nursing Home.

Mrs. Koehlmoos was baptized and later on was confirmed in the Lutheran Church.

On May, 7, 1914, she married Herman Koehlmoos of Pilger. They had three sons and two daughters.
After their marriage they located on a farm north of Pilger in Stanton County. This was her home for the rest of her life. In January, 1931, her husband died.

In recent years she was stricken with an illness which caused her to be a shut-in.

She leaves her five children, August, Wisner; Ernest, DeSmet, South Dakota; and William, Pilger; Edna Koehlmoos, Pilger; and Elsie (Mrs. Delbert Nathan), Randolph; three brothers, Willie Duesterbach, August Duesterbach and John Duesterbach, all of Lake Norden, South Dakota; one sister, Mrs. Tena Rieck, Estelline, South Dakota; and six grandchildren.

She was preceded in death by her parents and one sister.

Herman Koehlmoos obituary unavailable

Descendants of Herman Koehlmoos (father of Heinrich) by Donald W. Adams

3 Herman Phillip Karl August Koehlmoos b: May 10, 1873 in Cook County, Illinois d: January 12, 1931 in Norfolk, Nebraska Number of children: 5
.... +Anna Marie Tena Duesterback b: February 23, 1885 in Kingsbury County, South Dakota m: May 27, 1914 in Wayne County, Nebraska d: August 11, 196
  Nebraska Number of children: 5
.... 4 August Henry Frederick Koehlmoos b: October 31, 1915 in Stanton County, Nebraska Number of children: 1
.... +Lena Bertha Caroline Heller b: February 3, 1918 in Cuming County, Nebraska m: February 15, 1951 in Cuming County, Nebraska Number of child
.... 5 Lyla Marie Koehlmoos b: September 8, 1956
.... 4 Ernest Henry George Koehlmoos b: November 11, 1917 in Stanton County, Nebraska Number of children: 3
.... +Lydia Minnie Stolpe b: February 3, 1928 in Kingsbury County, South Dakota m: September 14, 1958 in Kingsbury County, South Dakota Number
.... 5 Norman Ernest Koehlmoos b: August 12, 1963 Number of children: 1
.... +Julaine Kriesel m: July 7, 1984 Number of children: 1
.... 6 Melanie Koehlmoos b: September 22, 1987
.... 5 LeRoy Herman Koehlmoos b: September 14, 1965
.... 5 Karen Bertha Koehlmoos b: September 20, 1966
.... 4 Edna Minnie Koehlmoos b: October 30, 1919 in Stanton County, Nebraska
.... 4 William Henry Koehlmoos b: November 1, 1921 in Stanton County, Nebraska
.... 4 Elsie Lizzie Louise Koehlmoos b: January 26, 1925 in Stanton County, Nebraska Number of children: 3
.... +Delbert Carl Nathan b: August 27, 1923 in Rural Lindsay, Nebraska m: October 4, 1953 in Pilger, Nebraska Number of children: 3
.... 5 Terry Lee Nathan b: March 12, 1955 in Norfolk, Nebraska Number of children: 7
.... +Kathy Rice b: December 8, 1954 m: August 15, 1975 in Osmond, Nebraska Number of children: 2
.... 6 Chad James Nathan b: January 22, 1979
.... 6 Gregory Lee Nathan b: January 18, 1985
.... *2nd Wife of Terry Lee Nathan:
.... +Kerry Weber Mattson m: July 26, 1980 Number of children: 1
.... 6 Adam Carl Nathan b: June 12, 1981
.... *3rd Wife of Terry Lee Nathan:
.... +Kerry (Weber) Mattson m: July 26, 1980 Number of children: 4
.... 6 Cory Mattson
.... 6 Heather Mattson
.... 6 Adam Carl Nathan b: June 12, 1981
.... 6 Gregory Lee Nathan b: January 18, 1985
.... 5 Randy Lynn Nathan b: March 26, 1957
.... 5 Cindy Sue Nathan b: March 21, 1958

Carolina (Lena)

Born March 15, 1875, at Coopers Grove, Illinois

Married to Adolph Ferdinand Woockman

Housewife

Died May 18, 1901, at age 26 plus three days

No photograph available

Records from First Trinity Lutheran Church, Altona, list the couple's marriage date as 1900. No written record is given of Lena's death, even though she is buried in the church cemetery.

Note: Carolina died after falling in a hay rake. The horses spooked and drug her, inside the rake, for a ways. She was pregnant at the time, and married only a year. I was told by someone in the family that it was such a tender funeral, with Lena holding the little baby in her arms. I asked my Grandmother Louisa (Lena's sister) and she said this was not so. The baby was born dead and in pieces, she said. Lena is buried alone at the First Trinity Lutheran Church Cemetery at Altona. (LaRayne {Gemelke} Topp)

The typical early horse-drawn hay rake was a dump rake, a wide two-wheeled implement with curved steel or iron teeth usually operated from a seat mounted over the rake with a lever-operated lifting mechanism. This rake gathered cut hay into windrows by repeated operation perpendicular to the windrow, requiring the operator to raise the rake, turn around and drop the teeth to rake back and forth in order to form the windrow. In some areas, a sweep rake, which could also be a horse-drawn or tractor-mounted implement, could then be used to pick up the windrowed hay and load it onto a wagon. *Wikipedia*

Descendants of Herman Koehlmoos (father of Heinrich) by Donald W. Adams

.... 3 Carolina (Lena) Koehlmoos b: March 15, 1875 d: May 18, 1867
.... +Adolph Ferdinand Woockmann b: September 13, 1867 in Wesselburen, Hoostin, Germany m: May 1900

Adolph died February 8, 1951, in Norfolk, Nebraska. His second wife was Anna Maria (Mary) Reuter

Note: This death date is incorrect in *Descendants of Herman Koehlmoos*. The death date on her gravestone is 1901. First Trinity Lutheran Church records show the death of Wiebke Woockmann and Marie Woockmann in 1901.

Lena listed on 1900 Census

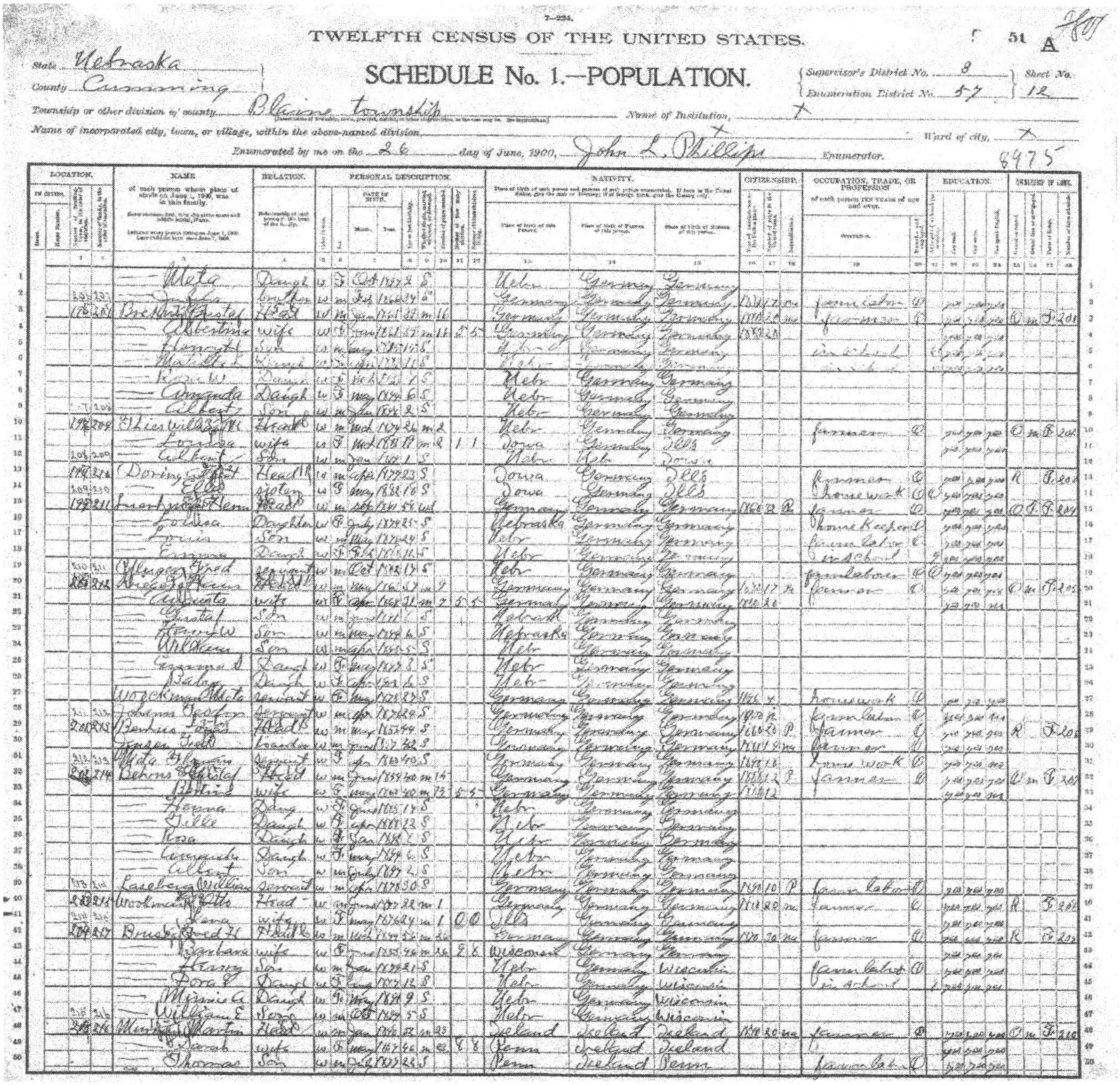

TWELFTH CENSUS OF THE UNITED STATES.

SCHEDULE No. 1.—POPULATION.

State: Nebraska. County: Cumming. Township or other division of county: Blaine township. Name of Institution: x. Name of incorporated city, town, or village, within the above-named division: Ward of city: x. Supervisor's District No. 3. Enumeration District No. 57. Sheet No. 12. 51 A.

Enumerated by me on the 26 day of June, 1900, John L. Phillips, Enumerator.

Line	Dwelling	Family	Name	Relation	Color	Sex	Month	Year	Age	Marital	Yrs married	Children born	Living	Birthplace	Father	Mother	Occupation
1			— Meta	Daugh	w	F	Oct	1897	2	S				Nebr	Germany	Germany	
2	201	202	— Julius	brother	w	m	Feb	1866	34	S				Germany	Germany	Germany	farm labor
3	176	203	Brechmann? Gustaf	Head	w	m	Jan	1861	39	m	16			Germany	Germany	Germany	farmer
4			— Albertina	wife	w	F	Jan	1861	39	m	16	5	5	Germany	Germany	Germany	
5			— Henry H	Son	w	m	May	1885	15	S				Nebr	Germany	Germany	in school
6			— Mathilda	Daugh	w	F	Apr	1888	11	S				Nebr	Germany	Germany	in school
7			— Rosa W	Daugh	w	F	Feb	1893	7	S				Nebr	Germany	Germany	
8			— Amanda	Daugh	w	F	May	1894	6	S				Nebr	Germany	Germany	
9		208	— Albert	Son	w	m	Jan	1898	2	S				Nebr	Germany	Germany	
10	198	209	Ellies William	Head	w	m	Mch	1874	26	m	2			Nebr	Germany	Germany	farmer
11			— Louisa	wife	w	F	Mch	1880	19	m	2	1	1	Iowa	Germany	Ills	
12	208	200	— Albert	Son	w	m	Jan	1899	1	S				Nebr	Nebr	Iowa	
13	199	210	Doring Alfred	Head	w	m	Apr	1877	23	S				Iowa	Germany	Ills	farmer
14	209	210	— Ella	sister	w	F	May	1882	18	S				Iowa	Germany	Ills	housework
15	199	211	Lienhard? Henry	Head	w	m	Sep	1841	58	wd				Germany	Germany	Germany	farmer
16			— Louisa	Daughter	w	F	July	1874	25	S				Nebraska	Germany	Germany	housekeeper
17			— Louis	Son	w	m	May	1876	24	S				Nebr	Germany	Germany	farm labor
18			— Emma	Daugh	w	F	Feb	1888	12	S				Nebr	Germany	Germany	in school
19	210	211	Ulmzen? Fred	servant	w	m	Oct	1882	17	S				Nebr	Germany	Germany	farm laborer
20	200	212	Kriege? Hans	Head	w	m	May	1863	37	m	9			Germany	Germany	Germany	farmer
21			— Augusta	wife	w	F	Apr	1868	31	m	7	5	5	Germany	Germany	Germany	
22			— Gustaf	Son	w	m	Jan	1891	7	S				Nebrask	Germany	Germany	
23			— Henry W	Son	w	m	May	1894	6	S				Nebraska	Germany	Germany	
24			— William	Son	w	m	Apr	1895	5	S				Nebr	Germany	Germany	
25			— Emma S	Daugh	w	F	May	1897	3	S				Nebr	Germany	Germany	
26			— Baby	Daugh	w	F	Apr	1900	[illegible]	S				Nebr	Germany	Germany	
27			Woeckmann? Meta	servant	w	F	May	1878	23	S				Germany	Germany	Germany	housework
28	211	212	Johannes Joseph	servant	w	m	Apr	1876	24	S				Germany	Germany	Germany	farm labor
29	200	213	Bartels Louis	Head	w	m	May	1855	44	S				Germany	Germany	Germany	farmer
30			Jaeger Fred	boarder	w	m	June	1857	42	S				Germany	Germany	Germany	farmer
31	212	213	Meta Hermann	servant	w	F	Apr	1860	40	S				Germany	Germany	Germany	housework
32	201	214	Behrns Gustaf	Head	w	m	June	1859	40	m	14			Germany	Germany	Germany	farmer
33			— Bertina	wife	w	F	May	1860	40	m	13	5	5	Germany	Germany	Germany	
34			— Henna	Daug	w	F	June	1883	17	S				Nebr	Germany	Germany	
35			— Tille	Daugh	w	F	Apr	1888	12	S				Nebr	Germany	Germany	
36			— Rosa	Daugh	w	F	Jan	1888	8	S				Nebr	Germany	Germany	
37			— Amanda	Daugh	w	F	May	1894	6	S				Nebr	Germany	Germany	
38			— Albert	Son	w	m	July	1897	2	S				Nebr	Germany	Germany	
39	213	214	Laseberg William	servant	w	m	Apr	1878	20	S				Germany	Germany	Germany	farm labor
40	203	215	Woolmann? Otto	Head	w	m	June	1877	22	m	1			Germany	Germany	Germany	farmer
41	214	215	— Lena	wife	w	F	May	1876	24	m	1	0	0	Ills	Germany	Germany	
42	204	217	Brush? Fred H	Head	w	m	Mch	1844	56	m	26			Germany	Germany	Germany	farmer
43			— Barbara	wife	w	F	June	1855	46	m	26	8	8	Wisconsin	Germany	Germany	
44			— Henry	Son	w	m	Jan	1879	21	S				Nebr	Germany	Wisconsin	farm labor
45			— Dora E	Daugh	w	F	Aug	1887	12	S				Nebr	Germany	Wisconsin	in school
46			— Minnie A	Daugh	w	F	May	1891	9	S				Nebr	Germany	Wisconsin	
47	215	216	— William E	Son	w	m	Oct	1894	5	S				Nebr	Germany	Wisconsin	
48	205	216	Murphy? Martin	Head	w	m	Jan	1848	52	m	23			Ireland	Ireland	Ireland	farmer
49			— Sarah	wife	w	F	May	1867	46	m	23	8	8	Penn	Ireland	Ireland	
50			— Thomas	Son	w	m	July	1877	22	S				Penn	Ireland	Penn	farm labor

Maria
Born at Coopers Grove,
Illinois
Died in infancy
about two weeks

Sophia
Born at Coopers Grove,
Illinois
Died in infancy,
about one week

*Maria Caroline Wilhelmine, 05-01-1877 to 05-13-1877

*Sophia, 12-02-1878 to 12-08-1878

*(Ancestry.com)

Wilhelmina – Minnie

Born March 17, 1881,

at Coopers Grove, Illinois

Married February 27, 1908

Housewife

Died December 16, 1966

Wedding day, February 27, 1908 George
Daum and Minnie (Koehlmoos)
Back row, from the left: Lizzie
(Dahlkoetter) Koehlmoos, Henry
Koehlmoos, Leonard Kamp and Louisa
(Koehlmoos) Gemelke

George and Minnie Daum family, April 1921. Front row, from the left: George Jr., George Sr. holding William, Ed, Minnie, Otto and Hildegard; back row: Amanda holding Amelia. Elmer not pictured.

George and Minnie Daum family, 1943. Front row, from the left: Minnie, Elmer, George; back row: William, Amanda, Hildegard, Otto, Amelia and Ed. George Jr. not pictured

Wilhelmina (Minnie) (George) Daum

Funeral services were conducted December 19, 1966, at St. John's Lutheran Church, Pilger, for Mrs. Minnie Daum, 85.

The Rev. H. M. Roth was in charge of the last rites and burial was in the family lot of the Pilger Cemetery.

Anthems were sung by the Ladies Choir of the Church, accompanied by Miss Trudi Pilger at the organ.

Pallbearers were Larry Daum of Walthill; Eldon Grashorn, Norfolk; Burnell Dreyer, Wisner; Michael Daum, Paullina, Iowa; Dennis Daum, Stanton; and Daryl Daum, Pilger.

Minnie Daum, daughter of Henry and Maria (Mindemann) Koehlmoos was born March 17, 1881, at Coopers Grove, Cook County, Illinois, and died December 16, 1966, at the Wayne, Nebraska, hospital. Her age was 85 years, eight months and 30 days.

Mrs. Daum was baptized and confirmed in the Lutheran faith. In 1884 she moved with her parents to a farm north of Pilger.

> ### Cpl. George Daum
>
> Cpl. George H. Daum (Jr.) was in a jeep accident in October during World War II which injured his knee and ankle. In his letter to his mother he stated: "I am feeling just fine. The weather in England was pretty nice but in Germany it was snowing when I left December 22." Cpl. Daum spent New Year's Day aboard ship en route to England. He was with General Patton's Third Army.

On February 27, 1908, she married George Daum at Trinity Lutheran Church, Altona. The ceremony was performed by the late Pastor F. Schaller. Mr. and Mrs. Daum were the parents of five sons and three daughters. They lived on a farm northeast of Pilger for a number of years. In May 1944 her husband died.

For the last six years she lived with her daughter, Mrs. Amanda Sedlak at Wayne.

Survivors include Otto Daum of Pilger, Edwin Daum of Stanton, George Daum of Paullina, Iowa, William Daum of Calumet, Iowa, Mrs. Amanda Sedlak of Wayne, Mrs. Richard (Hildegard) Dreyer of Wisner, and Mrs. Amelia Grashorn of Stanton; two sisters, Mrs. Dora Stuthman and Mrs. Louisa Gemelke, both of Pilger; one brother, Henry Koehlmoos of Pierce; 26 grandchildren; 17 great-grandchildren, besides other relatives and friends.

She was preceded in death by her parents, one son Elmer, three sisters and two brothers.

George Daum Rites Held Monday

George Daum was born on December 7, 1879, at Gubbersburg, Hessen-Darmstadt, Germany, the son of George and Katherine Daum. As a child, he was baptized in the German State church at Kirch-Gromback, Hessen-Darmstadt, Germany. After attending the Lutheran church school there, he was confirmed in May, 1894, in the Lutheran faith, to which he remained faithful to the end of his life.

In 1903, he followed his sister, Katharine, who had married Oscar Reinhardt, to America, arriving January 4, 1904. He worked for his brother –in-law on the latter's farm northwest of Altona. Here he remained until his marriage, February 27, 1908, to Minna Koehlmoos of Pilger. Pastor Schaller of Trinity Lutheran Church, Altona, performed the ceremony.

Mr. and Mrs. Daum now settled on the farm 2 ½ miles north and one mile east of Pilger, where they lived until his death.

As soon as he came to Wayne County, he became affiliated with Trinity Lutheran Church of Altona. Here he had his two children baptized and the older ones attended parochial school and confirmation instruction. The Lord blessed him and his wife with five sons and three daughters, all of whom survive their father. In 1930, he transferred his membership and that of his family to St. John's Lutheran Church of Pilger. Of this church he was a voting member until his death.

Mr. Daum had been ailing for a number of years so he was unable to do his own farm work. During the last year, he became steadily weaker, being affected especially with a dropsical condition that affected his heart. On Maundy Thursday of this year he was still able to partake of Lord's Supper at church. At that time, he realized that his end was near. This thought he repeated various times when the pastor visited him and his invalid son, Elmer. Last week, Friday, May 12, 1944, he retired in the afternoon, as other days, to his room to rest. When he did not respond to summons to supper, he was found to have passed away peacefully of a heart attack.

He attained the age of 64 years, five months and five days. He is survived by his bereaved wife, Mrs. Minna Daum of Pilger, five sons, Otto of Pilger, Edwin of Wayne, George, serving as corporal in the United States Army in England, William, a Pfc. in the United States Army on active service in Italy, and Elmer at home, three daughters, Amanda, Mrs. Alfred Sedlak, Winside, Hildegard, Mrs. Richard Dreyer of Pilger and Amelia, Mrs. Dick Grashorn of Wisner, nine grandchildren, a sister, Mrs. Oscar Reinhardt of Altona, and a brother, Heinrich of Germany, of whom, however, no word has been received for several years; also a host of other relatives and friends.

He received Christian burial on May 15, 1944, in services conducted at his home and in St. John's Lutheran Church of Pilger, with the pastor of that church, the Reverend Walter H. Koenig in charge. The funeral sermon was based on the words of Jesus, recorded in John 14:2. "In my Father's house are many mansions; if it were not so, I would have told you, for I go to prepare a place for you. And if I go and prepare a place for you, I will come again and receive you unto myself that where I am, ye may be also." I know that my Redeemer liveth.

Pallbearers were: Herman Husmann, Peter Hallstein, Gustav Gemelke, William Dohren, Lars Petersen and Henry Thies. Committal was in the Pilger cemetery.

Relatives from Iowa who attended the funeral were Mrs. John Tesch, Granville, Mrs. Wm. Daum, and Mrs. C. C. Otte, Sutherland.

Memories of Minnie Daum

Although Grandma Daum lived in my parents' (Otto and Luella Daum) farm home, she had her own living space. She did her own cooking on her side of the house. She got our Norfolk Daily News when we were done reading it, and she took care of her son Elmer. His arthritis was so painful that wires were stretched over him so the sheets wouldn't touch his body. The shades were also pulled in his room. Grandma Daum slept in the room with him; otherwise, she was in her front room/kitchen. Mom had ten kids, so when Grandma had a stroke she moved to the home of her daughter, Amelia Grashorn, to care for her. After Elmer died, she lived with her three daughters and ended up in Wayne at the home of Amanda Sedlak. (Judy {Daum} Allvin)

Minnie and Elmer moved to Stanton in 1958 to stay with Amelia Grashorn. He died that summer. After that, Minnie took turns staying with her children, Amanda Sedlak at Wayne; Hildegard Dryer in Wisner; Amelia Grashorn in Stanton; George and Kathleen Daum in Paullina, Iowa; and Bill and Marie Daum in Calumet, Iowa. Near the end, she was living with Amanda. She died at the hospital in Wayne.

More memories of Minnie Daum

Elmer's arthritis became so bad that he was unable to even roll over in bed. In his last days he laid on his left side in a fetal position. He was unable to wear clothes, and no one could turn him. He could drink through a straw, and held a foot-long ruler to use to scratch himself. The radio was beside him. When he died, they had to break his bones to put his body in the coffin. (Daryl Daum)

Grandma Daum lived in two rooms across the end of our house, a kitchen and living room in one, and a bedroom. Company sat in the bedroom when they came to see her. (Daryl Daum)

In the evening she would come to our side of the house to visit and bring the newspaper. (Mary {Daum} Steffens)

Grandma (Minnie) hardly left the house. She washed her and Elmer's clothes and hung them out on the clothesline. Rags used for Elmer were hung to dry over the fence. Occasionally, she went to church or attended a funeral. She had probably three dresses, one for good and two for every day. She always wore an apron. The pastor would come and give her communion, and her family came from Iowa. (Daryl Daum)

A garage near the house at the Daum farm was the building where Grandma and Grandpa (Minnie and George Daum) first lived and raised their kids. (Judy {Daum} Allvin)

Grandma (Minnie) had an area on the farm where she grew flowers, and she had me pull weeds. She gave me a silver dollar for doing that; I still have it. Her spirea bushes, iris, peonies, lilacs and tulips were on the west side of the sidewalk, and mom's (Luella) flowers on the other side. (Mary {Daum} Steffens)

(Marlene and her parents Bill and Mary Daum lived in Calumet, Iowa). We would pull up. She'd come out; I ran to her and she hugged us. Yellow roses were blooming on the fence. She called my dad "Boy." One time after her stroke she motioned with her fingers to come to her. "Take" she said to me, and it was a hankie. (Marlene {Daum} Vanderpol)

She (Minnie) wore black, black everything. I remember her sitting in a chair or a wheelchair at the Daum farm, not talking, with her hands folded in her lap. Later I remember she lived with Amanda (Sedlak) in an apartment at Wayne. The apartments were along a hallway. All the doors were open with screen doors. I could smell the food they were cooking. Everyone who lived in the apartments shared a bathroom at the end of the hall. There was a tiny kitchen, dining room with a tv and couch, and bedrooms. I don't know how we all got in for Christmas and birthdays. Us kids ate in the hallway. Grandma had a parakeet, and I remember a Christmas cactus on an old sewing machine cabinet, and starched crocheted swans on the buffet. (Cindy {Daum} Janssen)

I remember her in a chair in a black dress. I don't remember her talking. (Christy {Daum} Noelle)

Only Larry and Harley of Otto and Luella Daums' children were the only ones born when Grandpa Daum was alive. (Mary {Daum} Steffens)

Grandpa (George) had something they called dropsy. He went into town to play cards. When he came home he laid down to rest, and Grandma (Minnie) found him dead. (Marlene {Daum} Vanderpol)

When his dad died, Otto quit school after just the 6th grade to stay home and farm. (Daryl Daum)

Descendants of Herman Koehlmoos (father of Heinrich) by Donald W. Adams

3 Wilhelmina (Minnie) Koehlmoos b: March 17, 1881 in Cook County, Illinois d: December 16, 1966 Number of children: 8

..... +George Daum b: December 7, 1879 in Gubbersburg, Hessen, Darmstadt, Germany m: February 27, 1908 d: May 15, 1944 Number of children: 8

.... 4 Amanda Daum b: July 20, 1908 in Wayne County, Nebraska Number of children: 3

.... +Alfred Sedlak b: March 31, 1905 in Altenhain, Germany m: July 24, 1929 Number of children: 3

.... 5 Harry Sedlak b: December 10, 1929 d: August 6, 1933

.... 5 Helen Sedlak b: April 30, 1931 in Wayne, Nebraska d: July 12, 1989 Number of children: 3

.... +LeRoy Barner b: October 4, 1931 in Wayne, Nebraska m: June 24, 1951 in Winside, Nebraska Number of children: 3

.... 6 Peggy Lea Barner b: March 9, 1952

.... 6 Ricky Lee Barner b: March 12, 1955 in Wakefield, Nebraska Number of children: 2

.... +Barbara Boyd b: December 16, 1954 in Spencer, Iowa m: September 21, 1975 in Winside, Nebraska Number of children: 2

.... 7 Christopher Adam Barner b: April 8, 1976

.... 7 Amy Barner b: November 20, 1977

.... 6 Darrin Dee Barner b: September 17, 1966

.... 5 Hazel Sedlak b: February 28, 1933 in Wayne, Nebraska Number of children: 3

.... +William Farris b: November 28, 1930 m: September 19, 1956 Number of children: 3

.... 6 Kelly Jo Farris b: December 5, 1958 Number of children: 2

.... +Ferris Number of children: 2

.... 7 Mindy Ferris

.... 7 Rocky Ferris

.... 6 Tracy Allan Farris b: December 25, 1959

.... 6 Penny Renee Farris b: October 12, 1963 Number of children: 1

.... +Glen Smith Number of children: 1

.... 7 Nickolas Raymond Smith

.... 4 Otto Henry Daum b: November 29, 1909 in Stanton County, Nebraska d: May 10, 1973 Number of children: 10

.... +Luella Minnie Koehlmoos b: April 16, 1919 in Granville, Iowa m: September 15, 1940 in Germantown, Iowa d: February 3, 1988 Number of children: 10

.... 5 Larry Otto Daum b: February 22, 1943 Number of children: 3

.... +Karla Kay Schuldt b: May 12, 1945 m: December 14, 1963 in Emerson, Nebraska Number of children: 3

.... 6 Bryan Larry Daum b: September 7, 1964 Number of children: 1

.... +Teresa ? Number of children: 1

.... 7 Shelby Lynae Daum b: October 12, 1993

.... 6 Tarry Lee Daum b: September 11, 1967

.... 6 Douglas Ray Daum b: February 28, 1982

.... 5 Harley Dale Daum b: May 10, 1945 Number of children: 4

.... +Jeanne Ann Harder b: August 27, 1943 m: October 9, 1965 in Wayne, Nebraska Number of children: 4

.... 6 Denise Marie Daum b: August 16, 1970

.... 6 Deanna Lynn Daum b: September 17, 1971

.... 6 David Harley Daum b: September 20, 1972

.... 6 Jeremy LaVern Daum b: March 4, 1977
.... 5 Daryl Dean Daum b: April 15, 1946 Number of children: 3
.... +Karen Ann Hankins b: March 16, 1945 m: June 6, 1970 d: April 16, 1982 in Sioux City, Iowa hospital Number of children: 3
.... 6 Tatia Jaylene Daum b: November 12, 1967 Number of children: 1
.... +Shaffer Daum Number of children: 1
.... 7 Maggie Ann Daum b: July 1987
.... 6 Britni Michala b: March 29, 1972
.... 6 Megann Chanelle b: July 19, 1974
.... 5 Judy Ann Daum b: January 14, 1948
.... +Jerry Allvin m: May 3, 1980
.... 5 Mary Jane Daum b: August 11, 1949 Number of children: 1
.... +Delvin Meyer b: November 17, 1946 m: April 18, 1969 Number of children: 1
.... 6 Angela Marie Meyer b: July 26, 1971 Number of children: 1
.... +Aaron Schnoes m: May 15, 1993 in Cherokee, Iowa Number of children: 1
.... 7 Anthony Aaron Schnoes b: May 23, 1994
.... *2nd Husband of Mary Jane Daum:
.... +Thomas Lee Steffens b: May 4, 1952 m: December 10, 1976
.... 5 Roger Lee Daum b: October 30, 1954 Number of children: 3
.... +Cindy Howard b: August 12, 1956 m: April 16, 1977 Number of children: 3
.... 6 Aaron Dale Daum b: April 1, 1983
.... 6 James Lee Daum b: March 4, 1985
.... 6 Anne Marie Daum b: March 14, 1986
.... 5 Loren Henry Daum b: March 10, 1956 d: April 27, 1988
.... 5 Ida May Daum b: June 28, 1957 Number of children: 3
.... +David Emil Rehder b: January 22, 1954 m: February 11, 1978 Number of children: 3
.... 6 Justin Burette Rehder b: August 3, 1980
.... 6 Kelli Jo Rehder b: September 6, 1982
.... 6 Michala Jean Rehder b: June 8, 1985
.... 5 Randall Gene Daum b: July 4, 1958 Number of children: 4
.... +Brenda Clayton b: March 10, 1961 m: April 7, 1978 Number of children: 4
.... 6 Joseph Otto Daum b: November 7, 1978
.... 6 Jason Lawrence Daum b: September 28, 1979
.... 6 Jeffery Randell Daum b: May 31, 1981
.... 6 Jennifer Luella Daum b: October 2, 1988
.... 5 Arlen Ray Daum b: August 30, 1959 Number of children: 3
.... +Renee Lynn Biery m: October 5, 1985 Number of children: 3
.... 6 Amanda Lynn Daum b: February 24, 1986
.... 6 Ashley Marie Daum b: July 25, 1987
.... 6 Nicholas Otto Daum b: September 6, 1988
4 Hildegard Daum b: December 14, 1911 in Stanton County, Nebraska Number of children: 2
... +Richard Theodor Dreyer b: January 10, 1909 in Menfro, Missouri m: February 12, 1933 d: January 27, 1992 in Wisner, Nebraska Number of children: 2
.... 5 Bernice Dreyer b: August 5, 1934 Number of children: 4
.... +Kieth Kindschuh m: 1954 Number of children: 4
.... 6 Roxann Denice Kindschuh b: January 25, 1952 Number of children: 4
.... +Barry Meyer b: February 14, 1951 m: August 1, 1970 Number of children: 4
.... 7 Kandi Lynn Meyer b: April 24, 1972
.... 7 Brandi Leigh Meyer b: October 4, 1974
.... 7 Kiley Robert Meyer b: October 5, 1977
.... 7 Kasy Jo Meyer b: February 4, 1981
.... 6 Randy Kieth Kindschuh b: July 16, 1956 Number of children: 2
.... +Jeaneen Dozler m: August 13, 1977 in Elgin, Nebraska Number of children: 2
.... 7 Hilary Jean Kindschuh b: November 29, 1982
.... 7 Tate Jonathan Kindschuh b: August 6, 1987
.... 6 Rodney Gene Kindschuh b: September 28, 1957 Number of children: 2
.... +Kristie Holder m: April 16, 1983 Number of children: 2
.... 7 Desarae Denise Kindschuh b: January 25, 1984
.... 7 Tyler Nathaniel Kindschuh b: August 19, 1986
.... 6 Royce Laine Kindschuh b: May 18, 1965
.... 5 Burnell E. Dreyer b: March 25, 1940 Number of children: 2
.... +Karen F. Jurgensen b: November 20, 1944 m: June 23, 1963 in Wisner, Nebraska Number of children: 2
.... 6 Dean Leonard Dreyer b: March 20, 1966 Number of children: 1
.... +Lyson Ann Hohl m: March 5, 1982 Number of children: 1
.... 7 Ashley Ann Dreyer b: June 12, 1988
.... 6 Brenda Jane Dreyer b: September 26, 1968 Number of children: 1
.... 7 Megan Lynn Dreyer b: January 16, 1991
4 Edwin Daum b: September 10, 1913 in Stanton County, Nebraska Number of children: 4
... +Elsie Awiszus b: May 28, 1920 in Iroquios, South Dakota m: December 28, 1939 Number of children: 4
.... 5 Connie Sue Daum b: December 29, 1942 in Wayne, Nebraska Number of children: 2
.... +Leon George Schulz b: July 13, 1938 in Pierce, Nebraska m: October 7, 1962 in Norfolk, Nebraska Number of children: 2
.... 6 Lori Schulz b: September 16, 1965
.... +Ricardo Santos m: June 16, 1990

.... 6 Ryan Schulz b: November 26, 1975
.... +Sandra Paullin m: June 4, 1994 in Norfolk, Nebraska
.... 5 Dennis Daum b: February 27, 1948 Number of children: 1
.... +Lanaya Van Doren b: January 16, 1955 in St. John's, Newfoundland, Canada m: August 23, 1977 in Springfield, Illinois Number of children: 1
.... 6 Flisha JoLene Daum b: June 23, 1986
.... 5 Cindy Cecelia Daum b: June 30, 1953 in Wayne, Nebraska Number of children: 2
.... +Clayton Eugene Janssen b: April 2, 1951 in Norfolk, Nebraska m: May 29, 1971 in Norfolk, Nebraska Number of children: 2
.... 6 Jennifer Jill Janssen b: March 28, 1975
.... 6 Jacylan Joy Janssen b: June 20, 1978
.... 5 Christi Lu Daum b: June 9, 1957 in Wayne, Nebraska Number of children: 2
.... +Michael Anthony Smith b: December 5, 1952 in Neligh, Nebraska m: December 11, 1976 in Norfolk, Nebraska Number of children: 1
.... 6 Jessie Michael Smith b: October 15, 1979
.... *2nd Husband of Christi Lu Daum:
.... +Andy Noelle m: July 9, 1988 Number of children: 1
.... 6 Angela Beth Noelle b: August 17, 1989
 4 George Daum b: May 10, 1915 in Stanton County, Nebraska d: April 28, 1991 Number of children: 2
... +Catherine Alvina Steichen b: October 30, 1926 m: March 29, 1946 in Dakota City, Nebraska Number of children: 2
.... 5 Michael George Daum b: January 3, 1949 Number of children: 3
.... +Jane Schlicht m: September 17, 1977 Number of children: 3
.... 6 Jim Schlicht Daum b: November 1966
.... 6 Michael Schlicht Daum b: December 1969
.... 6 Matthew Lee Daum b: April 20, 1978
.... 5 Elaine Daum b: April 22, 1954 Number of children: 1
.... 6 Michelle Lea b: September 2, 1972
 4 William E Daum b: May 30, 1917 in Stanton County, Nebraska Number of children: 2
... +Marie A. Otte b: February 24, 1923 in Sutherland, Iowa m: November 2, 1943 in Sutherland, Iowa Number of children: 2
.... 5 Marjo M. Daum b: April 5, 1949
.... 5 Marlene K. Daum b: September 4, 1952 in Cherokee, Iowa Number of children: 3
.... +Galen D. Vander Pol b: April 11, 1949 in Primghar, Iowa m: January 27, 1973 Number of children: 3
.... 6 Darcey M. Vander Pol b: March 26, 1973
.... 6 Danee A. Vander Pol b: March 26, 1973 Number of children: 1
.... +Douglas Snyder m: December 26, 1993 Number of children: 1
.... 7 A Son b: June 13, 1994
.... 6 Tracy D. Vander Pol b: March 26, 1975
 4 Amelia Daum b: May 7, 1919 in Stanton County, Nebraska d: August 27, 1989 Number of children: 5
... +Dick Grasshorn b: March 22, 1915 m: September 9, 1940 d: April 4, 1985 Number of children: 5
.... 5 Erwin Grasshorn b: November 2, 1940 Number of children: 4
.... +Gladys Mack m: September 6, 1965 Number of children: 4
.... 6 Erwin Grasshorn, Jr. b: September 17, 1965
.... 6 Gary Lee Grasshorn b: July 8, 1970
.... 6 Larry Dean Grasshorn b: July 8, 1970 d: November 9, 1970
.... 6 Vilean May Grasshorn b: August 15, 1974
.... 5 Elden Ray Grasshorn b: December 19, 1942 Number of children: 3
.... +Sharlyn Hausman m: February 3, 1960 Number of children: 3
.... 6 Tammy Sue Grasshorn b: July 18, 1963 Number of children: 3
.... +Mike Mefford m: August 6, 1983 Number of children: 3
.... 7 Tonya Marie Mefford b: October 11, 1981
.... 7 Landon Michael Mefford b: July 20, 1984
.... 7 Casey James Mefford b: April 1, 1991
.... 6 Todd Allen Grasshorn b: April 5, 1966
.... 6 Tim Vernon Grasshorn b: August 25, 1973
.... 5 Walter Grasshorn b: February 25, 1945 d: September 20, 1970
.... 5 Alice Grasshorn b: March 16, 1946 Number of children: 3
.... +Dennis Patterson m: May 16, 1965 Number of children: 3
.... 6 April Sue Patterson b: August 18, 1966 Number of children: 2
.... +Denis Reese m: October 5, 1985 Number of children: 2
.... 7 Adam Elijah Reese b: April 12, 1987
.... 7 Bethany Amelia Reese b: July 28, 1990
.... 6 Brenda Marie Patterson b: February 3, 1969
.... 6 Shane Walter Patterson b: October 26, 1971
.... 5 Lola May Grasshorn b: June 6, 1949
 4 Elmer Henry F. Daum b: December 5, 1922 d: June 30, 1958

Dorothea -- Dora
Born May 10, 1883,
at Coopers Grove, Illinois
Married February 14, 1902
to Henry Ernst Carl Stuthman
Housewife
Died October 27, 1969,
at Norfolk, Nebraska
Burial in Pilger Cemetery

Front row, from the left, Dora, Ernest, Leona (Nelson) Henry Jr., Henry Sr.; back row: Alma (Stradley), Carl, Elsie (Tietgen), Arnold, Olga (Dreyer), Albert and Clara (Stunkel)

Dora and Henry Stuthman

Wedding day

February 14, 1902

Golden Wedding anniversary

1952

Dorothea (Henry) Stuthman

Funeral services for Mrs. Dorothea Stuthman, 86, were held October 30, 1969, in St. John's Lutheran Church at Pilger. The Rev. H. M. Roth officiated. Music was furnished by Mrs. William Jacobs and Mrs. John Goeller Jr.

Burial was in the Pilger Cemetery. Pallbearers were William Koehlmoos, Fred Koehlmoos, Emil Gemelke, Arnold Koehlmoos, Edwin Daum and Wilbert Stuthman.

Dorothea Stuthman, daughter of Mrs. and Mrs. Henry Koehlmoos Sr., was born May 10, 1883, in Cook County, Illinois. She died October 27, 1969, in a Norfolk nursing home.

She came to Stanton County in infancy with her parents. She grew up and spent most of her life in the Pilger vicinity.

On February 14, 1902, she married Henry Stuthman of Pilger in Trinity Lutheran Church of Altona. They lived on farms north of Pilger until 1946 when they retired and moved to Pilger. They observed their golden wedding anniversary in 1952.

Mrs. Stuthman lived in Pilger until January, 1968, when failing health made it necessary for her to be taken to Norfolk for medical care.

She was a member of St. John's Church, the Ladies Aid and LWML.

Survivors include five daughters, Mrs. Elsie Tietgen of Wisner, Mrs. Arthur (Olga) Dreyer and Mrs. Clara Stunkel, both of Norfolk, Mrs. Clarence (Alma) Stradley and Mrs. Ivil (Leona)Nelson, both of Wayne; five sons, Carl and Henry Jr., both of Pilger, Ernest of Norfolk, Albert of West Point and Arnold of Wisner; one sister, Mrs. Louisa Gemelke of Stanton; one brother, Henry Koehlmoos of Stanton; nine grandchildren and 28 great-grandchildren.

She was preceded in death by her husband in June, 1960; two brothers and two sisters.

Mr. Henry Stuthman Sr.

Born in Heemsen, Hanover, Germany, November 15, 1877. Son of Dietrich Fredrick Stuthman and Louisa Bierman. He was educated in Germany, Douglas County and Stanton County District 18. He came across when he was 14, with his brother, William, to Omaha and lived with his sister for several years.

From 1892-96 he was employed on farms in Douglas County. From 1896-97 he was with Herman Mahler, his brother-in-law, in building irrigation ditches near Hot Springs, South Dakota. Between 1897-1902, he was employed on farms in Stanton County. From 1902-1910, he operated a 240-acre grain and stock farm in Stanton County, then owned and operated a 320-acre grain and stock farm. He bred and fed approximately 250 purebred Duroc hogs per year, and topped the hog market in Omaha four times in 1937. In 1915-16, he entered stock in the National Swine Show in Omaha and at Nebraska State Fairs and won second and third in classes. He was director of Farmers Union Co-op, board member of District 18, member of St. John's Church, and was named in the 1940 Nebraska Who's Who. He retired to Pilger in 1946.

He married Dorothea (Dora) Koehlmoos February 14, 1902, in Altona, Wayne County. Dora was the daughter of Maria Mindemann and Henry (Heinrich) Koehlmoos Sr. Dora was born May 10, 1883, in Cook County, Illinois. She was a member of St. John's Church, Ladies Aid, LWML, and Sunshine Club. She gardened and had a *green thumb* for flowers. She did a lot of quilting.

They were the parents of ten children: Elsie (Hans) Tietgen, Carl (Bertha), Olga (Art Dreyer), Clara (Irvin Stunkel), Ernst (Pearl), Alma (Clarence Stradley), Albert (Elna), Arnold (Faith), Leona (Ivil Nelson), and Henry Jr. (Sally).

They celebrated their 58th anniversary in 1960. Henry passed away June 26, 1960, and Dora on October 27, 1969.

Note: Information on Ancestry.com states Henry arrived in 1892 from Hanover, Stadt Hanover, Niedersachsen, Germany.

Memories of Sally (Roenfeldt) Stuthman

Dora liked flowers in the house and outside, but in later years she didn't have as many outside. She liked to play cards. Henry raised Durocs. He was awful quiet.

Memories of Lucille (Stuthman) Gesell

Dorothea Stuthman, according to the genealogy listing, is my grandma. I never knew her as Dorothea or heard her called Dorothea. She was always Grandma. (My other grandma lived in Missouri so I never saw her very often.)

My grandma was the regular, hard-working, good-housekeeping, pleasant hostess, good cook, took-care-of-her-children kind of grandma. I and my sister, Lorene, were the oldest of 18 so we probably got the first grandchild treatment.

On Monday, one would find her washing clothes in the wash house, carrying huge buckets of water in and out. I would help put the clothes on the line and take them off. There were a long row of mulberry trees along the walk and lines so mulberry stains and birds' stains were a problem. But I loved the mulberries. (We did not have mulberries at our house.)

These trees lined the long walk along which was the deepest cave I have ever been in. Someone would go down before every meal to bring up butter, milk, and anything else that needed to be kept cool.

We would always eat in the dining room and had the regular meals, eggs and bacon, or oatmeal or pancakes. Dinnertime, noon, would be a meal of potatoes, meat, two vegetables and cake or cookies. Suppertime we would have the leftovers from dinner plus our supper items.

Grandma's dining room was special. Between the kitchen and dining room was a built-in, see-through china cabinet with nice things like a Shirley Temple blue cup and special dishes. The dining room had a flower window that extended out from the house. And she would have the most difficult-to-raise-and-get-to-bloom flowers that everyone (except me, I did not understand) would admire. She would bury a rose stem stuck through a potato and it would sprout. When one came into Grandma's house, the first thing one would smell is the geraniums. The back porch which one entered, was enclosed, had glass all around, and she had it lined with geraniums all blooming. Grandma had a yellow rose bush that many took a start from.

And she had a huge garden. We lived a few miles from them, so we would come up and help pick peas, strawberries, cucumbers and beans, and whatever was ready to harvest. We could look over the fence to see the huge, red Duroc hogs. (They must have provided the fertilizer for the garden.)

On Sundays, Grandma and Grandpa were always in church and whatever church event was around. I remember, especially, the Mission Services we attended. Every church in the area had guest speakers at their service. Everyone brought food for the noon meal. We would sing the familiar hymns like "From Greenland's Icy Mountains." We would enjoy seeing people we had not seen for a while. After the afternoon service, the ladies would pull out all the leftover food; ice cream was brought and we ate again. Pilger's services were held north of the public schoolhouse. We would sit on planks set on cement blocks or small saw horses.

We would always celebrate everyone's birthday at Grandma's house. The evening was spent playing cards: pitch. When we were little, we would go upstairs and play. Later we would play cards also. Later in the evening, pop was brought out and after playing cards we had lunch.

Everyone brought sandwiches and cake. Grandma would make more sandwiches and coffee. It was a big lunch.

I remember one Sunday night, one of the uncles and aunts had an anniversary celebration. It was winter time. It started snowing but no one realized how bad it was to get. Grandma had 30+ people she bedded that night and fed the next morning. We were able to get to Grandpa's and Grandma's corner and got stuck.

I remember the rail on my doll crib broke. Grandma took a tin can, cut a strip and nailed it and repaired it with that. I remember her covering a mouse hole with a piece of tin can.

I never had a close, loving, expressed relationship with Grandma or Grandpa, (I am not aware that any of her grandchildren did) but we all loved her, respected her and had a great model for how to be a Christian wife, mother and grandma.

I wish I had the opportunity to let her know now.

Henry and Dora Stuthman's 50th Anniversary party in February of 1952

The Stuthman children, from the left: Leona Nelson, Carl, Elsie Tietgen, Henry (Hank), Olga Dreyer, Arnold, Clara Stunkel, Ernest, Alma Stradley and Albert.

Descendants of Herman Koehlmoos (father of Heinrich) by Donald W. Adams

.. 3 Dorothea Koehlmoos b: May 10, 1883 in Cook County, Illinois d: October 27, 1969 in Norfolk, Nebraska Number of children: 10
...... +Henry Ernest Carl Stuthman, Sr. b: November 15, 1877 in Hanover, Germany m: February 14, 1902 in Wayne County, Nebraska d: June 26, 1960 in Norfolk, Nebraska
.... Number of children: 10
.... 4 Elsie Stuthman b: March 11, 1903 in Stanton County, Nebraska d: August 10, 1978
.... +Hans Tietgen b: May 23, 1888 in Fort Calhoun, Nebraska m: February 9, 1945 in Wayne, Nebraska d: May 23, 1958
.... 4 August Carl Stuthman b: July 18, 1904 in Stanton County, Nebraska d: February 20, 1987 in Pilger, Nebraska Number of children: 2
.... +Bertha Heinold b: December 30, 1914 m: February 27, 1938 in Stanton, Nebraska Number of children: 2
.... 5 Jeanette Faye Stuthman b: April 5, 1939 Number of children: 4

.... +Norman Glen Hoppman b: January 19, 1937 in Garden County, Nebraska m: July 31, 1960 in Wisner, Nebraska Number of children: 4
.... 6 Daniel Allen Hoppman b: October 2, 1961 Number of children: 2
.... +Elizabeth Gail Krause b: September 8, 1966 in Kansas City, Missouri m: June 6, 1987 in Concordia, Missouri Number of children: 2
.... 7 Paul Daniel Hoppman b: October 22, 1989
.... 7 Brandon Michael Hoppman b: April 13, 1995
.... 6 Jon Michael Hoppman b: November 8, 1963
.... +Theresa ? m: June 1997
.... 6 Karen Marie Hoppman b: October 7, 1964
.... 6 Sara Faye Hoppman b: July 9, 1968 Number of children: 2
.... +David Gene Oetting b: September 23, 1968 m: December 30, 1990 in Seward, Nebraska Number of children: 2
.... 7 Quinten Douglas Oetting b: December 22, 1993
.... 7 Payton Faith Oetting b: May 12, 1997
.... 5 LaFay Phyllis Stuthman b: August 31, 1941 in Pilger, Nebraska Number of children: 4
.... +Jerry Lee Weyhrich b: June 17, 1939 m: May 27, 1962 in Pilger, Nebraska Number of children: 4
.... 6 Randall Lee Weyhrich b: May 13, 1964 Number of children: 1
.... +Heather Elaine Nichols b: January 6, 1965 m: May 25, 1991 in Chickasha, Oklahoma Number of children: 1
.... 7 Seth Lee Weyhrich b: September 13, 1995 in Chickasha, Oklahoma
.... 6 Rhonda Faye Weyhrich b: December 15, 1965
.... +Ronald Alan Pingilley b: May 6, 1965 m: June 4, 1994 in Chickasha, Oklahoma
.... 6 Renee Marie Weyhrich b: May 22, 1967 Number of children: 2
.... +Kenyon Lee Bush b: July 22, 1966 m: June 25, 1998 in Chickasha, Oklahoma Number of children: 2
.... 7 Bethany Marie Bush b: July 11, 1990
.... 7 Brittany Nicole Bush b: October 20, 1993
.... 6 Roger Alen Weyhrich b: April 15, 1969 in Sidney, Nebraska Number of children: 1
.... +Lora Marie Franetovich m: August 12, 1995 in Chickasha, Oklahoma Number of children: 1
.... 7 Braeden Alesis Weyhrich b: December 2, 1997 in Ames, Iowa
    4 Olga Henni Marie Stuthman b: March 24, 1906 in Stanton County, Nebraska d: June 26, 1994 in Norfolk, Nebraska Number of children: 2
.... +Arthur Frederick Dreyer b: September 2, 1902 in Altenburg, Missouri m: December 11, 1927 in Wayne County, Nebraska d: January 10, 1998 in Norfolk, Nebraska Number of children: 2
.... 5 Lucille Lorraine Dreyer b: June 7, 1931 in Pilger, Nebraska Number of children: 6
.... +Marvin William Gesell b: March 10, 1930 m: July 26, 1953 in Christ Lutheran Church, Norfolk, Nebraska Number of children: 6
.... 6 Rebecca Lynn Gesell b: April 26, 1954 in Norfolk, Nebraska d: June 23, 1955 in Norfolk, Nebraska
.... 6 Pamela Jane Gesell b: October 15, 1955 in Norfolk, Nebraska Number of children: 2
.... +Terry Lee Dede b: April 13, 1957 m: October 3, 1976 in Norfolk, Nebraska Number of children: 2
.... 7 Jennifer April Dede b: April 15, 1977
.... 7 Catherine Lee Dede b: February 5, 1981
.... 6 Thomas Arthur Gesell b: March 6, 1957 Number of children: 3
.... +Vicki Lynn Matthies m: June 4, 1977 in Norfolk, Nebraska Number of children: 3
.... 7 Timothy Arthur Gesell b: August 20, 1980
.... 7 Nicole Lynn Gesell b: February 9, 1982
.... 7 Michael Thomas Gesell b: November 9, 1993
.... 6 Scott Lawrence Gesell b: November 16, 1958 Number of children: 2
.... +Betty Reinhart b: March 13, 1959 Number of children: 2
.... 7 Jonathan Gesell b: June 11, 1986
.... 7 Joshua Gesell b: April 11, 1989
.... 6 Gregory Howard Gesell b: July 18, 1960 in Spokane, Washington Number of children: 2
.... +Jodean Lynn Meisinger b: February 1, 1960 in Omaha, Nebraska m: May 26, 1985 in Plattsmouth, Nebraska Number of children: 2
.... 7 Arianne Lynden Gesell b: August 24, 1993
.... 7 Ian William Gesell b: May 22, 1996
.... 6 Phillip John Gesell b: March 2, 1962 Number of children: 2
.... +Luanne Darby b: December 13, 1959 m: March 24, 1984 Number of children: 2
.... 7 Erin Darby Gesell b: August 25, 1988
.... 7 Tanner John Gesell
.... 5 Lorene Lois Dreyer b: February 6, 1935 in Pilger, Nebraska Number of children: 3
.... +Donald William Adams b: October 12, 1927 in Beatrice, Nebraska m: September 22, 1956 in Christ Lutheran Church, Norfolk, Nebraska Number of children: 3
.... 6 Jeffrey Alan Adams b: January 24, 1959 in Omaha, Nebraska Number of children: 3
.... +Julie Diane Hinchman m: May 16, 1981 in Omaha, Nebraska Number of children: 3
.... 7 Kylie Elizabeth Adams b: March 8, 1984
.... 7 Drew William Adams b: February 10, 1986
.... 7 Darren Michael Adams b: December 22, 1989
.... 6 Craig Steven Adams b: June 25, 1960 in Omaha, Nebraska Number of children: 3
.... +Laura Jean Meyer b: June 3, 1961 in Tawas City, Michigan m: May 22, 1982 in Lincoln, Nebraska Number of children: 3
.... 7 Tyler William Adams b: December 23, 1991
.... 7 Zachary Joseph Adams b: May 18, 1994 in Pella, Iowa
.... 7 Jennifer Anne Adams b: February 23, 1997 in Pella, Iowa 4:54 AM
.... 6 Mark William Adams b: June 23, 1967 in Omaha, Nebraska d: December 21, 1984 in Omaha, Nebraska
    4 Clara Stuthman b: March 12, 1908 in Stanton County, Nebraska Number of children: 1
... +Irvin Stunkel b: February 26, 1909 m: March 5, 1933 in Wayne County, Nebraska d: September 24, 1934 in Stanton County, Nebraska Number of children: 1
.... 5 Marlene Stunkel b: March 27, 1935 Number of children: 4
.... +Merlin Timm b: January 31, 1931 m: June 28, 1953 in Norfolk, Nebraska Number of children: 4

.... 6 Beverly Ann Timm b: April 9, 1956 in Brownton, Minnesota Number of children: 2
.... +Tim Lannon b: in Grand Forks, North Dakota m: October 19, 1990 in Brownton, Minnesota Number of children: 2
.... 7 Molly Kate Lannon b: July 15, 1991
.... 7 Mallory Clare Lannon b: May 11, 1995
.... 6 Karen Jean Timm b: February 15, 1958 in Brownton, Minnesota Number of children: 3
.... +Alan Buckentin b: June 11, 1959 in Lewiston, Montana m: August 2, 1980 in Brownton, Minnesota Number of children: 3
.... 7 Matthew Alan Buckentin b: October 2, 1983
.... 7 Christopher Merlin Buckentin b: September 5, 1986
.... 7 Nicole Jean Buckentin b: May 13, 1989
.... 6 Sheryl Kay Timm b: November 14, 1962 in Brownton, Minnesota
.... 6 Connie Lou Timm b: September 21, 1966 in Brownton, Minnesota
  4 Ernst Stuthman b: January 18, 1910 in Stanton County, Nebraska d: February 18, 1982 in Norfolk, Nebraska Number of children: 2
.... +Pearl Evans b: February 8, 1919 m: June 20, 1937 Number of children: 2
.... 5 Eldon Ray Stuthman b: March 27, 1938 Number of children: 2
.... +Virgene Gay Brummond b: February 9, 1939 m: December 18, 1960 in Wisner, Nebraska Number of children: 2
.... 6 Jon Anthony Stuthman b: December 16, 1962 Number of children: 3
.... +Elaine Ritter m: January 1982 Number of children: 1
.... 7 Jessica Kay Stuthman b: July 23, 1982
.... *2nd Wife of Jon Anthony Stuthman:
.... +Debbie Akers m: June 12, 1992 in Las Vegas, Nevada Number of children: 2
.... 7 Katherine Rene Stuthman b: November 23, 1993
.... 7 Lydia Rose Stuthman b: August 16, 1995
.... 6 Terry Ray Stuthman b: December 4, 1963
.... 5 Clifford Ernst Stuthman b: November 14, 1939 Number of children: 1
.... +Katherine Hellmick m: April 3, 1966 Number of children: 1
.... 6 Timothy John Stuthman b: November 19, 1974 Number of children: 1
.... +Angela Lynn Sims b: July 31, 1975 Number of children: 1
.... 7 Alycia Ann Stuthman b: August 15, 1997
  4 Alma Stuthman b: December 7, 1911 in Stanton County, Nebraska Number of children: 2
.... +Clarence Stradley b: February 19, 1915 m: September 19, 1942 d: August 19, 1981 in Norfolk, Nebraska Number of children: 2
.... 5 Marilyn Jean Stradley b: November 26, 1943 Number of children: 3
.... +Theodore Reeg, Jr. b: June 15, 1941 m: December 1, 1963 in Pilger, Nebraska Number of children: 3
.... 6 Terry Lee Reeg b: July 18, 1967 Number of children: 3
.... +Lisa Lynn Workman Reynolds m: September 25, 1993 in Omaha, Nebraska Number of children: 3
.... 7 Michael Reynolds b: June 5, 1982
.... 7 Heather Reynolds b: November 22, 1985
.... 7 Zachary Reeg b: November 10, 1985
.... 6 Brian Alan Reeg b: July 24, 1971
.... 6 Brenda Sue Reeg b: May 22, 1973
.... 5 Dennis Lynn Stradley b: November 9, 1947 Number of children: 1
.... +Cindy Jaros m: June 21, 1983 Number of children: 1
.... 6 Brandon Jaros Stradley b: July 12, 1984
  4 Albert Stuthman b: December 15, 1913 in Stanton County, Nebraska d: August 28, 1980 in West Point, Nebraska Number of children: 3
.... +Elna Wendt b: October 19, 1917 in Cuming County, Nebraska m: December 11, 1938 in Cuming County, Nebraska Number of children: 3
.... 5 Deon Dean Stuthman b: May 7, 1940 Number of children: 2
.... +Judith Anny Mikkleson b: October 13, 1940 in Omaha, Nebraska m: June 24, 1962 in Omaha, Nebraska Number of children: 2
.... 6 Deborah Ann Stuthman b: November 26, 1963 Number of children: 2
.... +Steven Paul Plager m: July 5, 1986 in Minneapolis, Minnesota Number of children: 2
.... 7 Michael Steven Plager b: December 29, 1990
.... 7 Nicholas Dean Plager b: November 10, 1993
.... 6 Julie Diane Stuthman b: April 13, 1965 in Minneapolis, Minnesota Number of children: 1
.... +Timothy Peter Anderson m: June 25, 1991 in Minneapolis, Minnesota Number of children: 1
.... 7 Maren Elizabeth Anderson b: March 9, 1996
.... 5 LaJean Ann Stuthman b: August 26, 1941 Number of children: 2
.... +Larry Eugene Rinker b: April 14, 1942 m: June 27, 1965 in West Point, Nebraska Number of children: 2
.... 6 Barbara Lynn Rinker b: July 28, 1970
.... +Carl Ray Fiegenbaum b: November 12, 1967 m: March 11, 1995 in Wichita, Kansas
.... 6 Jeffery Scott Rinker b: July 5, 1974
.... 5 DeVern Albert Stuthman b: October 30, 1948
.... +Ronda McIntyre m: January 12, 1989
  4 Arnold Stuthman b: March 9, 1916 in Stanton County, Nebraska Number of children: 3
.... +Faith Granger b: August 31, 1921 m: August 18, 1940 Number of children: 3
.... 5 Sharon Kay Stuthman b: November 25, 1941 Number of children: 3
.... +Stanley Gene Walde b: January 16, 1936 m: August 3, 1962 in Wisner, Nebraska Number of children: 3
.... 6 Turena Sue Walde b: August 3, 1964 Number of children: 2
.... +Mark Edwin Ehlers b: May 9, 1964 m: April 19, 1986 Number of children: 2
.... 7 Heath Gene Ehlers b: December 7, 1988
.... 7 Brandon Mark Ehlers b: June 14, 1991
.... 6 Cynthea Kay Walde b: August 18, 1965 Number of children: 1
.... +Steven Keith Wagner b: September 21, 1960 m: November 27, 1993 in Columbus, Nebraska Number of children: 1
.... 7 Jasmine Rose Wagner b: October 25, 1996

.... 6 Paul Donovan Walde b: February 24, 1968 Number of children: 1
.... +Debra Lee Harlless b: October 23, 1970 m: October 25, 1989 Number of children: 1
.... 7 Brittany Elizabeth Walde b: June 30, 1992
.... 5 Merle Norman Stuthman b: May 19, 1944 Number of children: 2
.... +Katherine Mary Hipp b: December 19, 1947 m: August 19, 1967 in Yankton, South Dakota Number of children: 2
.... 6 Larell Lynn Stuthman b: June 28, 1972
.... +Brent Arnold Frahm b: June 17, 1971 m: August 21, 1992 in Norfolk, Nebraska at Our Savior Lutheran
.... 6 Wendy Lyn Stuthman b: February 27, 1977
.... +John Boeshart m: October 11, 1997 in Norfolk, Nebraska at Our Savior Lutheran
.... 5 Warren Lee Stuthman b: August 11, 1945 Number of children: 3
.... +Sheila Gayle Race m: August 20, 1977 in Norfolk, Nebraska Number of children: 3
.... 6 Minda Rae Stuthman b: April 3, 1979
.... 6 Bryon Lee Stuthman b: January 6, 1981
.... 6 Janeen Faith Stuthman b: November 1, 1987
.. 4 Leona Stuthman b: June 13, 1919 in Stanton County, Nebraska Number of children: 1
...... +Harold N. Tiedtke b: February 1, 1918 m: June 22, 1942 d: October 11, 1944
.. *2nd Husband of Leona Stuthman:
...... +Ivil E. Nelson b: October 4, 1919 in Stanton County, Nebraska m: March 10, 1949 in Pilger, Nebraska d: April 3, 1995 in Wayne, I
     children: 1
.... 5 Lyle Eugene Nelson b: November 16, 1951
.. 4 Henry Stuthman b: September 6, 1922 in Stanton County, Nebraska Number of children: 3
...... +Marcella Roenfeldt b: August 18, 1925 m: September 29, 1946 Number of children: 3
.... 5 Steven Dale Stuthman b: May 16, 1950 Number of children: 2
.... +Karen Wasserman b: June 13, 1951 m: April 27, 1974 in Arlington, Virginia Number of children: 2
.... 6 Paul Michael Stuthman b: February 19, 1975
.... 6 Ann Marie Stuthman b: July 1, 1977
.... 5 Stuart Duane Stuthman b: August 11, 1953 Number of children: 3
.... +LeAnna Cox b: May 24, 1957 m: September 28, 1974 Number of children: 3
.... 6 Matthew Stuthman b: March 17, 1976
.... 6 Christopher Allen Stuthman b: September 6, 1977
.... 6 Sarah Jane Stuthman b: November 25, 1978
.... 5 Gayle Raymond Stuthman b: April 30, 1961 Number of children: 3
.... +Ida Jean Johnson m: January 7, 1978 Number of children: 3
.... 6 Jennifer Marie Stuthman b: September 23, 1980
.... 6 Kelly Sue Stuthman b: October 21, 1981
.... 6 Jessica Lynn Stuthman b: July 2, 1987 in West Germany

Heinrich Karl Hermann Koehlmoos

Born March 7, 1886

Farmer

Married September 8, 1910

to Lizzie Dahlkoetter

Died November 20, 1971

Henry Koehlmoos Sr. was born in 1886 north of Pilger on the original 1884 Koehlmoos homestead. This is the Adolph Koehlmoos family (ALK) farm, once the home farm of Adolph and LeRoy Koehlmoos families. Lizzie (Dahlkoetter) Koehlmoos was born in 1889 in Arlington. In 1904, at the age of 15, Lizzie came with her parents to Stanton County, locating on a farm north of Pilger. Rumor has it that Henry Sr. and Lizzie may have met at a barn dance, although their family farms were in close proximity of one another. Henry Koehlmoos and Elise (Lizzie) Dahlkoetter were united in marriage on September 8, 1910, at Trinity Lutheran Church in Altona. Later, Henry Sr. and Lizzie were faithful charter members of St. John Lutheran Church, Pilger. Henry Sr. was one of nine men to sign the adopted constitution on August 15, 1915, of the newly formed St. John Lutheran Church. Lizzie was active in St. John Lutheran Ladies Aid and LWML.

For thirty-eight years the couple made their home and farmed north of Pilger before retiring to Pilger. The farm home is now occupied by Gary and Kathy Koehlmoos. Arnold Koehlmoos and Gary Koehlmoos families have resided there over the past years. To Henry Sr. and Lizzie's union were born ten children, five sons and five daughters. Elmer, Rosetta, Clarence, Adolph, Esther, Ella, Henry Jr. (Hank), Arnold, Emilia (Arlene) and Lillian. The eldest son, Elmer Koehlmoos, was killed in action in Germany on November 30, 1944. Rosetta, the second daughter, died in infancy. The third son, Clarence, never married. The sixth daughter, Ella (Koehlmoos) Klawonn and her young daughter perished in the Madison County tornado on June 5, 1954. *(Pilger Herald-Enterprise/Wisner News-Chronicle,* July 25, 2018)

The wedding of Heinrich Karl Hermann Koehlmoos and Elise (Lizzie) Fredrike Maria Dahlkoetter; back row: William Dahlkoetter, Ernst Gemelke, Annie Dahlkoetter (Mrs. Oscar Aurich) and Louisa (Koehlmoos) Gemelke. The ceremony took place at First Trinity Lutheran Church in Altona, Nebraska, on September 8, 1910.

The family begins....

To the right, front row from the left: Adolph Koehlmoos, Esther Koehlmoos Heller, Clarence Koehlmoos; back: Elmer Koehlmoos.

…until the family's complete.

Pictured above, front row from the left: Arlene, Lizzie, Henry Sr., Henry Jr.; back row, from the left: Adolph, Clarence, Esther, Ella, Lillian and Arnold. Pictured below, from the left: Lillian, Arlene, Ella, Esther, Lizzie, Henry Sr., Clarence, Adolph, Henry Jr., and Arnold. Elmer was a casualty of World War II by this time.

Sample of records from St. John's Lutheran Church, Pilger, listing life events of Heinrich Koehlmoos, photographed by Lynn (Heinold) Koehlmoos before the June 16, 2014, tornado leveled St. John's.

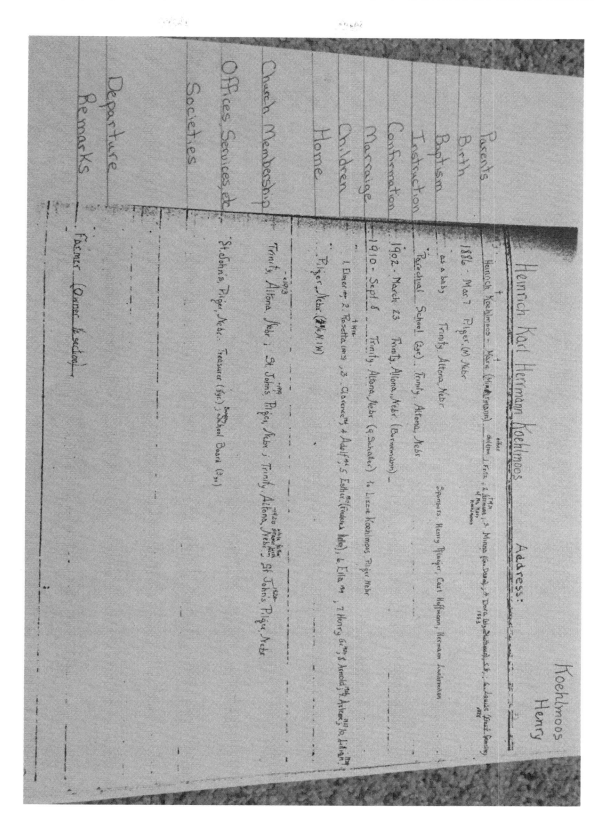

Sample of records from St. John's Lutheran Church, Pilger, listing life events of Lizzie Koehlmoos, photographed by Lynn (Heinold) Koehlmoos before the June 16, 2014, tornado leveled St. John's.

Henry Koehlmoos

Funeral services for Henry Koehlmoos, 85, of Pilger were held at 2 p.m . Tuesday in St. John's Lutheran Church at Pilger with the Rev. H. M. Roth officiating in the absence of the Rev. Eugene Juergensen. Burial was in the Pilger Cemetery.

Henry Koehlmoos, son of Mr. and Mrs. Carl Koehlmoos, was born March 7, 1886, at Pilger and he died Saturday, November 20, at the Stanton Nursing Home.

On September 8, 1910, he married Lizzie Dahlkoetter at Altona and they farmed most of his life in the Pilger area. He was a charter member of the St. John's Church.

Survivors include four sons, Clarence of Wisner, Adolph and Arnold of Pilger, and Henry Jr. of Tempe, Arizona; three daughters, Mrs. Frederick (Esther) Heller of Beemer, Mrs. LeRoy (Arlene) Lundahl of Emerson and Mrs. Leo (Lillian) Penn of Nevada, Missouri; 22 grandchildren and four great-grandchildren.

He was preceded in death by his wife in 1963; one son, two daughters and one grandchild.

Mrs. Koehlmoos Sr. buried on Monday

Funeral services were conducted Monday afternoon, July 29, 1963, at St. John's Lutheran Church, Pilger, for Mrs. Henry Koehlmoos Sr. 73. Her pastor, the Rev. H. M. Roth, officiated and burial was in the family plot of the Pilger Cemetery.

A ladies trio, Mesdames H. M. Roth, John Sokol and Richard VonSeggern, sang "Asleep in Jesus" and "Nearer My God to Thee," accompanied at the organ by Miss Letha Tobias.

Pallbearers were C. P. Christensen, Herman Willers, Gustav Gemelke and Lloyd Schneider, all of Pilger, Henry Reuter and Carl Schiermeier of Wisner.

Elise (Lizzie) Friederika Marie Koehlmoos, daughter of Herman Dahlkoetter and Maria Laaker was born at Arlington, Nebraska, on December 31, 1889, and passed away at her home in Pilger Friday morning, July 26, 1963. Her age was 73 years, six months and 26 days.

Mrs. Koehlmoos was baptized and confirmed in the Lutheran Church in the town of her birth. She was a charter member of St. John's Lutheran Church, a member of the Ladies Aid and LWML.

In 1904, at the age of 15, she came with her parents to Stanton County, locating on a farm north of Pilger. While living here she was united in marriage with Henry Koehlmoos of Pilger on September 8, 1910. They were married at the Trinity Lutheran Church of Altona by the late Rev. F. G. Schaller.

After their marriage they lived on a farm north of Pilger for 38 years. They were the parents of ten children. In 1948 they retired to Pilger where they have since lived. In 1960, they observed their golden wedding anniversary.

Survivors include her husband, Henry Sr.; four sons, Clarence, Adolph and Arnold of Pilger, and Henry Jr. of Mesa, Arizona; three daughters, Mrs. Fred Heller (Esther) of Wisner, Mrs. Arlene Pipal of Emerson, Mrs. Leo Penn (Lillian) of Emporia, Kansas; three sisters, Mrs. Oscar Aurich of Gurley, Mrs. Edward Glaubius of Wisner, and Mrs. Martha Aurich of Beemer; two brothers, William Dahlkoetter of Norfolk and Walter Dahlkoetter of Stanton. There are 22 grandchildren. She was preceded in death by her parents, one son Elmer, two daughters, Rosetta and Ella, and one grandchild.

Family hardships

Four of the Koehlmoos sons served simultaneously in the U. S. military during World War II: Sgt. Adolph Koehlmoos, a mechanic with an armored tank division, who was sent to England and France; Pvt. Elmer Koehlmoos, who was stationed for 20 months at Camp Carson, Colorado, sent to England in 1944, and then to France; Pfc. Clarence Koehlmoos with the ordnance ammunition company who was given a medical discharge in 1943; and Pvt. Henry Koehlmoos with the fleet marine force.

In addition, Cpl. Laurence Klawonn, a son-in-law and engineer with the Treadway Bridge Company, was stationed in France.

Pfc. E. Koehlmoos originally reported as missing in action on November 30, 1944, had been killed in action in Germany on that date.

Pvt. Koehlmoos left for military service July 8, 1942, and was stationed at Camp Carson, Colorado, for some 20 months. He then participated in maneuvers in Louisiana and at Camp Roberts, California, before being sent to Fort Meade, Maryland, and then to England in July 1944.

Information from the local newspaper had this to say: *He had been in the service two years and six months, the last six months being overseas. Yes, another Stanton County young man in the prime of his life, has made the supreme sacrifice. He gave his life for his country and its citizens. And how little we are doing!*

We bow in memory of you, Pfc. Elmer Koehlmoos, and all the other Stanton County men who have given their lives that freedom may prevail in the world.

In addition, in May of 1954, the Koehlmooses' daughter and granddaughter were killed as the result of a tornado in the Madison and Newman Grove areas. Tornadoes also killed three other children and injured at least 20 others in the path of the storm. Initially, among the list of the dead were Lynelle Klawonn who was eight years old at the time. At least seven farms were hit by two tornadoes, and torrential rains ranging up to 3 ½ inches made side roads impassable, sent streams over their banks, and blocked highways.

After hitting nearby farms, according to reports of the day, "The tornado then hopped across the highway to the Lawrence Klawonn farm, killing Lynelle Klawonn, 8, and injuring her parents. The farmhouse was leveled…. Wayne Wells, news director of Station WJAG of Norfolk, said the Klawonn farm was "The worst sight I ever saw. All the buildings were ripped out. Two-foot thick cottonwoods were twisted off like toothpicks."

Ella Klawonn and Lynelle Klawonn were the daughter and granddaughter of Henry and Lizzie Koehlmoos.

Note: My dad (Emil) said the rescuers couldn't find Lawrence's wife, Ella Klawonn, and after a thorough search found her in a pile of corn. She lived for several days in the hospital. Kernels of corn began to sprout beneath her skin, causing tremendous pain before her death. (LaRayne {Gemelke} Topp)

Note: Sixty years later five tornadoes followed a similar path to the 1954 tornadoes, with the first beginning in the Madison area, and the remainder attacking Pilger, along with the countryside around Stanton, Pilger, Wisner and Wakefield. The tornado hitting Pilger destroyed the home of LeRoy and Lynn Koehlmoos; LeRoy is a grandson of Henry and Lizzie Koehlmoos and son of Adolph and Lorraine Koehlmoos. He was in another building that was destroyed, and Lynn was at the Koehlmoos home. Neither were injured. Great-grandson Kory Koehlmoos (son of Gary and Kathy Koehlmoos, and grandson of Arnold and Betty Koehlmoos) was one of two firemen who risked their lives to manually sound the tornado alarm so residents would be safe. (LaRayne {Gemelke} Topp)

Memories of Lillian (Koehlmoos) Penn, written by her daughter Kathy Quinn…..

Lizzie Dahlkoetter (originally from Arlington, Nebraska) met Henry Koehlmoos (of Pilger) at a barn dance. Grandpa Henry Koehlmoos commissioned the building of their house on the farm property which has been held by the Koehlmoos family all throughout these years and is currently home to Gary and Kathy (Podany) Koehlmoos of Pilger. Lizzie and Henry had ten children together: Elmer, Rosetta, Clarence, Adolph, Esther, Ella, Henry Jr. "Hank," Arnold, Arlene, and Lillian. Rosetta died in infancy of sleeping sickness. Elmer was killed in Belgium during WWII and Ella (along with her only child, Lynelle) was killed in a tornado that hit their farm in Madison County, Nebraska in May of 1954.

Before going into the Army, Elmer worked as a field hand for a neighbor Henry Willers. Every Sunday, he would come back home and keep his mother Lizzie in stitches with various stories of things that had happened over there throughout the week. Elmer and Lizzie were always very, very close. After Elmer was killed, Grandpa Koehlmoos arranged to have his body returned to Pilger for burial in the cemetery which Lizzie always referred to as "Side Hill." My mom still remembers that day, telling us "the train was late and the family was already seated in St. John's Lutheran Church waiting for the train to arrive with Elmer's casket. As the train approached the station, it blew its whistle which prompted Grandma Lizzie to burst into loud tears. A child never forgets seeing his/her mom cry."

Lizzie would make ten big loaves of homemade bread every week, and oftentimes she would also make big pans of homemade sweet rolls with the same dough. She would make some kind of filling from crushed pineapple and powdered sugar and my mom said they were absolutely scrumptious! They would be fresh from the wood-fueled stove/oven when they'd come home from school and they (the kids) could eat as many as they wanted before setting out to do their farming chores. Mom was always very skinny, but she could eat five or six of them with no problem!

The family didn't celebrate the 4th of July with fireworks, instead, Grandpa Koehlmoos would take Arlene, Lillian, and Lorraine (Adoph's wife) into town where they would go into a tavern/ice cream parlor and eat big bowls of ice cream that were called "Clowns." Again, Mom said Grandpa would let them eat as many as they wanted and she would always eat several Clowns before she'd had her fill. Lorraine (Hilbers) Koehlmoos was wife to Adolph Koehlmoos and she and baby Franceil lived with Lizzie and Henry while Adolph was overseas in the Army during WWII. Franceil would be two years old before Adolph would ever see her. Grandma and Grandpa loved having Lorraine and Franceil live with them.

Mom remembers that Grandma always had a pot of homemade soup simmering on the back of the stove. During the Depression, she remembers numerous vagabonds coming by their house asking if they had any work for them to do. Grandma would always tell them to wait outside and she would give them soup and a piece of bread to eat before they went on their way.

Lizzie loved her flowers both inside (African violets) and outside (peonies). She was known to throw egg shells on her flower beds for compost, which is something I've noticed whenever I visit Amish communities. I've often wondered if Lizzie's heritage didn't come from the part of Germany closest to Switzerland as many of her mannerisms, beliefs, customs, and recipes seem to mirror that which I know to be rooted in the Amish way of life.

Lizzie had beautiful long, white hair which she always wore in a bun. She always wore house dresses, heavy black shoes and tiny wire-framed glasses. She spoke with a thick German accent. When we would come to visit from Omaha, we remember her saying "Who tink you come?" By this time, Grandma and Grandpa had moved from the farm into a house in town. We lived in Omaha and would come to visit every couple of months. Grandpa would always be sitting on the front porch swing holding a pipe in one hand, and a fly swatter in the other. My two older brothers would run inside to get the Chinese Checkers board and I was to ask Grandma for the marbles. She would keep the marbles in an empty coffee can and tell us to be sure we picked up all the marbles when we were done. There was a white picnic table and benches in the kitchen where we'd eat our lunch. I remember the wallpaper in the front room - it was a greenish gray background with big white and pink flowers. There were pocket doors to the parlor, but no one was allowed to go into the parlor (none of us kids anyway).

Gary Koehlmoos told me he remembers when they would bring Grandma to our house in Omaha where my mom would then take her for her cancer treatments. I was only four years old at that time, so don't remember too much about that. Grandma died when I was only 5 years old. Esther and Arlene took turns staying with Grandma in her last days. The day before she died, she requested Esther wash her hair, which she did. In one of her moments when she was awake, Grandma told Esther her bedroom was "filled with angels who were singing 'so loud.'" She left us the next day to be with Jesus. Grandma was always a devout Christian (Lutheran denomination), attending St. John's Church in Pilger all throughout her married life. I believe all of the Koehlmoos children (except Rosetta) were confirmed at St. John's Lutheran Church.

In modern day, we would probably refer to him (Henry) as the "Horse Whisperer." Mom said Henry Koehlmoos was a horse breeder as well as a farmer. She said he owned a big stallion named Jupiter who would sire foals with mares from near and far. (I believe there was a racetrack somewhere near Pilger.) Henry Koehlmoos bought a retired (and gentler) race horse for his children to ride. This horse's name was Belle. Dee Pinkelman has a photo of three or four young Koehlmoos children sitting bareback on this horse.

Additional memories of Henry and Lizzie Koehlmoos from their grandkids....

❖ After Grandpa moved to town, he came out to the farm to visit about three times a year. Mostly he came to watch baseball because he didn't have a tv set. Ours was a little black tv and there we sat in a row, Grandpa, dad (Adolph/Adolf) and me. Dad was a chain smoker and Grandpa smoked a cigar, so I could barely see the tv through the smoke. (Leon "Butch" Koehlmoos)

❖ Grandpa Koehlmoos and Ed Coley were neighbors in Pilger and played checkers under a shade tree between their houses. (Gary Koehlmoos)

❖ When the grandkids went to visit Grandpa and Grandma Koehlmoos in Pilger he was always in his chair by the front door. The grandkids pushed an ottoman by his chair and gather around it where they played cards and Chinese checkers. The parlor was closed off in Henry and Lizzie's house in Pilger, so when the doors were opened it smelled musty. The grandkids would sneak in there to have pillow fights. (Gary Koehlmoos and Leon "Butch" Koehlmoos)

❖ Arnie Koehlmoos took Grandma Lizzie for treatments for cancer to a doctor in Omaha. They would stay the night at the home of his sister, Lillian. (Gary Koehlmoos)

❖ When I stayed with Grandma Lizzie, she brushed her hair each night. She had long hair which she wore pinned up; few saw it down. (Jane Koehlmoos Adamski-DeLozier)

❖ Henry and Ed Coley were really good friends and would talk every day. When Henry moved to the nursing home, he went to a nursing home in Pierce first because Ed was there. Later he moved to the Stanton Nursing Home (Gary Koehlmoos)

❖ The word Koehlmoos was spelled out in marbles in the cement on the front steps of Henry and Lizzie Koehlmoos's house in Pilger. I remember Grandpa yelling at us to "Stop picking out those marbles!" (Phyllis {Koehlmoos} Lindsay)

❖ Note: Grandpa would *not* let me win at Rummy. (Phyllis {Koehlmoos} Lindsay)

❖ Grandpa would sit in his chair in the living room; he hardly left it. A bench at the table in the kitchen is where Grandma sat. At one time when they weren't getting along so well, they had company who all went out to sit in the kitchen with Grandma. Everyone loved Grandma. Grandpa came in the kitchen so Grandma went to sit in the living room, and they all followed her out there until Grandpa came in.... (Marlene {Koehlmoos} Claussen)

❖ I still have one of the quilt tops "the neighbors" were helping Grandma with...during harvest... they would take apart old men's suits and cut into squares, place on the quilting stand and tie with red yarn. (Franki {Koehlmoos} Parde

❖ A man would come by selling fish. Grandma would get his leftover ice and would make homemade ice cream. (Kathy {Penn} Quinn)

❖ My mom said Lizzie made beer, but it was served warm. A man would come by and sell fish. Grandma would get his leftover ice and make homemade ice cream. (Kathy {Penn} Quinn)

❖ I can remember as a little girl on Saturdays after going to children's choir after grandma was mostly in bed, she had me write names on all the pictures she had stored - so "people" could remember who they all were - also I would get groceries for them, she would make a list and I would walk up to Miller's store (felt very important) and got a nickel for a candy bar for my work!!! It was a labor of love, miss her - she was a fine lady. (Marlene {Koehlmoos} Claussen)

❖ I got snowed in that one winter and had to stay almost a week. The part I remember is dating a boy and trying to "explain that" to my "rather old fashioned" grandparents... We stayed with them many, many times when very young...combing Grandpa's hair...he had a LOT of hair...and pouring "Rose Oil" on and giving him the "slick back" look. "Toots" (Marlene) and I learned "high card" from him...course, she remembered and that is probably why she is such a good Bridge Player today! (Franki {Koehlmoos} Parde)

Descendants of Herman Koehlmoos (father of Heinrich) by Donald W. Adams

```
.. 3 Henry Koehlmoos  b: March 7, 1886 in Stanton County, Nebraska  d: November 20, 1971  Number of children: 10
..... +Lizzie Friederike Marie Dahlkoetter  m: September 8, 1910  d: July 26, 1963  Number of children: 10
.......... 4 Elmer Heinrich Friedrich Koehlmoos  b: February 9, 1912 in Stanton County, Nebraska  d: November 30, 1944 in Germany
.......... 4 Rosetta Koehlmoos  b: 1913  d: 1914
.......... 4 Clarence Koehlmoos  b: November 24, 1914  d: March 9, 1979
.......... 4 Adolph Koehlmoos  b: April 10, 1916 in Stanton County, Nebraska  Number of children: 6
.......... +Lorraine Hilbers  b: August 23, 1923  m: July 6, 1942  Number of children: 6
................. 5 Franciel Mae Koehlmoos  b: April 5, 1944  Number of children: 2
.................. +David Carl Judke  b: July 20, 1944  m: August 29, 1965 in Pilger, Nebraska  d: December 3, 1970
.................. *2nd Husband of Franciel Mae Koehlmoos:
.................. +Merlyn Parde  m: October 4, 1971  Number of children: 2
..................... 6 Aleesa ReMae Parde  b: July 22, 1977
..................... 6 Aaron Patrick Parde  b: March 17, 1981
................. 5 Marlene Joyce Koehlmoos  b: October 5, 1947  Number of children: 2
.................. +Arthur Claussen  m: May 9, 1969 in Omaha, Nebraska  Number of children: 2
..................... 6 Matthew James Claussen  b: April 22, 1971
..................... 6 Leslie Ann Claussen  b: May 24, 1974
................. 5 Lynda L. Koehlmoos  b: July 29, 1950  d: July 29, 1950
................. 5 Leon Adolph Koehlmoos  b: May 6, 1952  Number of children: 3
.................. +Linda Handke  b: July 29, 1952  m: September 4, 1971 in Pilger, Nebraska  Number of children: 3
..................... 6 Loren Michael Koehlmoos  b: May 22, 1973
..................... 6 Lance Allen Koehlmoos  b: June 16, 1978
..................... 6 Lonnie Lee Koehlmoos  b: November 11, 1980
................. 5 LeRoy Loren Koehlmoos  b: January 28, 1954  Number of children: 3
.................. +Lynn Hienold  b: March 19, 1959  m: September 22, 1979  Number of children: 3
..................... 6 Kristin Kay Koehlmoos  b: October 8, 1982
..................... 6 Katie Lynn Koehlmoos  b: February 9, 1985
..................... 6 Kellie Marie Koehlmoos  b: July 29, 1989
................. 5 Phyllis Ann Koehlmoos  b: September 5, 1957
.................. +Thomas Henry Podany  b: January 29, 2957  m: May 28, 1977 in Pilger, Nebraska
.......... 4 Esther Marie Koehlmoos  b: July 11, 1917 in Stanton County, Nebraska  Number of children: 3
............... +Frederick Herman Carl Heller  b: September 19, 1915 in Cuming County, Nebraska  m: December 31, 1939 in Pilger, Nebraska  d: June 17, 1980  Number of children: 3
................. 5 Lloyd Frederick Heller  b: September 2, 1940  Number of children: 4
.................. +Diane Mandle  b: November 4, 1945  m: June 24, 1967 in Dodge, Nebraska  Number of children: 4
```

.... 6 Brian Allen Heller b: November 9, 1969
.... 6 Lori Ann Heller b: February 5, 1971
.... +Darin Urwiller m: June 9, 1990
.... 6 Tracy Lynne Heller b: January 9, 1973
.... 6 Kristi Kay Heller b: December 22, 1976
.... 5 Ronald Dean Heller b: August 29, 1943 Number of children: 3
.... +Donna Wegner m: December 31, 1977 in West Point, Nebraska Number of children: 3
.... 6 Bradley Wegner Heller
.... 6 Lou Ann Wegner Heller b: July 8, 1955
.... +Roger Adams b: July 8, 1955 m: April 18, 1977
.... 6 Amy Wegner Heller Number of children: 1
.... +Gregory Shulz m: September 30, 1978 Number of children: 1
.... 7 Jasmine Nicole Shulz b: September 1, 1980
.... 5 Dee Ann Esther Heller b: July 29, 1946
.... +Gelen George Pinkelman m: June 24, 1994
4 Ella Clara Koehlmoos b: December 19, 1919 in Stanton County, Nebraska d: May 30, 1954 Number of children: 1
.... +Lawrence Klawonn m: January 6, 1942 Number of children: 1
.... 5 Lynell Klawonn b: May 22, 1943 d: May 30, 1954
4 Henry Koehlmoos, Jr. b: January 31, 1922 in Stanton County, Nebraska Number of children: 2
.... +Helen Jensen b: February 5, 1925 m: February 16, 1946 Number of children: 2
.... 5 Michael Koehlmoos b: May 27, 1948 Number of children: 2
.... +Vickie Moss b: January 13, 1951 Number of children: 2
.... 6 Ernie Koehlmoos
.... 6 Michaela Rue Koehlmoos
.... 5 Jane Koehlmoos b: November 29, 1950 Number of children: 1
.... +Ken Goodwin m: July 1968 Number of children: 1
.... 6 Julie Ann Goodwin b: October 7, 1971
.... *2nd Husband of Jane Koehlmoos:
.... +Steve Blackford b: July 3, 1945 m: July 27, 1975
. 4 Arnold Koehlmoos b: January 30, 1926 in Stanton County, Nebraska d: October 25, 1988 Number of children: 3
..... +Betty Nissen b: February 24, 1930 m: May 2, 1948 in Pilger, Nebraska Number of children: 3
.... 5 Gary Eugene Koehlmoos b: April 21, 1950 Number of children: 4
.... +Kathleen Louise Podany b: September 19, 1949 m: February 28, 1970 in Pilger, Nebraska Number of children:
.... 6 Korey Kurtis Koehlmoos b: December 5, 1971
.... 6 Kasey Lynn Koehlmoos b: July 28, 1974
.... 6 Kyley Jo Koehlmoos b: May 9, 1979
.... 6 Kolby Ryan Koehlmoos b: July 24, 1984
.... 5 Danny Duane Koehlmoos b: October 10, 1953 in Norfolk, Nebraska Number of children: 1
.... +Karen Kaye LaFrenz b: June 15, 1953 m: May 15, 1976 in Creighton, Nebraska Number of children: 1
.... 6 Travis Koehlmoos b: December 30, 1977
.... *2nd Wife of Danny Duane Koehlmoos:
.... +Joan Louise Hupp m: August 20, 1982
.... 5 Dean Allen Koehlmoos b: November 16, 1961 Number of children: 2
.... +Debra Schutte m: May 24, 1985 Number of children: 2
.... 6 Eric Dean Koehlmoos b: August 14, 1990
.... 6 Austin Allen Koehlmoos b: March 12, 1994
. 4 Arlene Koehlmoos b: April 3, 1927 in Stanton County, Nebraska Number of children: 3
..... +Melvin Pipel m: January 14, 1951 d: February 15, 1958 Number of children: 3
.... 5 Randy Pipel b: April 10, 1952 Number of children: 2
.... +Donna Forsyth m: June 16, 1973 Number of children: 2
.... 6 Amanda Kay Pipel b: December 21, 1977
.... 6 Jacob Allen Pipel b: November 13, 1980
.... 5 Rickey Pipel b: November 23, 1955 Number of children: 1
.... 6 Steven Pipel
.... 5 Joey Pipel b: February 14, 1958
.. *2nd Husband of Arlene Koehlmoos:
..... +LeRoy Lundal m: July 27, 1967
.. 4 Lillian Koehlmoos b: July 21, 1929 in Stanton County, Nebraska Number of children: 6
..... +Leo Penn b: August 17, 1929 m: June 6, 1953 Number of children: 6
.... 5 Pat Penn b: October 16, 1954 Number of children: 1
.... +Julia Hinkle m: July 24, 1976 Number of children: 1
.... 6 John Christopher Penn b: July 30, 1982
.... 5 Michael Penn b: April 10, 1956
.... 5 Kathy Penn b: May 23, 1958
.... +James R. Tuinn m: July 2, 1982
.... 5 Timothy Penn b: May 16, 1959
.... +Becky Franz m: May 21, 1982
.... 5 Stephen Penn
.... 5 William Penn Number of children: 1
.... 6 Samantha Penn b: June 6, 1989

Louisa Katharina Koehlmoos

Born February 20, 1888

Housewife

Married Ernst Gemelke
March 9, 1911
at First Trinity Lutheran Church, Altona

Died November 13, 1979
Burial at Pilger Cemetery

Front row, from the left: Viola, Ernst, Louisa, Mildred;
back row: Anita, Gertrude, Herbert, Emil and Wilhelma

Louisa Gemelke

Funeral services for Mrs. Ernest (Louisa) Gemelke were held Saturday morning, November 17, 1979, at St. John's Lutheran Church in Pilger. The Rev. Willard Kassulke officiated with burial in the Pilger Cemetery.

Mrs. Louisa Gemelke was born on February 20, 1888, to Henry and Maria (nee Mindemann) Koehlmoos in rural Pilger in Stanton County, Nebraska. She was baptized and confirmed at Trinity Lutheran Church in Altona, Nebraska.

On March 9, 1911, she was given in marriage to Ernest Gemelke. To this union two sons and five daughters were born. Mrs. Gemelke and her husband were instrumental in the founding of St. John's Lutheran Church in Pilger which organized officially as a congregation in 1935 (of which she was a charter member.)

Mrs. Gemelke passed away suddenly on November 13, 1979, at the Stanton Nursing Home at the age of 91. She was preceded in death by her parents, her husband, one daughter, two grandchildren, three brothers and three sisters.

Survivors include her two sons, Emil of Pilger and Herbert of Byron, Minnesota; four daughters, Mrs. Viola Brueggeman of Norfolk, Nebraska, Mrs. Wilhelma Kemper of San Antonio, Texas, Mrs. Anita Reimnitz of Corsica, South Dakota, and Mrs. Mildred Janulewicz of North Platte; 19 grandchildren and 26 great-grandchildren

Ernst Gemelke

Ernst Gemelke was given Christian burial on Wednesday, June 28, 1944, in St. John's Lutheran Church of Pilger, with the former pastor, Walter H. Koenig in charge. The funeral address was based in Matthew 25: 19-21.

Ernst Friedrich Wilhelm Gemelke was the son of Heinrich Gemelke and his wife Sophie (nee Janicke). He was born on January 18, 1888, at Hainhaus, near Bissendorf, Province Hanover, Germany. As an infant, he was dedicated to the Lord through holy baptism in the German Lutheran Church at Bissendorf. Here, too, he was confirmed in 1902. For two years after, he continued to receive religious instruction.

He began training as an apprentice in the hotel business in Germany, but in 1904 he came to America to join his sister, Mrs. Alwine Leseberg, who lived near Altona, Nebraska, having also come from Germany two years earlier. He now worked on various farms, first near Altona and then near Pilger, for Henry Koehlmoos Sr. All this time, he was affiliated with the Trinity Lutheran Church of Altona.

In 1911, he was joined in holy wedlock with Miss Louisa Koehlmoos by Pastor Frederick Schaller of Trinity Lutheran Church of Altona. He now made his home with his bride on a farm 2 ½ miles north of Pilger. Soon after he acquired the quarter section directly west of here, where he built the home which the family used until the time of his death. The Lord blessed their home with seven children, all of whom survive their father.

Mr. Gemelke was very active in organizing a church of the pure word of God in Pilger. His efforts and persistence, joined with that of some of his relatives and friends, begun in 1911, finally in 1915 led to the organizing of St. John's Evangelical Church (U.A.C.) of Pilger, Nebraska. He was the first one to sign the constitution among the nine charter members. He was also chosen as the first secretary of the congregation. In this capacity he served the congregation until 1931, when he was elected as an elder of the congregation. This important office he held until the time of his death. He was also the able chairman of the meetings of the congregation for the last twelve years of his life.

In 1928 he was chosen as one of the members of a building committee, who were to see about the building of a church building for the small congregation, of which at that time he was one of the leading members. Nothing came of those plans. In 1933, he served on a similar committee, and again in 1935, when his dream of St. John's having a church of its own came true. In 1933, he also served on a committee to obtain a resident pastor for his beloved St. John's Church. In 1936, as first delegate to a Synodical Convention from St. John's of Pilger, he signed the constitution of Synod in the name of the congregation. In recent years, he was especially active in wiping out the church debt and procuring a new parsonage. St. John's of Pilger will certainly miss his unflagging interest in and consecrated work for its welfare. In all things, he showed himself an earnest, zealous Christian. He was also interested in civic and agricultural projects.

The last two years Mr. Gemelke had not been feeling well at all. Still it was a great shock to his family, his church and friends, when last Saturday morning, June, 24, 1944, he was stricken in Pilger, while he was fixing his tire at the filling station, with a severe heart attack, and passed to his reward in heaven. The Lord wished thus to take His servant home.

He attained the age of 56 years, five months and six days and is mourned by his devoted wife, Mrs. Louisa Gemelke of Pilger, his two sons, Herbert, a Pfc. in the military police of the U.S. Army stationed in Washington, D.C. and Emil at home; his five daughters, Gertrude (Mrs. Floyd Vollmer of Wisner, Nebraska), Wilhelma (Mrs. Ivan Kemper of Norfolk, Nebraska), Anita, Viola and Mildred, all still at home; also two brothers, Friederich, still living, when last heard of, in Germany, and Gustav of Pilger; also two sisters, Alwine, (Mrs. Leseberg of Canyon, Texas) and Ella (Mrs. Siemsglusz of Norfolk, Nebraska); also one granddaughter, Gloria Vollmer. His parents and one brother Herman preceded him into death.

Interment was in the Pilger cemetery. Pallbearers were: W. T. Burris, Paul Schneider, Ed Hasenkamp, Herman Ritze, Harvey Petersen, John Dohren and Herman Husmann.

Blessed are the dead, which die in the Lord, from henceforth; yea.

Descendants of Herman Koehlmoos (father of Heinrich) by Donald W. Adams

.... 3 Louisa Koehlmoos b: February 20, 1888 in Stanton County; Nebraska d: November 13, 1979 Number of children: 7

+Ernst Friedrich Wilhelm Gemelke b: January 18, 1888 in Hainhous, Bissendorf, Hanover, Germany m: March 9, 1911 in Wayne County, Nebraska d: June 24, 1944 Number of children: 7
.... 4 Herbert Henry Gemelke b: April 29, 1912 in Stanton County, Nebraska d: December 19, 1984 Number of children: 3
.... +Margaret Olive Price b: March 27, 1912 m: May 12, 1944 Number of children: 3
.... 5 Robert Ernest Gemelke b: February 26, 1945 in Swea City, Iowa Number of children: 3
.... +Louise Ida Engler b: March 11, 1946 m: July 15, 1967 Number of children: 3
.... 6 Trina Elizabeth Gemelke b: March 28, 1970
.... 6 Robert Ernest Gemelke, Jr. b: February 7, 1972
.... 6 Mark Robert Gemelke b: July 18, 1979
.... 5 Mary Cinda Gemelke b: March 8, 1949 in Norfolk, Nebraska Number of children: 4
.... +Charles Schneiter b: December 4, 1946 m: December 30, 1967 Number of children: 4
.... 6 Lisa Marie Schneiter b: July 21, 1968
.... 6 Patricia Ann Schneiter b: July 22, 1969
.... 6 Richard Charles Schneiter b: July 26, 1970
.... 6 Jeffrey Allen Schneiter b: June 6, 1972
.... 5 Richard Carl Gemelke b: January 22, 1951 d: July 10, 1954
.... 4 Gertrude Ell Gemelke b: June 18, 1915 in Stanton County, Nebraska Number of children: 2
.... +Floyd Vollmer b: May 23, 1914 m: April 3, 1938 in Pilger, Nebraska Number of children: 2
.... 5 Gloria Vollmer b: September 28, 1941 Number of children: 4
.... +Clifford Lee DuPras Number of children: 4
.... 6 Roger Lee DuPras b: February 3, 1964 d: February 3, 1964
.... 6 Michelle Nicole DuPras b: June 28, 1965 d: July 29, 1965
.... 6 Michael Antony DuPras b: April 25, 1966
.... 6 Brian David DuPras b: June 15, 1967
.... 5 Floyd Vollmer b: November 23, 1944
.... 4 Wilhelma Dorthea Gemelke b: May 21, 1917 in Stanton County, Nebraska
.... +Ivan Kemper b: December 25, 1910 m: March 9, 1937
.... 4 Emil Gustav Gemelke b: June 12, 1919 in Stanton County, Nebraska Number of children: 3
.... +Bernitha Frieda Hasenkamp b: March 23, 1923 in Stanton County, Nebraska m: August 30, 1944 in Pilger, Nebraska Number of children: 3
.... 5 Duane Edward Gemelke b: August 4, 1945 in Stanton County, Nebraska Number of children: 3
.... +Linda Kathleen Stewart b: March 22, 1948 m: January 22, 1967 in Pilger, Nebraska Number of children: 3
.... 6 Kristine Kay Gemelke b: November 14, 1968
.... 6 Michael Duane Gemelke b: March 5, 1972
.... 6 Nathan David Gemelke b: December 30, 1976
.... 5 Ronnie LeRoy Gemelke b: June 3, 1947
.... 5 LaRayne Marie Gemelke b: September 23, 1951 in Norfolk, Nebraska Number of children: 3
.... +Kevin Karl Meyer b: April 6, 1951 in West Point, Nebraska m: January 2, 1969 in Pilger, Nebraska Number of children: 3
.... 6 Trisha Jo Meyer b: August 8, 1969
.... 6 Brenda Marie Meyer b: November 3, 1971
.... 6 Clinton Kevin Meyer b: October 21, 1975
.... 4 Anita Alvine Gemelke b: December 6, 1923 in Stanton County, Nebraska Number of children: 8
.... +George Reimnitz b: February 22, 1924 m: June 20, 1948 in Pilger, Nebraska Number of children: 8
.... 5 Russell George Reimnitz b: May 8, 1949 Number of children: 3
.... +Judy Herman b: February 14, 1954 m: May 3, 1974 Number of children: 3
.... 6 Jaycent Reimnitz b: April 15, 1976
.... 6 Tawnna Ellen Reimnitz b: May 27, 1978
.... 6 Katrina Kay Reimnitz b: September 18, 1979
.... 5 Karen Louise Reimnitz b: May 13, 1950 in Parkston, South Dakota Number of children: 5
.... +Howard Mueller b: April 28, 1949 m: December 19, 1970 Number of children: 5
.... 6 Jeffery Paul Mueller b: October 24, 1974
.... 6 Gregg Howard Mueller b: March 23, 1977
.... 6 Kerry Louise Mueller b: February 27, 1979
.... 6 Melissa Kaye Mueller b: October 4, 1980
.... 6 Scott Philip Mueller b: September 23, 1983
.... 5 Marjean Marie Reimnitz b: July 31, 1951 Number of children: 4
.... +Vern Mathis b: November 30, 1948 m: June 29, 1973 Number of children: 4
.... 6 Angela Jean Mathis b: December 23, 1975
.... 6 Shawn Alvin Mathis b: December 19, 1977
.... 6 Marie Kathleen Mathis b: December 28, 1979
.... 6 April Louise Mathis b: August 29, 1984
.... 5 Douglas Paul Reimnitz b: October 23, 1952 Number of children: 3
.... +Bonnie Jean Klumb b: August 1956 m: October 10, 1975 Number of children: 3
.... 6 Joseph Paul Reimnitz b: October 12, 1979
.... 6 Leah Louise Reimnitz b: February 3, 1984
.... 6 Hannah Joy Reimnitz b: June 5, 1985
.... 5 Joyce Elaine Reimnitz b: July 1, 1955 Number of children: 6
.... +Ira Curtis van Drongelen b: February 21, 1952 m: July 23, 1976 Number of children: 6
.... 6 Kristie Joy van Drongelen b: January 22, 1977
.... 6 Stacie Lynn van Drongelen b: September 13, 1978
.... 6 Spencer Paul van Drongelen b: August 18, 1980
.... 6 Vickie Louise van Drongelen b: July 9, 1982

.... 6 Rachel Eileen van Drongelen b: February 3, 1984
.... 6 Carlyle Lee van Drongelen b: May 13, 1985
.... 5 David Ernest Reimnitz b: April 21, 1957 Number of children: 1
.... +Jane Hopper b: September 25, 1959 m: May 9, 1981 Number of children: 1
.... 6 Amber Daun Reimnitz b: May 28, 1984
.... 5 James Robert Reimnitz b: August 6, 1958 Number of children: 2
.... +Kristy Lou b: June 14, 1963 m: September 4, 1982 Number of children: 2
.... 6 Justine Louise Reimnitz b: January 28, 1983
.... 6 Joslyn Roana Reimnitz b: January 28, 1983
.... 5 Sheila Kaye Reimnitz b: March 1, 1969
. 4 Viola Marie Gemelke b: February 13, 1926 in Stanton County, Nebraska Number of children: 3
..... +Robert A. Brueggeman b: April 3, 1920 m: September 8, 1957 in Norfolk, Nebraska Number of children: 3
.... 5 Mark David Brueggeman b: April 28, 1959
.... 5 Corren Elizabeth Brueggeman b: July 22, 1960
.... +Jeffrey Thomas Carnes m: May 4, 1985
.... 5 Barbara Louise Brueggeman b: January 5, 1965
. 4 Mildred Irene Gemelke b: July 11, 1930 in Stanton County, Nebraska Number of children: 2
..... +Leo Janulewicz b: September 27, 1924 m: October 14, 1961 in Omaha, Nebraska Number of children: 2
.... 5 Renae Jeanine Janulewicz b: April 10, 1963
.... 5 Jolene Janulewicz b: June 19, 1968

Sophia (Sophie)

Born December 19, 1896
in Stanton County, Nebraska

Housewife

Married John Tesch
September 14, 1919

Died April 25, 1950
Germantown, Iowa

Confirmation 1910
First Trinity Lutheran Church
Altona

Wedding Day, September 14, 1919
John Tesch and Sophie Koehlmoos

Front row, from the left: Margaret Tesch Byers, Melvin Tesch; back row: Marilyn (Merlon's wife), Mildred Tesch Krambeck, Merlon Tesch, Dorothy Tesch (Melvin's wife).

From left: George Daum, John Tesch, Sophie (Koehlmoos) Tesch and Minnie (Koehlmoos) Daum (Sophie's birth mother, although raised by her grandparents, Henry and Maria Koehlmoos)

John K. and Sophie Tesch

John K. Tesch was born June 12, 1896, in Cook County, Illinois. He came to America at age five, attended school at St. John Lutheran in Germantown, and was confirmed there. John was a veteran of WWI.

He married Sophie Koehlmoos September 14, 1919. She was born December 19, 1896, in Stanton County, Nebraska. Their children are Margaret (Byers) in 1920, Melvin in 1923, Mildred (Krambeck) in 1924, Merlon in 1926 and Mardella.

(Paullina, Iowa 1883 – 1983)

Note: The first four Tesch children were married in the Paullina and Germantown, Iowa, areas and raised families there, with the exception of two children. Myrtle was born in Granville, Iowa, on May 14, 1928, and died June 2, 1928, at the age of 19 days. Mardella was born April 17, 1932, and died at the age of 11 in August, 1943, from a shooting accident.

Mrs. John Tesch Is Buried Thursday, May 4, 1950, from *Paullina Times*, Paullina, Iowa

Funeral services were held on Thursday afternoon at 2 p.m. at St John Evangelical Lutheran church, Germantown, for Mrs. John Tesch, who passed away April 25, 1950, at St. Joseph hospital in Sioux City. Interment was in St John cemetery. Rev. G. B. Eschenbacher officiated.

Sophie Koehlmoos Tesch was born December 19, 1896, and raised by Henry and Maria Koehlmoos in Stanton County, Nebraska.

On September 14, 1919 she was united in marriage with John Tesch, and moved to a farm three miles southwest of Germantown, Iowa, where she spent her married years.

Death came early Tuesday morning after an illness which extended over several months. She had reached the age of 53 years, 4 months and six days.

She leaves to mourn, beside her widowed husband, two sons, Melvin and Merlon, two daughters, Mildred and Mrs. Vernon Byers, (Margaret). Also three sisters, Minnie Daum, Louisa Gemelke and Dora Stuthman and one brother, Henry Koehlmoos, all of Pilger, Nebraska.

Three daughters and one son preceded their mother in death.

Pallbearers were Orlynn Koehlmoos, Burnell Koehlmoos, Elwood Koehlmoos, Leland Koehlmoos, Francis Koehlmoos and Wesley Kuester.

Services Held Saturday for John Tesch, 78

Funeral services for John K. Tesch were held Saturday, April 26, 1975, at St. John's Lutheran Church in Germantown, Iowa. Mr. Tesch passed away Wednesday, April 23, 1975, at Veterans Hospital in Sioux Falls, South Dakota.

The Rev. Charles Kramer officiated at the services Saturday morning. Pallbearers were Keith Tesch, Kevin Tesch, Terry Tesch, Robert Tesch, Eldon Krambeck, James Krambeck and Lewellyn Byers.

The congregation sang three hymns with Mrs. Charles Brockmann as organist.

Burial was in St. John's Lutheran cemetery at Germantown.

John K. Tesch was born on June 12, 1896, in Cook County (Chicago), Illinois to Martin and Maria Henrietta (Krause) Marschalek. He came to the Germantown area in 1900. He was baptized, confirmed and educated in the Lutheran faith at St. John's.

In September of 1919 he was united in marriage to Sophia Koehlmoos. To this union eight children were born.

John farmed in the Germantown area for many years and retired in 1966. He had been in failing health the past couple of years and passed away at the Veteran's hospital in Sioux Falls, South Dakota, at the age of 78 years, 10 months and 11 days.

He leaves to mourn his passing two daughters, Margaret (Mrs. Vernon Byers) of LaPuente, California, Mildred (Mrs. Eldon Krambeck) of Galva, Iowa; and two sons, Melvin of Granville, Iowa, and Merlon of Hartley, Iowa. He is also survived by 18 grandchildren, 13 great-grandchildren and the following brothers and sisters: Dora (Mrs. Albert Gaudian), Olga (Mrs. Carl Gaudian), Hulda (Mrs. Emil Pauling), Selma (Mrs. Ray Fiddelke) and Herbert Tesch, all of Paullina, Iowa.

His parents and one sister, Ella, preceded him in death.

Above, John and Sophie Tesch with children,
from the left: Merlon, Melvin, Mildred and Margaret.
Left: Sophie and baby Mardella.

Memories of Mildred (Tesch) Krambeck

Mildred's mother, Sophie, was a real farm lady. She raised a big garden. Her kids had to pull the weeds. Sophie did lots of canning, and made sauerkraut in the fall. She also made root beer.

In early spring they shook mulberries, spreading out a sheet below and knocking the purple or white berries into it. They picked cherries, and Sophie made lots of pies, in addition to lots of cookies, bread, cakes and doughnuts.

Sophie baked a lot of bread, six loaves at a time. She often made bismarcks which were sweet rolls with apricots in the center. They were shaped like a doughnut, with apricot filling in the center, topped with more dough and deep-fried.

They had no running water, going to the well for water where they'd first have to prime the pump. They had a coal heater in the dining room, and a cookstove in the kitchen. A reservoir on the back kept water warm.

Sophie raised 500 chickens in the spring, which they cleaned and sold. She kept 200 laying hens. "Eggs and cream was our grocery money," Mildred said.

John had a threshing machine and went from place to place, threshing grain. Sophie and the kids cooked for the threshers and neighbor men who helped when they came to the Tesch farm.

Sophie didn't drive; she was a "home person," Mildred said, who wasn't in Ladies Aid or any clubs. She was usually home. Mildred enjoyed riding the horse to get the mail.

John farmed, milked cows—fourteen cows—and raised many hogs. They separated the milk, taking the cream in to town to sell. Mildred remembered washing all the little plates from the separator.

Sometimes gypsies traveled by, riding in an enclosed wagon or buggy, pulled by one or two horses. "One would come by the door and talk to Mom, and another would go to the chicken house and get a chicken and some eggs. We kids were scared and ran to the house," Mildred recalled. They would also take old car batteries that were sitting around. "They'd grab them up and take them. I don't know what they were good for."

The Tesch kids played softball in the pasture, played with a kids' wagon, and played in the haymow. They had a swing in the barn to play on until the barn was filled with hay. "In the summertime we had a good time until they put the hay in," Mildred said.

The Tesch family traveled to Nebraska every summer, spending one night with all the aunts and uncles. "Aunt Minnie (Daum) was our favorite. She was lots of fun, and I liked to go by Henry and Lizzie too. It was fun there," Mildred said. They played with their cousins, and also played card games.

In the dry years of 1932-1933, they tied a bedspring between trees to sleep on; it was cooler in the trees than in the house. Pigs died, it was so hot. They dug a trench by the corncrib where they buried the dead pigs and covered them with dirt, repeating the process the next day. "It was terrible hot, 110 all the time," Mildred said.

Descendants of Herman Koehlmoos (father of Heinrich) by Donald W. Adams

```
... 3 Sophia Koehlmoos  b: December 19, 1896  d: April 25, 1950 in Stanton County, Nebraska  Number of children: 6
....... +John Tesch  b: June 12, 1896 in Parsonage, Germany  m: September 14, 1919  Number of children: 6
............. 4 Margaret Tesch  b: March 25, 1921  Number of children: 7
................... +Vernon T. Byers  b: July 27, 1920  m: December 30, 1945  Number of children: 7
.................... 5 Sharon Lee Byers  b: October 30, 1946  Number of children: 1
.................... +Duane B. Henson  b: January 4, 1944  m: March 5, 1966  Number of children: 1
.................... 6 Brian D. Henson  b: October 20, 1971
.................... 5 Charlotte Marie Byers  b: October 30, 1946  Number of children: 2
.................... +David Bruce  b: August 23, 1945  Number of children: 2
.................... 6 Lisa Marie Bruce
.................... 6 Rhonda Lee Bruce
.................... 5 Vernon L. Byers  b: September 26, 1949
.................... 5 Sheryl Lorie Byers  b: March 25, 1954
.................... +Dave MaConell  b: December 11, 1948  m: February 11, 1978
.................... 5 Charmaine Mareen Byers  b: April 10, 1956
.................... 5 Eric Guy Byers  b: October 18, 1971
.................... 5 Cora Elizaeth Ann Byers  b: July 11, 1974
............. 4 Melvin Tesch  b: March 28, 1923  Number of children: 5
............. +Dorothy Dobbertin  b: May 10, 1916  m: January 23, 1949 in St. John German Lutheran Church  Number of children: 5
.................... 5 Melvin Keith Tesch  b: March 27, 1950  Number of children: 1
.................... +Macrina Currans  b: April 10, 1951  m: April 20, 1974 in Ruthvan, Iowa  Number of children: 1
.................... 6 Nathan Keith Tesch  b: January 26, 1978
.................... 5 Dorothy Denise Tesch  b: July 1, 1952
.................... +Robert Edgar  b: October 1, 1951  m: May 10, 1976 in GermanTown Church
.................... 5 Kevin Gene Tesch  b: April 24, 1954
.................... +Lisa Pluim  b: September 26, 1958  m: March 28, 1978 in Orange City, Iowa
.................... 5 Terry Lynn Tesch  b: October 31, 1955  Number of children: 1
.................... +Terri Finley  b: September 21, 1957  m: July 8, 1977 in Julesburg, Colorado  Number of children: 1
.................... 6 Michelle Lynn Tesch  b: September 19, 1986
.................... 5 Glenda Fay Tesch  b: December 1, 1943  Number of children: 1
.................... +Robert Perry  b: May 24, 1947  m: July 21, 1967 in Tuscon, Arizona  Number of children: 1
.................... 6 Thomas Christopher Perry  b: May 30, 1974
............. 4 Mildred Ida Tesch  b: August 13, 1924  Number of children: 6
............. +Eldon Paul Krambeck  b: June 19, 1923  m: July 2, 1950 in GermanTown Lutheran Church  Number of children: 6
.................... 5 Milan Wayne Krambeck  b: October 23, 1945  Number of children: 4
.................... +Joan Lytle  b: June 15, 1938  m: June 2, 1972 in Elizabeth City, North Carolina  Number of children: 4
.................... 6 Donald Edward Krambeck  b: December 21, 1957
.................... 6 William Roy Krambeck  b: January 7, 1959
.................... 6 Daniel Lytle Krambeck  b: May 15, 1960
.................... 6 Robert Allan Krambeck  b: October 7, 1961
.................... 5 Linda Faye Krambeck  b: September 6, 1952 in Sutherland, Iowa  Number of children: 3
.................... +Allan Arthur Peterson  b: November 21, 1947  m: July 25, 1970 in St. John Church Galva, Iowa  Number of children: 3
.................... 6 Scott Allan Peterson  b: May 4, 1971
.................... 6 Jason Wayne Peterson  b: August 7, 1974
.................... 6 Michael Paul Peterson  b: March 12, 1977
.................... 5 Elden Gene Krambeck  b: December 21, 1954 in Galva, Iowa  Number of children: 1
.................... +Paula Rae Presott  b: October 27, 1954  m: June 1974 in St. Pauls Luth. Church, Holstein, Iowa  Number of children: 1
.................... 6 Bobbie Jo Krambeck  b: March 22, 1976
.................... 5 Ellen Jane Krambeck  b: December 21, 1954  Number of children: 2
.................... +Gailen Henry Wessel  b: September 10, 1950  m: April 17, 1971 in Ida Grove, Iowa  Number of children: 2
.................... 6 Gale Kevin Wessel  b: October 3, 1971
```

.... 6 Brent Michael Wessel b: March 9, 1977
.... 5 Susan Reva Krambeck b: February 20, 1957
.... 5 James Karl Krambeck b: January 4, 1960
. 4 Merlon Tesch b: July 3, 1926 Number of children: 3
..... +Marilyn Virginia Sampson b: April 30, 1930 m: October 3, 1948 in Methodist Church, Hartley, Iowa Number of children: 3
.... 5 Cindy Sue Tesch b: June 14, 1951
.... 5 Steven Tesch b: April 14, 1954 d: May 31, 1954
.... 5 Robert John Tesch b: July 13, 1956
.. 4 Myrtle Tesch b: May 14, 1928 d: June 2, 1928
.. 4 Mardelle Tesch b: April 17, 1932 d: August 1943

Taking another step back.....

Descendants of Herman Koehlmoos (father of Heinrich) by Donald W. Adams

Descendants of Herman Koehlmoos

1 Herman Koehlmoos Number of children: 4
.... 2 Heinrich Koehlmoos b: June 1, 1848 in Germany d: February 18, 1918 Number of children: 8
...........:... +Maria Mindemann b: March 1, 1848 m: in Coopers Grove, Cook County, Illinois d: December 9, 1916 Number of children: 8

. 2 Maria Koehlmoos Number of children: 3
..... +Fred Meyer, Sr. Number of children: 3
.... 3 Maria Meyer
.... 3 Fred Meyer, Jr.
.... 3 Kurt Meyer
. 2 Ehler Koehlmoos Number of children: 8
..... +Mary Brooks Number of children: 8
.... 3 Emil Koehlmoos b: July 15, 1904 in Caledonia Township, O'brien County, Ia. d: March 29, 1982 in Primghar, Iowa Number of children: 3
.... +Adele Meyer m: December 19, 1928 in Paullina, Iowa Number of children: 3
.... 4 Vernice Koehlmoos
.... 4 Orlynn Koehlmoos
.... 4 Dennis Koehlmoos
.... 3 Fred Koehlmoos
.... 3 William Koehlmoos
.... 3 Henry Koehlmoos
.... 3 Hilda Koehlmoos
.... 3 Edwin Koehlmoos
.... 3 Minnie Koehlmoos
.... 3 Emma Koehlmoos
.. 2 Dorothea Koehlmoos Number of children: 15
..... +Julius Hoger Number of children: 15
.... 3 Herman Hoger
.... 3 Sophia Hoger
.... 3 Bertha Hoger
.... 3 Louise Hoger
.... 3 Wilhelm Hoger
.... 3 Henry Hoger
.... 3 August Hoger
.... 3 Albert Hoger
.... 3 Emil Hoger
.... 3 Anna Hoger
.... 3 Otto Hoger
.... 3 Dorothea Hoger
.... 3 Mathilda Hoger
.... 3 Martha Hoger
.... 3 Ernest Hoger

A number of the children of Henry and Maria Koehlmoos attended and were married at First Trinity Lutheran Church at Altona. This is the second building, on the north side of the road, dedicated in the latter part of 1911. The original church, on the south side of the road, is pictured on page 5.

History of the Church *(First Trinity Lutheran Church, Altona, Nebraska, 1881-1981)*

On Trinity Sunday, June 12, 1881, first Trinity Evangelical Lutheran Church, Altona, Nebraska, was organized under the leadership of the Rev. G. Bullinger at the home of Carl Erxleben, Sr. The Erxleben home was located one and one-half miles east and two miles north from the present church. The following were charter members: Christian Bastian, Wm. Wieland, Wm. Thies, Herman Brundieck, Herman Luehrmann, Henry Pflueger, John and Philipp Gruenwald.

It is not possible to determine from early church records exactly where worship services were held during the first six years, 1881-1887. It is believed members met for worship in their homes, then in a public school in the area. It is also thought that a room was later constructed on the Erxleben home for the purpose of holding worship services.

The first church building was erected in 1887 with the rear of the building serving as parsonage. This was located on the south side of the road across the road from the present church. In 1897 the first parsonage was built located to the west of the present parking lot. The first church building served the members of First

First Altona Church - Built in 1887

Trinity until 1911 when the present church was built. In 1912 the pipe organ was installed and was pumped by hand before the electrical era. With the building of the present church in 1911, the old church building served as a parochial school.

That same year, W. R. Schmidt was called by the congregation to serve as teacher. Prior to that time, the Pastor also did the teaching. Mr. Schmidt served as teacher until 1916. In 1917 the first teacherage was built.

After the church's Golden Jubilee celebration in 1931, a new school building was built. Men of the congregation brought their work horses with scrapers and excavated the basement. With the help of carpenters, masons and electricians the congregation completed the school in time for the fall semester. The first teachers in the new school were C. E. Germeroth and Miss Florence Zastrow.

Note: This is the church the Koehlmoos family attended. Once Ernst and Louisa were married, they were instrumental in establishing a new church in Pilger. They met first in the homes, a school, and the United Methodist Church basement in Pilger until they built a new church. (LaRayne {Gemelke} Topp)

Rural Church in 100th year by Florence Roggenbach (*Norfolk Daily News*)

The small community of Altona, 8 ½ miles south and one east of Wayne, might be considered a "ghost town," but the First Trinity Lutheran Church there is very much alive as it approaches its 100th anniversary.

The congregation was organized on Trinity Sunday, 1881, in the home of Carl Erxleben, 1 ½ miles east and two north of the present church. The church is now located one-half mile east of Altona. The congregation will celebrate its 100th anniversary Sunday, May 24, 1981.

First Trinity is the oldest Lutheran church in Wayne County and the second oldest of all churches in the county. The congregation erected its first church on the south side of the road across from its present location in 1886. The original church bell cost $25. The rear part of the building served as the parsonage until 1897 when the first parsonage was built.

Parochial School was held in the church on weekdays with the pastor teaching until 1911 when the first teacher was called.

The church had two coal burning stoves. Lights were kerosene lamps in brackets on the side walls. For many years during church services the men sat on the left side, the women on the right and school children in front.

The present church was built in 1911, with dedication services on December 18, 1911. The organ was installed in the spring of 1912, at a cost of $1,200. The building cost of the church was not over $3,500.

The original building was used as a school until 1931 when it was torn down and a new school built.

The congregation today has 115 baptized members and 90 communicant members. Although this is down from the high of over 300 members in the '30's, it does show an increase in recent years.

Altona itself has lost all of its businesses—and most of its residents. There are three families still residing in the small community. One couple, Mr. and Mrs. Walter Wesemann, are also members of the church.

The hamlet itself was founded in 1898, at one time "booming" with a general merchandise store being its first business; later having a bank, post office, blacksmith and a scattering of other small businesses.

The congregation includes two four-generation groups. Six generations of the Reinhardt family have been affiliated with the church, four generations still members: Mrs. Emil (Ella) Reinhardt; her daughter, Mrs. Les (Pearl) Youngmeyer; the latter's son, Jim; and his son, Matthew. All are of Wayne. Deceased family members are John and Oscar Reinhardt. The other four-generation group consists of Wayne residents Mrs. Anton (Mabel) Pflueger, grandmother; her son, Harris; his son, Terry; and Terry's children. The Pfluegers have had five generations as members.

Dr. Oswald Hoffmann of the Lutheran Hour radio program will be the speaker for the 10:30 a.m. worship service. Dr. Hoffmann is originally from Snyder. The Rev. Paul Jackson will be liturgist. A tent with closed-circuit television will be set up in the parking lot to handle the extra numbers of church-goers expected that day.

A noon meal will be catered by a Norfolk restaurant, followed at 1:30 p.m. with an organ recital by Dr. Anthony Garlick of Wayne State College.

The afternoon worship service will be at 2 o'clock with the Rev. Eldor Meyer, president of the Nebraska District, Missouri Synod, as speaker.

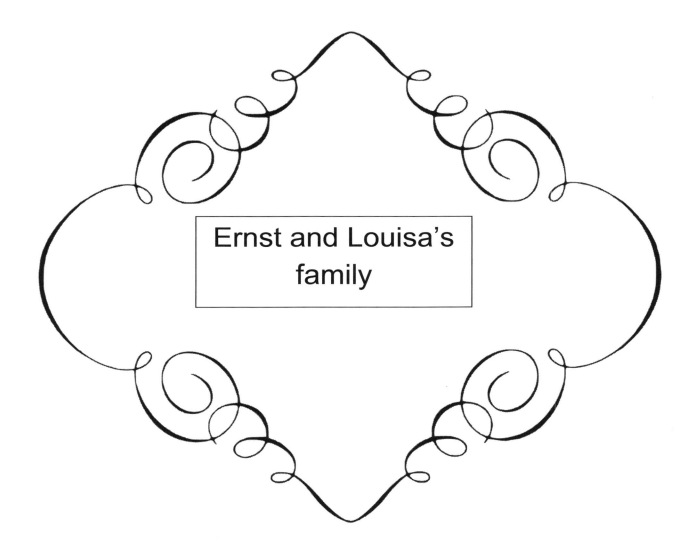

Ernst and Louisa's family

Gemelke, Ernst and Louisa by Emil and Bernitha Gemelke and LaRayne {Gemelke} Topp, *Pilger, Nebraska, Century Edition, 1887-1987*

Ernst Gemelke was born in Hainhous, Bissendorf, Hanover, Germany, in 1888. He worked as a waiter in Germany in a train depot café. The people were served in the train cars; if they weren't finished with their meal when the train was ready to leave, the waiters rode with the passengers to the next stop to retrieve the plates. He became confident at balancing five plates up one arm with the other arm free to open the door.

Ernst came to America at age 17. He told his friends he planned to buy a ticket to go to America and to prove it, he had to actually buy one. At that point, with his money spent, he had no choice but to come here. He rode on the train to Wisner where his sister lived, stepped off the train and into a mud puddle and was ready to go back to Germany.

He worked as a hired man for Heinrich Koehlmoos and married the *Farmer's Daughter*, Louisa Koehlmoos, in 1911. She was the daughter of Heinrich and Maria (Mindemann) Koehlmoos, and was born in 1888. She and her parents and brothers and sisters lived on what is now the Adolph Koehlmoos farm, north of Pilger.

Ernst and Louisa lived on what is now the Emil Gemelke farm north of Pilger and raised seven children: Herbert (Margaret Price), Gertrude (Floyd Vollmer), Wilhelma (Ivan Kemper), Emil (Bernitha Hasenkamp), Anita (George Reimnitz), Viola (Robert Brueggeman) and Mildred (Leo Janulewicz). Ernst and Louisa were instrumental in starting St. John's Lutheran Church of Pilger. Ernst served on the Farmers Union Oil Board from start to finish, and also served on the Humbug Local, Farmers Union Board and the District 43 school board.

The farm they lived on was bought from Louisa's parents with one dollar plus love and affection as a wedding gift. According to an early plat book, it was known as Cedar Knoll Farm. A second quarter section, immediately to the east, was bought around 1919. Ernst raised all red polled cattle and his first tractors were Fordson and Case. A tractor was used mainly, at first, to plow. The rest of the work was done with horses, as it was felt that tractors would pack the earth. Cream was shipped in cans, by train, to Lakeville, Minnesota, to be sold.

The present house was built around 1915. During the building of the house, the carpenters lived with the family in the old house. It was one of the few places around with carbide lights in the house and out buildings. They even had a carbide yardlight. Carbide crystals and water were combined in the light plant. The resulting gas from this combination was piped into the buildings where it was lit with a flint from gas jets on the walls.

A soft water cistern under the house held runoff rain water which seeped through a soft brick filter and was used for washing. Once a week, water pressure was built up with a single piston pump and pumped from the pressure supply tank into the cookstove. The water was piped into the water jacket around the cookstove; if the stove was heated, so was the water. Drinking water was provided by a pitcher pump by the sink and a wind charger kept the battery charged for the radio.

Ernst passed away in 1944, and Louisa moved into Pilger in 1945. She lived in Pilger until she moved to the Stanton Nursing Home in 1970. She lived there until her death in 1979.

Farm north of Pilger owned by Louisa and Ernst Gemelke

Note: I believe the photograph above was taken with an early day camera set up in the pasture by Gustav Gemelke. I estimate it sometime in the late 1910s, as I think the first three children had been born at the time the new house was built. See the horse barn on the right which caught on fire when Herb and Margaret Gemelke lived on the farm. (LaRayne {Gemelke} Topp)

View of the farm looking north

The house on the 160-acre farm "sold" to Louisa by her father on April 23, 1918, "in consideration of one dollar." (South West ¼, Section No. 15, township No. 24, North, Range 3.) Ernst bought the east bordering farm. (South East ¼, Section No 15, township 24, North, Range 3.) Both farms were homesteaded through a land grant process in the early 1870's, with ownership gained in exchange for five years of cultivation and improvements in exchange for the deed of title from Hans Bonck and wife.

A different house was on the place at first and the lane was west or its current location. Grandma Louisa said that the previous homeowners sat on the front porch and target shot into a boxelder tree which was just east of the house pictured. It was hollowed out from all the shooting, and when Dad (Emil) burned it years later, the smoke curled out of all the branches. Carpenters stayed at the home as they built the new house and their children were young; Grandma and Grandpa gave them room and board. Later on, a porch was built on the west side when Dad was a young boy. One of the carpenters at that time asked Dad for a broom, and he brought a water basin, as broom in German is *besen*. "*Dummkopf* (dumb head)", the carpenter said. (LaRayne {Gemelke} Topp)

Our house had carbide lights throughout as well as the barns and the yardlight. Carbide crystals were poured into an underground tank in the houseyard where they were mixed with water to create a gas which was piped to the house and outbuildings. A sparker or flint, much like a cigarette lighter, ignited the flame at each outlet. Two flames burned like a welder's flame. (Emil Gemelke)

When the REA (Rural Electrification Administration) came around to get farmers to sign up for REA, Grandpa Ernst wasn't interested because he had carbide lights, but he agreed for the neighbors' sake. (LaRayne {Gemelke} Topp)

I remember the tornado that hit our home in 1932. Herb, Dad and I tried to hold the west door shut, but could not. After it was over, the horse barn leaned about 18" over. Looked like it was going to fall over. We cut long poles and braced it up until it got fixed. (Emil Gemelke)

The "honeymoon cottage" on the 160-acre farm bordering it to the east, also owned by Ernst and Louisa Gemelke. Many couples, just starting out after their marriage, lived in this house until they could find a home of their own. When Mom and Dad lived in it after they were first married it had no indoor plumbing or electricity, a hardship as Mom grew up with a generator and Dad grew up with carbide lights. They carried water from the pasture to the farmplace.

In 1954, the farm was hit by a tornado when Emil and Bernitha and family lived there. They had to reach the cellar via the outside cave door, at the same time the tornado was hitting the grove west of the farmstead. Ron couldn't find his shoes, and when he finally found them, Dad carried him downstairs. Mom said they floated down the steps.

When we went to the cave or basement for bad weather we had to be fully dressed with coat and shoes. Dad prepared for tornadoes such that we would have what we needed if we were hit. When Dad was a young man, he, Herb and Grandpa Gemelke were working in the field as a tornado headed for the west farm on which they were living. Grandma had taken the girls to the cave by the time the three men got to the place. Dad said he, Herb and Grandpa came to the house and it took the three of them to hold the porch door shut as the wind worked to blast its way in. The tornado took out a portion of the grove. (LaRayne {Gemelke} Topp)

Places of Worship

Meetings and instructions held in the Henry Siemsglusz home from 1924- 1933

Present home of Leonard and Cynthia Raabe

Methodist Church
Services held here from 1920 - 1935

St John's Evangelical Church
Services held here from 1936 1960

St. John's Evangelical Lutheran Church
Services held here from 1961 to June 16, 2014

Note: Once Ernst and Louisa were married, and moved several miles south of the home of her parents, it became too far to drive to Altona for church services with a horse and buggy. At that time, Louisa and Ernst were instrumental in establishing a new church in Pilger. They met first in the homes, a school, and the United Methodist Church basement in Pilger until they built a new church. (LaRayne {Gemelke} Topp)

History of St. John's Lutheran Church, *Pilger, Nebraska, Century Edition, 1887-1987*

As early as 1890, Lutheran services were conducted in the Pilger area by the Rev. Brandt of Stanton. In 1906, the Rev. H. A. Hilpert, pastor of St. Matthew's Lutheran Church southeast of Pilger, conducted services in the old frame public school building in Pilger. He was followed by the Rev. Schaller, pastor of Trinity Lutheran Church of Altona.

On the afternoon of December 26, 1911, the Rev. H. R. Bohlsen, pastor of St. Paul's Church in Wisner, conducted his first service in the home of Mrs. Otelia Mahlke. The services were continued in the homes every two weeks. Herbert Gemelke, son of Mr. and Mrs. Ernst Gemelke, was the first baby baptized. After a short illness, the Rev. Bohlsen died April 21, 1913, at the age of 41 years.

In the summer of 1913, the Rev. Jahn, pastor of St. Matthew's conducted several services. In 1914, the new pastor of St. Paul's, Wisner, the Rev. Martin M. Leimer continued conducting services in the homes. On August 15, 1915, under the Rev. Leimer's leadership, St. John's Evangelical Lutheran Church of Pilger was organized. The adopted constitution was signed by nine men: Ernst Gemelke, Henry Gemelke, Nicklaus Dohren, Henry Koehlmoos Sr., Henry H. Peters, William Dohren, John Dohren, Gustav Gemelke and Herman Kilchenmann. Pastor Leimer continued to serve the congregation until shortly after the United States entered the World War in 1917.

In June, 1919, when the Rev. J. H. Tegeler was called to Wisner, he also took charge of St. John's. The services were conducted in the Pilger Methodist Church. Meetings and instruction classes were held in the Henry Siemsglusz (Aunt Ella) home from 1924 to 1933. In June, 1931, the Ladies Aid Society was organized at the home of Mrs. Albert Pilger, and a Sunday School was started about this time with 20 pupils enrolled.

In 1933, St. John's called a seminary graduate, Walter H. Koenig of Clarence Center, New York. He was ordained and installed as the first resident pastor of the congregation on July 2, 1933. For two years services were continued at the Pilger Methodist Church. The following years were years of rapid growth. The Sunday School was reorganized into five classes with 40 pupils enrolled. A young people's society was organized September 1933 with 29 charter members.

In 1935, the congregation resolved to build a new church building in order to have its own house of worship. Construction began in the fall at an estimated cost of $4,500. Much labor was donated by members of the congregation, and the church was dedicated January 14, 1936. A parsonage directly west of the church was purchased at a cost of $942.

In 1936, English services were to be conducted every Sunday. Many of the services before this time were conducted in the German language. On August 17, 1936, St. John's was taken into voting membership in Missouri Synod at the convention of the Northern Nebraska District.

Pastor Koenig served the congregation until 1944. When he left for Pekin, New York, the congregation had 278 members. Pastor O. E. Schlecht of St. Paul's Wisner served as vacancy pastor until November 5, 1944, when the Rev. A. I. Bernthal was installed. A larger house, located directly north of the present church was purchased to serve as a parsonage.

In 1950 a new Wurlitzer electronic church model organ was purchased for $2,300. The Rev. Bernthal served the congregation until January 1951, when he left for Minnesota.

Pastor Schlecht of Wisner again served as vacancy pastor until the Rev. H. M. Roth of Gordon, Nebraska, was installed April 29, 1951.

Continued growth pointed the need for new church facilities. Construction began in September 1960. On May 7, 1961, the completed church was dedicated at an estimated cost of $55,000 and donated labor and materials amounting to $33,000. The congregation observed its 50th anniversary on September 12, 1965. The debt on the new church was paid April 9, 1969.

The parsonage purchased in 1944 was torn down during September, 1969. The new parsonage was dedicated on May 24, 1970. On the same day, the congregation commemorated the 50th anniversary of Pastor Roth at which time he preached his farewell sermon before he and Mrs. Roth moved to Norfolk, Nebraska, to live in retirement.

On June 7, 1970, the Rev. Eugene Juergensen of Liberal, Kansas, was installed as the congregation's fourth resident pastor. A bell tower was completed for the church in the spring of 1971 for the bell that had been at the old church. In 1974, the choir loft and a new Allen computer organ were dedicated. In 1975, Pastor Juergensen accepted a call to Lafayette, Colorado.

The Rev. Willard Kassulke was installed as pastor by vacancy pastor Clarence Stenbeck on April 20, 1975. In 1977, the new educational unit which included six new classrooms was dedicated. In 1980 a church library was started. The Rev. Kassulke accepted a call to Altenburg, Missouri, in June 1982.

The Rev. Walter Pinnt of Stanton served as vacancy pastor until the Rev. Michael Gruhn of Lincoln, Nebraska, was installed on January 30, 1983. The church has continued to develop new programs and activities to help its ministry and mission for Jesus Christ.

Memories

Early years of church meant sleeping on my dad's lap. It was always in German. The women always sat on the other side of the church. (Emil Gemelke)

Anita played the pump organ for a funeral for the parents and brother killed in a train wreck at Omaha. Only two young boys remained who were home that day on the family farm north of Pilger. Their family name was Buss. People were seated at the first wooden church and the school across the street. In those days after the funeral, the congregation went outside and those who wanted to came through and viewed the deceased again. Anita played the organ the entire time, for more than an hour as people processed through. "I played a long time," Anita said. "That's how come I got bowlegged."

I sat in the car with Grandma Louisa before services the morning the new church was to be dedicated in 1961. She'd cried that morning, she said, to think that Ernst wouldn't be there. (LaRayne {Gemelke} Topp)

Several from the family are pictured in this photograph of St. John's Ladies Aid. Front row, farthest left is Minnie Daum, third from the left is Louisa Gemelke, and to the right of her is Ernst's cousin, Frieda (Gemelke) Hallstein.

BEST-EVER SALAD DRESSING
2/3 cup sour cream
2 eggs
3 tablespoons sugar
1/2 teaspoon pepper
1/3 cup vinegar
1/2 teaspoon mustard
1 teaspoon salt
1/2 teaspoon celery salt
Mix altogether and cook until thick. Will keep for days if kept cool. May be thinned with sweet or sour cream when used, if liked.

Mrs. Louisa Gemelke

From Vegetables – Salads section of 1950 St. John's Ladies Aid Cookbook

From 1950 Cookbook, compiled by St. John's Lutheran Ladies Aid

Front row, beginning with second from left, are Bernitha and Ron Gemelke, Margaret Gemelke, Lorraine and Marlene Koehlmoos. Louisa Gemelke is directly behind Lorraine.

Group Picture of St. John's Ladies' Aid

THE CHARTER MEMBERS
Left to Right: Mrs. Louisa Gemelke, Mrs. Heneritta Siegert, Mrs. William Tohren, Mrs. John Tohren, Mrs. William Waite, Mrs. William Pobanz.

Excerpt from *Eighty-one Seconds: The Attack and Aftermath as Tornadoes Hit Pilger, Stanton, Wakefield and Wisner, Nebraska* by LaRayne M. Topp

The tornado grievously sinned against four of the five church buildings at Pilger. It was particularly wicked to two, both with ties to St. John's Lutheran Church. It wiped both from the face of the earth. It did the same with the former United Methodist Church, serving as a private home. St. Peter's Church, on the south side of the tornado's hell-bent course through town was beaten up but not to death. The fifth, the former Baptist Church, was filled with historical items and memorabilia as the Pilger Museum of The Historical Society of Stanton County. Located in the northwest corner of town, it received relatively minor exterior damage.

The first of St. John Lutheran Church's two worship centers was built in 1935. A wooden frame building on the east part of town, at the time of the tornado it had been extensively remodeled into the home of Tim and Betty Maly. Betty loved the home so much, she often commented that if she ever moved away from Pilger she'd want to take the house with her.

The church was originally built without a bell tower, but when the Rev. Carl Koenig served as the pastor he felt all churches should have a bell. A bell tower was built over the front entryway, and the youth group at that time, the Walther League, purchased a bell. As the story liked to be told, the heavy cast iron bell was loaded in the back of a little Ford pickup belonging to member Ed Hasenkamp, with some strong, young men seated on the front fenders as a counterweight.

In 1961, a new brick and wooden-beamed church was built directly across the street, again without a bell tower. Ten years later, those who were in youth group at the time the bell was purchased for the old church, asked that their bell be used once again. A short but sturdy bell tower was built outside, around one of the church's stained glass windows.

As the tornado roared through town, it stole away the first church building. And the second. And the parsonage. The only thing left standing, amidst all the rubble, was the bell tower and, within it, the Walther League's bell.

Fortunately, the church records were stored in drawers beneath the tower and those remained when the tornado hightailed it out of town. Several computer towers were recovered along with their files. All of those records were doubly important as the congregation was in the planning stages for its 100th anniversary in 2015. As Celia Siecke stood at the living room window of her farm home, watching Pilger and her beloved St. John's Church get hit, the church was foremost in her mind. She'd spent months gathering information for a history book of the congregation in time for its centennial celebration. So dedicated was she, that she held in her hand the jump drive with all the information about the church's upcoming celebration. If a tornado hit their farm, and rescue workers found her body, she said, St. John's members would have the information and could carry on.

Once the church was hit members gathered the next Sunday at their sister congregation, First Trinity Lutheran Church at Altona, a dozen miles away. A voters meeting followed at which members decided to rebuild. Orphan Grain Train ministries, a Missouri-Synod Lutheran-based relief organization with its main offices in Norfolk, offered to build a mobile chapel for the church to use until their new sanctuary was completed.

That afternoon about 100 people gathered near the bell tower: St. John's members, former parishioners, First Trinity Lutheran congregants and volunteer workers. The community of Laurel was hit by fierce storms a day after Pilger was hit. Even so, a Laurel man, Morris Ebmeier, brought along a portable altar he'd built more than 50 years ago. It was used during the worship service along with paraments and two candelabra located among the rubble.

A church pew had been rescued, one side torn away, but still containing its red pew cushion. It rested under the bell tower along with a Bible, discovered amidst the debris of the building and opened to Psalm 84. The familiar psalm opens with the words, "How lovely is thy dwelling place."

Hymnals found scattered among the debris were distributed, a little wet and dirty, smeared with leaves and mud. Members wiped them off, and turned the pages to sing. The Rev. Terry Makelin, robed in white vestments and the green stoles of Pentecost, began the service with a light-hearted comment about seeming to have misplaced his church, setting the tone for a service both cheerful and tearful.

Rural School District 43 by Virgie Burris Frerichs (friend of Wilhelma and Gertrude), *Pilger, Nebraska, Century Edition, 1887-1987*

District 43 was organized February 21, 1891. It was formed from territory detached from Districts 7, 18 and 25. Courthouse records show descriptions of boundary lines and valuations and inventories of those three districts in order to make fair distribution of tax and property apportionments. Petitioners were members of the school boards and legal voters of Districts 7, 18 and 25. Of course, residents of the newly formed District 43 were among those petitioners. The declared value of the buildings and contents is a bit shocking.

The census for 1891, taken by Director James Doty, was 16 males and 11 females. In 1892 it showed 12 males and 19 females. In 1894 Margaret Matheson taught the school for $30 per month.

Our early records seem to have disappeared and courthouse information is scanty. We have to rely on memories and a few family records for the information we have. County superintendents' records vary also. Some are adequate and some pages are blank.

From an 1897-98 report card, we know a full range of subjects was taught: reading, writing, arithmetic, spelling, geography, language or grammar, physiology and history. Around 1900, one of our teachers taught algebra and English to a couple of interested pupils that weren't going to be able to attend high school. In 1912, geography of Nebraska, mental arithmetic, composition, agriculture, civics, domestic science, drawing, manual training, vocal music and modern orthography were listed on the records. All pupils ages 5 through 21 were encouraged to attend. There was no Kindergarten.

During the earliest years, school was in session no more than six months for the school year. Our district had a few families with several *big* boys (Foote, Glaubius, Koehlmoos, Duncan, Longcor and Willers families, to name a few). Enrollments ranged upwards to 30 and 40 pupils at times. We have several snapshots of school groups showing that many. That number didn't attend regularly. Sometimes school was not held during the worst winter weather. Most early years, the older boys helped their father at planting and harvest time and many of those boys only had from three to five months of schooling per year.

We had two teachers that taught five years. Luella Matheson in early 1900's and Marvel Waxe, 1933 to 1938. A resident of the district never taught our school but all (or most) were from Stanton County. That means the teacher stayed with one of the local families and paid room and board. It was usually a family not too far from the schoolhouse that kept the teacher because walking was the only way to get there. Grades were first through eighth.

Spelling bees were a popular learning tool. It seems we had a spell-down every week or two. Every child had his or her own slate, chalk, tablet, pencils and colors. Most of the desks were double. If you were lucky, you could choose the person you wanted to share your desk with, but not always. There was a long recitation bench at the front of the rows of desks. Each class took their place there when it was their turn for class. Opening exercises included flag salute or Pledge of Allegiance and singing. There was a lot of patriotic emphasis then. There was no basement and the building was heated by a big, old, round stove that burned cobs, wood or coal. We had a good storm cellar that didn't have to be used very often. In later years a basement and furnace were added.

In 1928, there were 34 pupils and Ethel Lueninghoener was the teacher. Again in second semester, 1958, enrollment was more than 30. Greta Iverson Bowder was the teacher. Twice, there were only five pupils but that changed quickly. Most years each grade was well represented. During the years 1934 through 1968 where we have records, it shows there were 22 Petersens, 15 Koehlmooses and 12 Gemelkes that went to District 43.

Four of the families living here prior to 1900 have descendants still farming or living in the district: Ellis, Foote, Koehlmoos and John Petersen.

Our last day of school in District 43 was actually October 23, 1968. We had only five pupils that fall and one was in seventh grade. We agreed he would benefit by going to Junior High at Wisner-Pilger so that left only four. We contracted our four students to Wisner-Pilger elementary at Pilger.

We closed officially July 1, 1970, as required by Nebraska legislative bill #1377. A 79-year tradition was lost to the ages.

Church and Sunday School services were held regularly in District 43 during those earlier years. The exact years are uncertain. They were held every Sunday at 2:00 p.m . Various ministers or persons had charge of the services. Ed Whisman was Sunday School superintendent at one time. Preachers and everyone came by horse and buggy. Revival meetings were held in the evenings occasionally. The Rev. Senniff, a Methodist minister from Pilger, served often. Mrs. Foote taught Sunday School. It was a cooperative effort and appreciated by the families. Lutheran families went to Altona to church most of the time. Families who attended regularly were Foote, Rennick, Cary, Willers, Pierce, Wells, Wilson, Rhudy, Taylor, Whisman, Petersen, Ellis, Burris, Longcor and Glaubius kids and Gemelke kids. A couple of ladies would stay and clean up and put desks back in place after services. We aren't sure when they disbanded but it was probably after cars became common.

Special programs were presented each Christmas season and were the absolute highlight of the year. They were simultaneously the most frightening and the most wonderful thing we could have experienced. Poor, bashful, little country kids…so happy and so proud when they were given their *parts* for the program. It was so awful when the time came and we had to stand up there in front of what seemed like half the world and fear that the words wouldn't come or the minds wouldn't work and the embarrassment would be more than we could handle. In spite of all that, there was such magic in those Christmas programs.

Quite often the programs were followed by a Box Social but sometimes there was just a bag of treats for each child. How wonderful those treats were…that was the only time of the year most of us had *store bought* fruit plus the nuts and candies. Again I say…such magic!

Another highlight was the picnic at the end of the school year. Every family brought their favorite foods and it was like something out of a storybook. Memories of picnics such as those must have been the origin of the fabulous buffet meals we see in some of our restaurants today. The earliest years I remember didn't include very many of the fathers. They were usually in the fields. Sometimes they would come to eat but leave immediately afterwards to get back to the field.

The mothers and children would stay until mid-afternoon or so and let the children play. I'm sure the mothers appreciated the chance to visit with neighbors, too. It was a glorious time. Quite often, picnic day was opening day of the season for going barefoot. After the picnic, go home and take off the shoes and socks and you were officially launched for the summer ahead!

Memories

Dad (Emil) said that kids were several years behind in their studies until the arrival of Mrs. Marvel Waxe. She quickly caught everyone up. If I remember correctly, one of the older boys got mouthy or did something she didn't approve of and she hit him into the wall. He slumped down, but she never missed a beat. "This is what will happen to the rest of you," she said, if you don't behave. The school had a floor furnace with the fire from the furnace's belly roaring only a few feet beneath the floor. The older boys took the register cover away and young Einar Jensen, not knowing they had done so, took a step backwards. He fell into the register and caught himself by his elbows. Dad pulled him out, much to Einar's gratitude, if you can imagine. (LaRayne {Gemelke} Topp)

School was 1 ½ miles from home. We walked most of the time. Sometimes we cut through the pasture. Mom didn't care much about that; sometimes we hooked our pants on the fence. I started to school in short knee-length pants and long stockings. I was very proud when I got my first long pants. (Emil Gemelke)

I had Marvel Waxe for six years. She was pretty strict. (Anita {Gemelke} Reimnitz)

Marvel Waxe had a ring she'd hit us with. (Millie {Gemelke} Janulewicz)

Dad (Emil) told a story about how strict Mrs. Waxe was, a story that he was always ashamed to tell (but I loved it). He was playing baseball on the ballfield south of the school with the big boys while the little boys were playing Marbles by the front door. He hit a ball and it crashed through the schoolhouse window. He could see Mrs. Waxe get up from her desk and knew he would be in big trouble. But when she got outside he was playing Marbles with the little boys. All the big boys got marched into the schoolhouse, and had to stay after school. No one ever told on him. (LaRayne {Gemelke} Topp)

I never went to high school. I kinda wanted to, but my older sisters and brother didn't. I had to say home and do the things that were necessary, like cleaning the barn, etc. (Emil Gemelke)

Pilger's Main Street, looking north, 1929

Family picture, early 1920, clockwise, from the left: Louisa, Gertrude, Herbert, Ernst, Emil and Wilhelma

Note: My dad (Emil) said this was his favorite photo because he was the youngest, the baby, before three more sisters came along. (LaRayne {Gemelke} Topp)

Above, front row, from the left: Viola, Ernst, Louisa, Millie; back row: Anita, Gertrude, Herbert, Emil and Wilhelma.

Below, taken same day, from the left: Gertrude, Anita, Herbert, Viola, Emil, Millie, Wilhelma

Gemelke children took the names of sponsors as middle names

Ernst Friedrich Wilhelm
Herbert Henry
Gertrude Ella
Wilhelma Dorothea
Emil Gustav
Anita Alvina Louise
Viola Marie
Mildred Irene

Gemelke family standing at the back porch, left, and kitchen windows on the farm. Front: Mildred (Millie); middle row, from the left: Viola (Vi), Ernst, Louisa, Anita; back row: Gertrude (Gertie), Emil, Herbert (Herb) and Wilhelma (Willie). Notice the striped socks.

Herbert Henry

Oldest child of Ernst and Louisa Gemelke

Born April 29, 1912

Married Margaret Olive Price

Died December 1984 at Byron, Minnesota
at age 72

Buried at Rochester, Minnesota

Married Margaret Olive Price

Born March 27, 1912

to Milton and Cinda Price

Died October 23, 2004

Confirmation class, 1928, front from the left:
Elsie Siemsglusz, Rev. J. H. Tegeler;
back row: Elmer Koehlmoos, Herbert Koehlmoos,
Alvin Siemsglusz, Ellen Gemelke

Right, Ellen (Gemelke) Glover (daughter of
Herman and Emma Gemelke) and Herbert
Gemelke

Herbert Gemelke and Margaret Price
Married in Washington D.C., May 12, 1944

Former Resident Is Married To PFC. Herbert Gemelke— After A Visit In New York They Will Make Their Home in Washington

Mr. and Mrs. M. T. Price of Swea City, Iowa, announce the marriage in Washington, D.C., of their daughter, Margaret, formerly of this city, to PFC Herbert Gemelke, son of Mr. and Mrs. Ernest Gemelke of Pilger, Nebraska.

A church wedding, the ceremony took place May 12, 1944, at four o'clock in the afternoon with the Rev. Ernest Pruden officiating.

The bride wore a light blue frock with a shoulder-length veil of pink. She carried a colonial bouquet of mixed flowers tied with white streamers.

Miss Mary Elizabeth O'Connor of Washingon, D.C., daughter of Mr. and Mrs. Emmett O'Connor, was the bride's only attendant.

She wore a pale pink frock of crepe with a blue veil, shoulder-length, and carried a nosegay of mixed blossoms tied with colored streamers.

George Zinell of Washington, D.C. served as groomsman.

Both men are on duty with the White House police.

After a wedding trip to New York City, PFC. Gemelke and his bride returned to Washington to make their home.

Before going to Washington to accept a civil service appointment, the former Miss Price was employed in Fort Dodge. She attended Fort Dodge-Tobin Business College here.

Many pre-nuptial courtesies were given for her by Washington friends.

From the Ft. Dodge, Iowa, newspaper

Herb was a White House guard in 1943. He was pictured in the newspaper with fellow guards, Joe Jura of Stanton and LeRoy Mumm of Norfolk, adding up to 642 pounds of White House guard. In a letter, Jura wrote, "Nebraska is well represented in the White House guard, there being ten of us, all over six feet. Besides we three, one is from Bancroft, another from Omaha and the other five are from the western part of the state. So you see we are proud of Nebraska where men are men. Besides attending the league baseball games at Griffin stadium, we also have an opportunity to see many of the notables visiting here, such as Churchill, Benes, Madame Chiang Kai-shek, etc."

Note: Later in life, Herb visited the changing of the guards at Arlington National Cemetery. When he told them he'd once served as a White House guard, they asked for identification, and when they returned they gave him the honor of placing the wreath on the Tomb of the Unknown Soldier. (LaRayne {Gemelke} Topp)

Hardship

Mrs. Louise Gemelke received word that her grandson, Spec. 5 Robert Gemelke, son of Mr. and Mrs. Herbert Gemelke, was wounded in combat May 12 in Vietnam. Spec. Gemelke was wounded in the left leg, left arm and suffered a fractured left elbow. He was treated in a hospital in Vietnam and was later transferred to a hospital in Illinois. (Year not given.)

His wife is the former Louise Engler, Currier, Minnesota. The Gemelke family formerly resided on a farm north of Pilger, and now resides at Byron, Minnesota.

Top left: Robert and Mary; top right: Pvt. Herbert Gemelke guarding the White House; bottom left: Margaret, baby Bobby and Herb; and bottom right: Mary and baby Richard Gemelke who died in a truck accident when he was three.

Second Farm Fire Strikes Near Pilger

The second serious farm fire to strike the same vicinity north of Pilger in four days occurred Monday afternoon at the Herbert Gemelke place, four miles north of town. The barn, garage and tool shed were destroyed, as well as 150 bales of straw and 50 bales of alfalfa in the barn, and tools in the shed. Mrs. Louisa Gemelke of Pilger owns the farm. (Year not listed, in early 1950's)

Last Saturday afternoon, a fire caused similar damage at the Fed Schneider farm, only three-quarters of a mile south of the Gemelke farm.

The Gemelke fire was discovered by Mr. and Mrs. Gemelke between 4:30 and 5 o'clock in the afternoon. As they were returning home from town they saw smoke pouring from the barn. The blaze started in the barn hayloft and was believed caused by defective electric wiring.

Fireman responded to the alarm from Pilger, Stanton and Wisner. They were still on the job well after dark Tuesday evening because of the smoldering hay and straw. A strong wind hampered efforts to control the fire, but the flames were kept away from the house although the wind was blowing toward the house.

Note: Dad (Emil) said the pasture was on fire and many neighbors came with rugs and shovels to put it out. Several men carried out a fuel barrel from behind the burning tool shed. Had they known it was nearly empty, they remarked later, they would not have attempted it. (LaRayne {Gemelke} Topp)

Herbert H. Gemelke

Funeral services for Herbert Gemelke of Byron, Minnesota, were held Friday, December 21, 1984, at Christ Lutheran Church at Byron, Minnesota, with the Revs. Ronald Huber and Victor Sorenson officiating. Burial was in the Grandview Memorial Gardens in Rochester with military graveside services conducted by the Byron American Legion Post.

Herbert Gemelke was born April 29, 1912, to Ernst and Louisa (Koehlmoos) Gemelke in Pilger where he lived and farmed until entering the Army in 1942, later serving in Italy. He married Margaret Price on May 12, 1944, in Washington, D.C. After his discharge from the service the couple farmed in Nebraska until moving to rural Byron in 1955, where they farmed until retiring. Mr. Gemelke died Wednesday, December 19, at the age of 72 years.

Survivors include his wife; a son, Robert (Louise) of Prior Lake, Minnesota; a daughter, Mrs. Mary Schneiter (Charles "Buddy")of Byron; seven grandchildren; a brother, Emil of Pilger; four sisters, Mrs. Wilhelma Kemper of San Antonio, Texas, Mrs. Anita Reimnitz of Corsica, South Dakota, Mrs. Viola Brueggeman of Norfolk, and Mrs. Mildred Janulewicz of North Platte.

He was preceded in death by a son and a sister.

Margaret Gemelke

Services for Margaret Gemelke, 92, Rochester, Minnesota, were October 27, 2004, at Our Savior's Lutheran Church in Rochester.

Formerly of Pilger, she died October 23, 2004, in Rochester.

She was born March 27, 1912, in Clarion, Iowa, to Milton and Cinda (Frazier) Price. She married Herbert Gemelke of Pilger, and the couple farmed near Pilger until they moved to Byron, Minnesota, in 1954.

She is survived by one daughter and son-in-law, Mary and Charles Schneiter of Rochester; daughter-in-law Louisa Gemelke of Prior Lake, Minnesota; seven grandchildren and 12 great-grandchildren.

She was preceded in death by her husband, two sons (Richard and Robert) and one great-grandchild.

Memories

The only thing I remember about Grandma was the house in town. Not sure why but Bob and I had to stay on the front porch when we went to visit. There was a thing you looked in (stereoscope viewer) and there was this double picture card you put in it. It then would be one picture. She had quite a few different cards. Also there was this board you could play different games on it. It had holes on the ends with a net. I remember playing checkers on it. (Mary {Gemelke} Schneiter)

Gertrude Ella

Born June 18, 1915, at Pilger, Nebraska

Married Floyd A. Vollmer

Died June 12, 1973, at Sacramento, California

Buried at Citrus Heights at age 57

From the left, in order of age: Gertrude, Wilhelma, Anita, Viola and Mildred

St. John's Lutheran Church Confirmation Class of 1929

Front row, from the left: Gertrude Gemelke, Clarence Koehlmoos, Rev. J. H. Tegeler, Walter Siemsglusz, Lawrence Steffens; back row: Irmagard Dohren, Ferdinand Siegert, Esther Peters, Lester Krueger, Elsa Dohren and Harold Krueger.

Page courtesy of Marlene (Vollmer) Hansen

Floyd & Gertrude

Gertrude Gemelke and Floyd Vollmer
April 3, 1938

Young Couple were Married During Week

The marriage of Miss Gertrude Gemelke, daughter of Mr. and Mrs. Ernst Gemelke, and Floyd Vollmer, son of Mr. and Mrs. Albert Vollmer of Wisner, took place Sunday afternoon at four o'clock, April 3, 1938, in the St. John's Lutheran Church at Pilger. The Rev. W. H. Koenig, pastor of the church, read the marriage lines, using the double ring ceremony. The bridal couple and their attendants, Miss Adaline Vollmer, sister of the groom, and Emil Gemelke, brother of the bride, entered the church to the strains of Lohengren's Wedding March, played by Anita Gemelke, sister of the bride.

The bride wore a powder blue dress trimmed with navy blue and wore blue accessories to match. She wore a shoulder corsage of roses and sweet peas. Her bridesmaid wore a rose pink dress with matching accessories, and wore a corsage of sweet peas. Both groom and best man wore dark suits.

A five o-clock dinner was served to immediate families. A large three-tier wedding cake adorned the table. Table waitresses were Miss Esther Siegert of Wayne and Miss Irmagard Dohren of Oak Park, Illinois. The house was decorated in the bride's colors of blue and pink. A reception was held in the evening for about ninety guests.

Mr. and Mrs. Floyd Vollmer will reside on a farm five miles south and 2 ½ miles east of Pilger.

Out of town guests were Mr. and Mrs. Albert Vollmer and family, Mr. and Mrs. Roy Vollmer, Mr. and Mrs. Fred Beerbohm, Miss Delores Norden, Mr. and Mrs. Rhudy Rabbass of Wisner; Mr. and Mrs. Arnold Geurn, Mr. and Mrs. Eugene Leimer of Wisner, Carl Walters and Ruth of Altona, Mr. and Mrs. Art Dreyer and family, Mrs. Ella Siemsglusz of Norfolk, Mrs. Wm. Blume and Frieda and Herbert of Armour, South Dakota, Bill and Marie Prien of Parkston, South Dakota.

Daughter Gloria, born 1941

Floyd Ernest Vollmer Jr.
Born November 23, 1943
Died November 24, 1943
Buried Wisner Cemetery
Wisner, Nebraska

*Infant daughter, 1942, unmarked grave, Ernst and Louisa Gemelke plot, Pilger Cemetery, Pilger, Nebraska
*Infant daughter, another Gemelke plot, Pilger Cemetery, Pilger, Nebraska
* Information Marlene (Vollmer) Hansen family history

Note: Dad (Emil) said Floyd and Ernst Gemelke built a casket for one of these baby's burials and Floyd carried the casket in his arms to the burial site. (LaRayne {Gemelke} Topp)

Floyd Albert Vollmer

Born May 23, 1912

Mason

Died January 29, 2001

Carmichael, California

Burial at Sacramento, California

Above, from the left: Bernitha with Duane, Gertrude with Gloria, Louisa and Millie. Center: Gertrude and Gloria. Bottom: Gertrude and Gloria at Louisa's living room in Pilger.

Memories

Gertrude practically raised me. I was pretty mad when Floyd married her. I was going to stay with Ivan and Wilhelma one time and got homesick and had to come home, but I never got homesick at Gertrude and Floyd's. (Millie {Gemelke} Janulewicz)

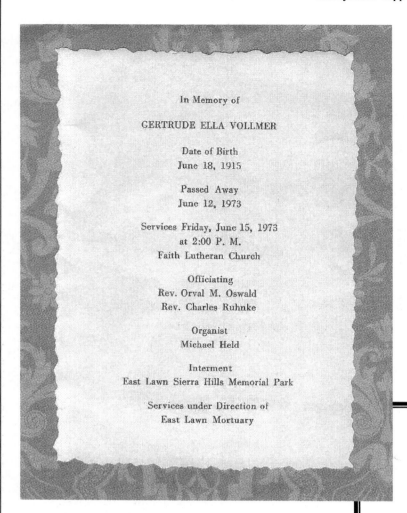

In Memory of

GERTRUDE ELLA VOLLMER

Date of Birth
June 18, 1915

Passed Away
June 12, 1973

Services Friday, June 15, 1973
at 2:00 P. M.
Faith Lutheran Church

Officiating
Rev. Orval M. Oswald
Rev. Charles Ruhnke

Organist
Michael Held

Interment
East Lawn Sierra Hills Memorial Park

Services under Direction of
East Lawn Mortuary

Vollmer, in Carmichael June 12, 1973, Gertrude Ella Vollmer. Beloved wife of Floyd A. Vollmer of Fair Oaks. Loving mother of Mrs. Gloria DuPras of Orangevale, California. Daughter of Mrs. Louisa Gemelke of Stanton, Nebraska. Sister of Wilhelma Kemper of San Antonio, Texas, Anita Reimnitz of South Dakota, Viola Brueggeman of Norfolk, Nebraska, Mildred Janulewicz of Omaha, Nebraska, Herbert Gemelke of Byron, Minnesota, and Emil Gemelke of Pilger, Nebraska. Grandmother of Michael M. and Brian DuPras. A native of Nebraska. Aged 57 years. Funeral at 2:00 p.m. in The faith Lutheran Church, San Juan Avenue and Fair Oaks Boulevard. Interment East Lawn Sierra Hills.

In Memory Of
Floyd Albert Vollmer

Born
May 23, 1912
A native of Nebraska

Passed Away
January 29, 2001
Carmichael, California

Memorial Services
Monday, February 5, 2001
At 10:00 A.M.
East Lawn Mortuary Chapel
5757 Greenback Lane
Sacramento, California

Officiating
Pastor John Herrmann

Interment
East Lawn Sierra Hills Memorial Park
Sacramento, California

Wilhelma Dorothea Gemelke

Born May 21, 1917

Married to Ivan Kemper March 9, 1937

Died June 22, 1999

Buried at Sunset Memorial Park, San Antonio, Texas

Gemelke women taken in Louisa Gemelke's living room in Pilger, sisters and sisters-in-law.

Front row from the left: Viola, Mildred; back row: Margaret, Gertrude, Wilhelma, Anita, Bernitha

Confirmation, St. John's Lutheran Church, Pilger, Nebraska, 1930

Front row, from the left: Mabel Siemsglusz, Adolph Siemsglusz, Inez Glaser;
back row: Esther Siegert, Esther Koehlmoos, Rev. J. H. Tegeler and Wilhelma Gemelke

Wedding day March 9, 1937

Attendants are Richard Stauffer
and Gertrude Gemelke

Wilhelma Gemelke Weds Pilger Man

At a very pretty church wedding Tuesday afternoon, March, 9, 1937, at St. John's Lutheran Church, Miss Wilhelma Gemelke became the bride of Mr. Ivan Kemper. The Rev. W. H. Koenig, pastor of the church, officiated, using the double ring ceremony.

The bridal couple and their attendants, Miss Gertrude Gemelke, sister of the bride, and Richard Stauffer, friend of the groom, entered the church to the strains of Lohengrin's Wedding March, played by Mrs. Walter Koenig.

The bride was gowned in a pretty dawn blue crepe dress with accessories to match. She wore a shoulder corsage of bride's roses and sweet peas. Her bridesmaid wore a green crepe gown with matching accessories and wore a corsage of pink sweet peas.

The bride is a daughter of Mr. and Mrs. Ernst Gemelke. She received her education in the Stanton County schools and has assisted her parents with the home work since. The groom is a son of Mr. and Mrs. Edward Kemper. He also attended rural schools of this county. For the past few years he has been engaged in farming.

Both of these young folks have a wide circle of friends who join us in extending congratulations.

In the evening a reception was held at the home of the bride's parents for about 100 guests. The house was decorated in the bride's colors, blue and white. A large wedding cake adorned the table as the centerpiece.

Mr. and Mrs. Kemper will reside on a farm three miles south and one east of Pilger.

Out-of-town guests attending the wedding and reception were Mr. and Mrs. John Tesch of Graindville, Iowa, Mr. and Mrs. Hans Paulson and family and Otto Daum of Boyden, Iowa, Mr. and Mrs. Rudy Rabbass, Mr. and Mrs. Henry Brundieck, Mr. and Mrs. Ernest Brundieck of Wisner.

Stanton Men Patent New Type Airplane

Ivan Kemper and Herman Blank built a new type of airplane, propelled by an auger-type propeller, which they invented and recently patented (1940). They estimate the speed of this type of plane at 700 miles per hour. The plane has all stiff rod controls, small wing spread and automatic control on the auger-type propeller. The pilot's cockpit is located in the front part of the plane for clear vision.

Note: I believe Ivan and his brother built a house in Stanton at 409 14th and Elm Streets. (LaRayne {Gemelke} Topp)

Ivan Kemper SF 1-C Arrives in Stanton

Ivan Kemper, SF 1-C, who spent 34 months in the service, 23 of them being overseas, has arrived home and he and his wife are now visiting with relatives and friends in Pilger and Stanton.

A member of the SeaBees, he landed in Hawaii in December 1943, where he was stationed nine months while a large naval receiving base was built. In October, 1944, the unit was shipped to Guam where they constructed Admiral Nimitz' headquarters. He sailed from Guan October 16th, and landed at San Diego October 31, and was discharged at Saint Louis, Missouri.

He wears the Asiatic-Pacific, Good Conduct and the American War ribbons. His plans for the future have not yet been made.

Note: Wilhelma told me they dried out farming and couldn't find work in the Pilger or Stanton area. Because they didn't want to be *on relief* (Welfare or Social Services assistance) they moved to Texas near his brother. Ivan worked as a civilian and a plumber on a military base at San Antonio, Texas. (LaRayne {Gemelke} Topp)

Wilhelma at the keyboard
at their San Antonio home

Joining in the singing are
Anita and George
Reimnitz (left) and Viola
Brueggeman

Memories

After Grandpa Gemelke died and Herb was in the service, Dad's sisters helped him farm. Grandma Louisa still lived on the farm at that time. Wilhelma was stacking hay in a field east of the house, using a car sweep which you had to drive backwards. Wilhelma accidentally drove into the ditch. Anita and Millie were sitting on the front of the car and Viola on the gas tank. They were fortunate they weren't killed, Millie said. They had to pull the sweep out of the ditch so their mother wouldn't find out, not realizing she was watching from the pantry window. When the four sisters got to the house, Louisa asked, "Was that car sweep heavy?" (Mildred {Gemelke} Janulewicz, Anita {Gemelke} Reimnitz, and Viola {Gemelke} Brueggeman)

Wilhelma D. Kemper

Date of birth: May 21, 1917

Entered into Rest: June 22, 1999

Services: Saturday, June 26, 1999, at Mt. Calvary Lutheran Church, San Antonio, Texas

Entombment, Sunset Memorial Park, San Antonio, Texas

Ivan Kemper

Ivan D. Kemper, age 93, died Thursday, December 16, 2004. He was born in Pilger, Nebraska, on December 25, 1910, to Herman and Mary Schowalter Kemper. He was a Veteran of the United States Navy and a member of Mount Calvary Lutheran Church. Mr. Kemper was preceded in death by his loving wife, Wilhelma Kemper. He is survived by several nieces, nephews, cousins and extended family and friends. The visitation will be held on Sunday, December 19, 2004, from 2:00 to 4:00 p.m. at Sunday Funeral Home, 1701 Austin Highway. The Funeral Service will be held on Monday, December 20, 2004, at 9:00 a.m. at Mount Calvary Lutheran Church, 308 Mount Calvary Road, San Antonio, Texas 78209, with the Rev. Kim DeVries officiating. The Entombment will follow in the mausoleum in Sunday Memorial Park.

Memories

We had a family reunion at the home place north of Pilger when Kevin and I lived there. We invited neighbors who knew the Gemelke kids when they were younger. Neighbor Virgie (Burris) Frerichs and Wilhelma had been best friends when they were girls. One of my favorite memories is of the two of them, listening to a game we were playing, Wilhelma standing behind Virgie (or perhaps the other way around), with her chin on Virgie's shoulder, their faces side by side. Below: Dad (Emil) did the driving for his sisters and the Burris girls until he began to date Mom (Bernitha). Anita explained it this way. "He would take us places; he would take us to dances. All of a sudden he quit. He went over the hill (to the Hasenkamp farm to see Mom). He had other places to go." That's Dad (Emil) behind the wheel, and Virgie standing on the fender. (LaRayne {Gemelke} Topp)

Emil Gustav

Born June 12, 1919

Farmer

Married August 30, 1944

Bernitha Hasenkamp

Died October 3, 2002

Buried at Pilger Cemetery

Note: Dad couldn't wait to get his photograph taken because he imagined an immense, beautiful studio. He was surprised and disappointed to see, instead, a corner of a room with cloth backdrops. (LaRayne {Gemelke} Topp)

Confirmation class of 1934, St. John's Lutheran Church, Pilger

Front row, from the left: Helen Husmann, Emelia Daum, Emil
Gemelke, Ella Koehlmoos, Doris Ritze; back row: Margaret Peters,
Rev. W. Koenig and Marie Pobanz.

Note: Dad (Emil) was always surrounded
by girls. One day, when I complained to
Dad about having two brothers and no
sisters, he said he knew just how I felt.
"Think of me," he said. The cousins his age
were girls, his Confirmation class was all
girls, plus he had five sisters. Five sisters!
But how he loved to farm. (LaRayne
{Gemelke} Topp)

Emil Gemelke and Bernitha Hasenkamp
August 30, 1944

Gemelke-Hasenkamp

The marriage of Miss Bernitha Hasenkamp, eldest daughter of Mr. and Mrs. Ed Hasenkamp, and Emil Gemelke, youngest son of Mrs. Louisa Gemelke, took place Wednesday evening at 7 o'clock, August 30, 1944, in the St. John's Lutheran Church at Pilger. The Rev. O. E. Schlecht of Wisner read the marriage lines using the double ring ceremony. The bridal couple and their attendants entered the church to the strains of Lohengrens Wedding March played by Mrs. Ivan Kemper, sister of the groom.

The bride wore an aqua blue street length dress with pink shoulder length veil held in place with pink roses. Her jewelry was two strand pearls, a gift of the groom, and she wore a corsage of talisman roses.

Her only attendant, Miss Anita Gemelke, sister of the groom, wore a street length blue crepe dress also with a pink shoulder length veil held in place with pink roses. Her corsage was of pink roses. Wilfred Hasenkamp, brother of the bride, served as best man. Both the groom and best man wore brown suits with white carnation boutonnieres.

A wedding reception was held at the home of the bride's parents for the immediate families. A three-tier wedding cake baked by Mrs. Ivan Kemper, sister of the groom, centered the table.

The rooms were decorated in the bride's chosen colors, aqua blue and pink. The three waitresses were Viola and Mildred Gemelke, sisters of the groom, and Luetta Hasenkamp, sister of the bride.

The young couple will reside on a farm three miles north of Pilger.

Memories

I had a small wedding during wartime. My sister, Anita, was bridesmaid and Bernitha's brother was my best man. We went to the church about four o'clock. Rained a small shower that day. Earlier that afternoon I had worked in the shop and knocked a saw off of a nail. It fell down on my lip so had a sore lip for my wedding. I backed the car out of the shed and backed into my folks' car. (Emil Gemelke)

Emil and Bernitha went to school together. "I drew his name for Christmas and Mom bought a pocket knife to give to Emil. I was in the first grade and Emil in the fourth. Can you imagine giving a pocketknife now? I knew German and not English when I started to school. The teacher would say something to do. I'd say in German, I don't know how to do that. So Wilhelma would tell me what to do. The teacher said to cut out a rooster. I never cut out a rooster before, and I was looking for a scissors. I said, *"Wo ist die shere?"* Wilhelma knew what I wanted. Of us four first graders, I had the worst looking chicken." (Bernitha {Hasenkamp} Gemelke)

"We were going to get married and Emil's dad died. We moved the wedding till later. We were going to have a shower the day he died. I wanted a June 1st wedding, but Mom (Beata Hasenkamp) said, "You can't. Merlin (brother) is in the service. He had a furlough the 21st, but then Emil's dad passed away. His Mom said she wasn't going to lose a son and a husband in the same week. The funeral was the day we were supposed to get married. We waited two months, until August 29th. The vacancy minister was going to take his son to the fair, and asked, "Can't you make it one day later?" So we got married on the 30th." (Bernitha {Hasenkamp} Gemelke)

"I remember that day very plain. We were going to have a bridal shower that day for Bernitha. Dad was going to take some feed to town. He came into the parlor to talk with us, and it seemed he didn't want to leave. Afterwards he was going to come back to take us girls to the shower. He had a flat tire, and after he dropped the grain off, he took the tire off, and didn't come back. He had a heart attack at the gas station. Dr. Reid called on the phone. Mom sat down in the rocking chair and said, 'Dad's gone. Send for Emil.'" I'll never forget that. (Millie {Gemelke} Janulewicz)

Gemelke, Emil and Bernitha (Hasenkamp) by LaRayne Meyer Topp, 1987, *Pilger, Nebraska, Century Edition, 1887-1987*

Emil Gemelke was born June 12, 1919, north of Pilger, to Ernst and Louisa (Koehlmoos) Gemelke. He attended District 43 country school and St. John's Lutheran Church, Pilger.

In August 1944, he married Bernitha Hasenkamp at Pilger. She is the daughter of Edward and Beata (Loewe) Hasenkamp. She was born north of Pilger and also attended St. John's Church and rural school Districts 43 and 25. They lived only a mile apart while they were growing up and have remarked that as they dated during the gas rationing time of World War II, Emil had only enough gas to go over the hill and so he married Bernitha.

They lived on Emil's father's farm which was eventually bought by Emil. They raised three children: Duane, currently of Minneapolis, Minnesota; Ron, Dallas, Texas; and LaRayne (Mrs. Kevin Meyer), Pilger.

In 1955, they moved to the farm directly west and farmed both places until 1983, when they moved to their present home in Pilger.

Bernitha grew up in a household which had its own generator for electricity for lights and a hand pump in the kitchen for water. Emil lived in a home with a carbide plant for lights, running water and a bathroom. After their marriage, they moved to the farm that had none of these advantages and had to adjust to kerosene lights and water carried from the well in the pasture.

Mostly German was spoken in Bernitha's home. When she started to school, she knew German only. One of the older students (Wilhelma Gemelke) in school translated to the teacher for her until she learned English. Her parents then decided they must speak only English at home for the sake of younger brothers and sister. However, when there was something they wished to talk about without the children understanding, they would resort to German, not realizing Bernitha still understood German.

When they lived on the east farm, Herb and Margaret and family lived on the west farm until Herb and family moved to Minnesota in 1955. The road which ran between the two farms they farmed was a cow trail. A Jeep was used to take the children to school.

Both Emil and Bernitha and their three children were delivered by Pilger's longtime physician, Dr. Reid. LaRayne was born on Dr. Reid's birthday.

Emil was involved with the Humbug local Farmers Union Board, the Telephone Board, and the District 43 school board. Bernitha is a charter member of the neighborhood Sewing Club which has continued for over 30 years and is active in St. John's Ladies Aid. They belong to St. John's Lutheran Church, its Lutheran Laymen's League and AAL group, and enjoy several Pitch and Sheephead card clubs.

In 1968, Emil received the Ak-Sar-Ben Good Neighbor Award for help given during the 1967 tornado that hit and severely damaged several neighboring farms.

Note: We played lots of games with Dad in the evenings: cards or a game with marbles called Chinese Checkers. He said he and his siblings and his mom sat around the kerosene lamp at the kitchen table and played a lot of games. When Grandma Louisa lived in the nursing home at Stanton, we would go and play Sheephead. She lived there for nine years and lost only two games of Sheephead that I remember. (LaRayne {Gemelke} Topp)

Gemelke kids, from left: Ronnie, Duane and LaRayne with much-loved
Cocker Spaniel Poochie, taken on the Gemelke farm.

To the left, Emil getting his mustache brushed by sister
Viola. To the left, top to bottom, are Millie, Wilhelma and
Anita. Below, Emil, left, visits with brother Herb.

Emil Gustav Gemelke

Emil Gustav Gemelke was born June 12, 1919, in Stanton County, Nebraska, to Ernst and Louisa (Koehlmoos) Gemelke. He was baptized on July 13, 1919, and later confirmed at St. John's Lutheran Church on May 13, 1934. Emil attended Stanton County rural school district #43.

On August 30, 1944, he was united in marriage to Bernitha Hasenkamp at St. John's Lutheran Church in Pilger. The couple farmed north of Pilger until retiring in October of 1983 when they moved into Pilger. In the Spring of 2000, Emil entered the Wisner Care Center. Emil passed away on Thursday, October 3, 2002, at the Wisner Care Center.

He was a lifelong member of St. John's Lutheran Church in Pilger, and has served as a trustee, elder, and was a member of its Lutheran Laymen's League. In 1968, Emil received the Aksarben Good Neighbor Award for assisting area farmers after a tornado struck in 1967.

Survivors include wife Bernitha Gemelke of Pilger; sons Duane and his wife Linda Gemelke of Brooklyn Park, Minnesota, and Ronnie Gemelke of Richardson, Texas; daughter LaRayne Meyer of Pilger; six grandchildren: Kristine and husband Steve Hanson of Madison, Wisconsin, Michael Gemelke of Portland, Oregon, Nathan Gemelke of Stanford, California, Trisha and husband William Lombard III of Inwood, Iowa, Brenda and husband Harold Breitkreutz of Ft. Thomas, Kentucky, and Clinton Meyer of Murphysboro, Illinois; five great-grandchildren: Ryan, Corinne and William Hanson, Tara Lombard and Ian Breitkreutz; sisters Anita and husband George Reimnitz of Corsica, South Dakota; Viola and husband Robert Brueggeman of Norfolk, Nebraska, and Mildred and husband Leo Janulewicz of Omaha, Nebraska; sister-in-law Margaret Gemelke of Rochester, Minnesota; and brother-in-law Ivan Kemper of San Antonio, Texas.

Emil was preceded in death by his parents, son-in-law Kevin Meyer, brother Herbert, two sisters Wilhelma Kemper and Gertrude and husband Floyd Vollmer.

Bernitha Gemelke

Bernitha Frieda Helena was born at rural Pilger to Edward and Beata (Loewe) Hasenkamp on March 23, 1923.

On April 22, 1923, she was baptized into the Lutheran faith at St. John's Lutheran Church, Pilger, where she attended Sunday School and Walther League, and was confirmed. She attended Stanton County rural schools districts #43 and #25, north of Pilger.

She was married to Emil Gemelke on August 30, 1944. The ceremony was held in the original St. John's Church, with their reception at the home of her parents. The couple farmed north of Pilger where they raised their family. Upon retirement, they moved to Pilger in the fall of 1983. The couple enjoyed playing cards in various card clubs and dancing. Bernitha also spent time sewing, quilting and doing crafts.

She was a member of the neighborhood Sewing Club and St. John's Ladies Aid and LWML for more than 60 years. She put up the monthly birthday board for many years at Pilger's Senior Citizens Center.

Emil passed away on October 3, 2002. Bernitha continued living in Pilger until she moved to Colonial Courts Assisted Living at Beemer in 2006. In May of 2018, at the age of 95, she moved to Colonial Haven Nursing Home.

She died June 1, 2018, at Colonial Haven.

Left to cherish her memory are son and wife Duane and Linda Gemelke of Brooklyn Park, Minnesota; daughter LaRayne Topp of Wisner; grandchildren and spouses Kristine (Steve) Hanson of Las Cruces, New Mexico, Trish (Bill) Lombard of Inwood, Iowa; Brenda (Harold) Breitkreutz of Wisner, Michael (Emily Strother) Gemelke of Portland, Oregon, Clinton (Hillary) Meyer of Indianola, Iowa, and Nathan (Edina Sarajlic) Gemelke of State College, Pennsylvania; two step-granddaughters, Trisha Johnson and Tracy Topp (Matthew Marsolek), all of Arlee, Montana; 11 great-grandchildren; 5 step-great-grandchildren and one great-great-grandson; sister Luetta Reuter of Norfolk; brother Wilfred Hasenkamp of Stanton; sister-in-law Joan Hasenkamp of West Point; brother-in-law Bob Brueggeman of Norfolk; and a host of nieces and nephews.

She was preceded in death by parents Edward and Beata Hasenkamp, in-laws Ernst and Louisa (Koehlmoos) Gemelke, husband Emil, son Ronnie, brother Merlin Hasenkamp, sons-in-law Kevin Meyer and Dale Topp; and in-laws Palma Hasenkamp, Calvin Reuter, Herb (Margaret) Gemelke, Gertrude (Floyd) Vollmer, Wilhelma (Ivan) Kemper, Viola Brueggeman, Anita (George) Reimnitz and Mildred (Leo) Janulewicz.

Anita Alvina Louise

Born December 6, 1923
at Pilger, Nebraska

Married June 20, 1948
to George Reimnitz

Died May 1, 2014
at Corsica, South Dakota

Married to George Robert August Reimnitz

Born February 22, 1924

Farmer

Died June 27, 2007

George Reimnitz came with his
family to Shirley Gemelke's
confirmation (daughter of
Gustav and Marie) Anita and
George started dating then. He'd
come down to Pilger to go to
movies or a dance.

Confirmation class of 1937, St. John's Lutheran
Church, Pilger, Nebraska

Front row, from the left: Irene Finkhouse, Betty Grenz,
Rev. W. Koenig, Bernitha Hasenkamp, Anita Gemelke;
back row: Neal Siecke, Norbert Husmann and Vernon
Putz. Not pictured: Samuel Burris and Ivan Kemper.

Reimnitz-Gemelke Wedding Sunday

St. John's Lutheran Church, Pilger, was the scene of an all-white wedding Sunday, June 20th, 1948, at 4 o'clock, when Miss Anita Gemelke, daughter of Mrs. Louisa Gemelke, became the bride of George Reimnitz, son of Mr. and Mrs. Paul Reimnitz, Mt. Vernon, South Dakota. The Rev. A. I. Bernthal performed the single ring ceremony.

Misses Luetta Hasenkamp, Shirley Gemelke and Lillian Koehlmoos sang, "Blest Be The Tie That Binds," and "The Lord is My Shepherd." James Karel accompanied them and also played the wedding marches.

The bride, given in marriage by her brother, Herbert, was attired in a gown of white marquisette with lace insertions in the skirt, extending into a two-yard train fashioned with a sweetheart neckline and long sleeves that came to a point at the wrist. She carried a bouquet of white roses tied with white streamers. She wore a single strand of cultured pearls, a gift of the bridegroom.

Miss Viola Gemelke, sister of the bride, acted as maid of honor. She was dressed in a gown of white cohana crepe.

Miss Lena Reimnitz, sister of the bridegroom, and Miss Mildred Gemelke, sister of the bride, and bridemaids were gowned in white marquisette and all wore corsages of pink roses and a string of pearls, their gift from the bride.

Darlene Reimnitz, niece of the bridegroom and flower girl was seen in a white marquisette dress and carried a colonial bouquet.

Roger Stahl, nephew of the bridegroom, acted as ring bearer and wore a white suit and carried the ring on a white satin pillow.

The bridegroom was attended by his brother Robert, as best man. Marvin Gemelke, Ivan Bialas, Louis Reimnitz and Merlin Hasenkamp were ushers. The bridegroom and his attendants wore white carnations in their lapels.

The bride's mother wore a light blue figured dress and the bridegroom's mother wore a dark blue figured dress. They each wore a corsage of white carnations.

A reception was held at Washington Hall, which was decorated with white and pink streamers. The three-tiered wedding cake baked by Mrs. Carl Schiermeier and Mrs. John Dohren was topped with a miniature bride and bridegroom.

Misses Shirley Gemelke, Lillian Koehlmoos, Delores Puepke, Elsie Koehlmoos, Wilma Schuette and Luetta Hasenkamp, waitresses, wore white aprons fashioned with tiny pink bows.

Mrs. Clifford Petersen and Mrs. Herbert Frerichs were responsible for the refreshments.

Miss Lenore Vonderohe, Norfolk, had charge of the guest book and Miss Doris Ritze, Wayne, and Miss LaVerne Harms, Norfolk, were in charge of the gift table.

Out-of-town guests from the following towns attended the wedding: Parkston, Mt. Vernon, Delmont, Armour, Corsica, Dimock, Mitchell, Ethan and Wessington Springs, all in South Dakota; St. Louis, Missouri; Happy Canyon and Amarillo, Texas; Norfolk, Wayne and Wisner, Nebraska.

The newlyweds will reside in Parkston, South Dakota.

Left: Anita and George
Center, from the left: Anita, Emil and Viola
Bottom: Anita

Above, front row: Karin, Anita, George, Russell;
and back row: James, David, Douglas, Marjean, Joyce and Sheila

Left: Anita and baby Karin

Note: Mom (Anita) had two middle names - Alvina and Louise. I was never real sure which one came first. A memory I have is going to Grandma's house in Pilger and sitting in the front porch and looking thru that contraption that had the pictures - two next to each other (a stereoscope). (Karin {Reimnitz} Mueller)

Note: Anita worked for the Hughes family in Norfolk after the farm sale and Louisa moved to Pilger. After Anita got married, Vi worked at the Hugheses. Anita, Vi and Wilhelma worked for Emil after Ernst's death until Herb came home from the war.

Anita Reimnitz

Anita Alvina Louise (Gemelke) Reimnitz was born on December 6, 1923, to Ernst and Louisa (Koehlmoos) Gemelke at Pilger. She was baptized and confirmed at St. John's Lutheran Church in Pilger and attended country school #43 in Stanton County.

She married George Reimnitz on June 20, 1948, at Pilger, Nebraska. Together they farmed west of Dimock, South Dakota, for 20 years. In 1967, they moved to a farm east of Corsica, South Dakota, where she lived until she moved to Prairie Villa in Armour, South Dakota, in 2012. George died on June 27, 2007.

Anita was a member of Immanuel Lutheran Church west of Dimock. She was a hard worker and was known for her huge gardens. She also enjoyed crocheting and reading. Her children and grandchildren will always remember her homemade salsa, pickles, cookies and chocolate brownies. In March of 2014, she became a resident of Good Samaritan Society in Corsica where she died on Thursday, May 1, 2014, at the age of 90.

She is survived by eight children: Russell (Gladys) Reimnitz, Mitchel, South Dakota; Karin (Howard) Mueller, Milbank, South Dakota; Marjean (Larry) Moeller, Mitchel; Douglas (Bonnie) Reimnitz, Corsica; Joyce (Ira) Van Drongelen, Harrison, South Dakota; David (Jane) Reimnitz, Sioux Falls, South Dakota; James (Dawn Steen) Reimnitz, Sioux Falls; and Sheila (Luke) Schafer, Gillette, Wyoming; sister, Mildred Janulewicz, Omaha; sister-in-law, Bernitha Gemelke, Beemer; brother-in-law Robert Brueggeman, Norfolk; 33 grandchildren; one step-grandchild; 26 great-grandchildren; and four step-great-grandchildren.

She was preceded in death by her parents; her husband George; two brothers Herbert and Emil Gemelke; and three sisters, Gertrude Vollmer, Wilhelma Kemper and Viola Brueggeman.

Services were held Tuesday, May 6, 2014, at Immanuel Lutheran Church, rural Dimock. Interment was in Immanuel Lutheran Cemetery, rural Dimock.

George Reimnitz

George Robert August Reimnitz was born on February 22, 1924, to Paul and Lena (Blume) Reimnitz in Davison County, South Dakota. He was baptized at Immanuel Lutheran Church near Dimock, South Dakota, where he was a lifelong member and held various positions. He attended country school in Davison County, South Dakota.

He married Anita Gemelke in Pilger, Nebraska, on June 20, 1948. They farmed in the Flensburg area for 20 years before moving to a farm east of Corsica, South Dakota, in 1967 where they have lived until his death. George enjoyed farming, hunting, fishing, gardening and flying kite with his great-grandchildren.

He died on June 27, 2007, on his farm near his home near Corsica, South Dakota, at the age of 83.

He is survived by his wife, Anita, Corsica, South Dakota; eight children: Russell Reimnitz and wife, Gladys, Corsica, South Dakota; Karin Mueller and husband Howard, Milbank, South Dakota; Marjean Mathis, Mitchell, South Dakota; Douglas Reimnitz and wife, Bonnie, Corsica, South Dakota; Joyce VanDrongelen and husband, Ira, Harrison, South Dakota; David Reimnitz and wife, Jane, Sioux Falls, South Dakota; James Reimnitz, Mitchell, South Dakota; and Sheila Schafer and husband, Luke, Gillette, Wyoming; a brother, Louis Reimnitz and wife Doris, Mitchell, South Dakota; three sisters: Dorothy Stahl, Mitchell, South Dakota; Lydia Sigmund, Mitchell, South Dakota; and Lena Bialas and husband, Ivan, Parkston, South Dakota; a sister-in-law Wilma Reimnitz, Corsica, South Dakota; 31 grandchildren, one step-grandchild, 20 great-grandchildren and one step-great-grandchild.

He was preceded in death by his parents, three brothers, Leonard, Robert and Paul Reimnitz, a sister-in-law, Beverly Reimnitz, and two brothers-in-law, Otto Stahl and Edwin Sigmund, Sr.

Viola Marie

Born February 13, 1926

Married Robert A. Brueggeman
September 8, 1957

Died July 2, 2011 at age 85
Norfolk, Nebraska

Anita, left, and Viola

Confirmation class of 1940,
St. John's Lutheran Church,
Pilger, Nebraska

Front row, from the left: Rev. W. Koenig,
Viola Gemelke, Frances Klima, Lavina
Schlecht, Oscar Gemelke; and back row:
Marvin Husmann, Arnold Koehlmoos,
Jerome Krutz and Delvin Krueger

Robert Brueggeman and Viola Gemelke
September 8, 1957
Attendants are Mildred Gemelke and Leo Schellpeper

Gemelke-Brueggeman

Miss Viola M. Gemelke, Norfolk, daughter of Mrs. Louisa Gemelke, Pilger, became the bride of Robert A. Brueggeman, son of Mrs. Martha Brueggeman, Norfolk, at two-o'clock Sunday afternoon, September 8, 1957, in the Christ Lutheran Church in Norfolk. The Rev. Wm. Hassold officiated.

Church decorations included candelabra and baskets of white gladioluses and pink carnations.

The bride was attired in a pink satin dress with matching accessories. She carried a bouquet of white gladioluses. Miss Mildred Gemelke, Omaha, served her sister as maid of honor. She wore a peacock blue satin dress with accessories to match with a corsage of pink carnations.

Leo Schellpeper, Norfolk, brother-in-law of the groom, was best man.

Mothers of the couple wore carnations complimenting their outfits. The bride's table was covered with white satin. It was centered with a four-tiered, all white cake, flanked by candles.

After the reception at Olson's Inn, the couple left on a wedding trip to Colorado. The bride is employed at Safeway Stores, Inc., and the bridegroom is employed at the Norfolk Post Office.

Memories

This is Viola's story: He came to my work at the store. First he came with his mother to get groceries, and I had my eye on him. He kept coming in. I started to walk home one evening, it was dark, and he wanted to know if I wanted a ride. Later on, I had to sell tickets to the race track. I had an extra ticket so I took him. He got in free. I was happy to get a city boy. Farmers work too hard.

This is Bob's story: She courted me.

Top left, from the left: Mildred, Louisa, Viola and Wilhelma.

Top right: Viola at farm home in front of parlor window. Note the violets.

Center: Viola at old Lutheran Hospital in Norfolk.

Bottom left, by Norfolk Hatchery: Anita, left, and Viola.

Bottom right: Viola working in the kitchen in Louisa's kitchen in Pilger.

Viola and Bob's three children, from the left: Mark, Coreen and Barbara

Viola Brueggeman

Services for Viola M. Brueggeman, 85, of Norfolk, Nebraska, will be at 1:30 p.m. Thursday, July 7, 2011, at Grace Lutheran Church in Norfolk with the Revs. Ray Wilke and Christopher Asbury officiating. Burial will be in Prospect Hill Cemetery, Norfolk.

She died Saturday, July 2, 2011, at Heritage of Bel Air.

Vi was born on February 13, 1926, in Stanton County, the daughter of Ernst and Louisa (Koehlmoos) Gemelke. She was baptized March 26, 1926, and confirmed on June 2, 1940, at St. John's Lutheran Church at Pilger. She was raised on the family farm and attended rural school.

Vi married Robert (Bob) A. Brueggeman on September 8, 1957, at Christ Lutheran Church in Norfolk. She worked at many various jobs as a young woman and at Safeway Grocery Store for several years prior to her raising her children.

Vi was active in the PTA while her children were growing up and was a member of Grace Lutheran Church, its ladies aid, and the quilting group.

Viola is survived by her husband, Bob Brueggeman of Norfolk; her son, Mark, and his wife Sadie Brueggeman of McAlister, Oklahoma; two daughters, Coreen Carnes of Lincoln, Nebraska, and Barbara Nave of Kansas City, Missouri; four grandchildren; two sisters, Anita Reimnitz of Corsica, South Dakota, and Mildred and her husband Leo Janulewicz of Omaha, Nebraska, and many nieces and nephews.

She was preceded in death by her parents, two brothers, Herbert Gemelke and Emil Gemelke, and two sisters, Gertrude Vollmer and Wilhelma Kemper.

At the time of this writing, Bob resides at the Veterans' Home in Norfolk, Nebraska.

Mildred (Millie) Irene

Born July 11, 1930

Married Leo Janulewicz
October 14, 1961, at Omaha

Died April 18, 2015

Interment in Calvary Catholic Cemetery
Omaha, Nebraska

Confirmation Class of 1944
St. John's Lutheran Church, Pilger, Nebraska

Front row, from the left: Darlene Thies, Mildred Gemelke;
back row: James Karel, Rev. W. H. Koenig, Wilfred Hasenkamp

Millie Gemelke and Leo Janulewicz

October 14, 1961

Miss Gemelke Is Bride of L. Janulewicz

Miss Mildred Gemelke became the bride of Leo Janulewicz in a 9 a.m. ceremony performed by Rev. Joseph Meyers at St. Phillip Neri Church in Omaha (1961).

The bride is the daughter of Mrs. Louisa Gemelke of Pilger. Mr. Janulewicz is the son of Mr. and Mrs. Floyd K. Janulewicz of Loup City.

The bride was dressed in a gown of white Chantilly lace over tulle and bridal satin. The fitted lace bodice was styled with a scalloped Sabrina neckline accented with sequins and seed pearls. Long lace sleeves tapered to a point at the wrists. The bouffant skirt repeated the re-embroidered scalloped lace on the aisle-wide chapel train and fashioned a butterfly bustle effect in the back. She wore an imported English illusion three-tier ballerina length veil, held by a queen's crown of iridescent hairbraid trimmed with Aurora crystal beads. Her bouquet was a cascade of red roses.

Mrs. Larry Willis of Blair was matron of honor. Her street length dress was green with matching accessories. She carried a cascade bouquet of bronze mums.

Ted Oseka of Omaha was best man.

A wedding dinner and reception was held at Napoleon's Restaurant.

After a wedding trip South, the couple will live in Omaha.

Uncle Leo came into the family when he married Aunt Millie, the only Polish Catholic in a family of German Lutherans. At first we liked this bigger-than-life man because he loved our Millie, but in the end, we loved him for himself—because how could you not? (LaRayne {Gemelke} Topp)

Photo at right: Leo, left, and brother-in-law Emil. Below: Bernitha teaching Leo how to crochet.

Top: Millie.
Center: Viola, left, and Millie.
Bottom, on a trip to South Dakota, front row from the left: Emil and sons, Duane, left, and Ronnie; and back row: Millie, Louisa, Anita and George.

Memories

"I went to polka dances on Sunday afternoons. The first time I went, I had my eye on someone else. When he went to sit down he missed the chair. He always blamed me for kicking it out. We lived in the same trailer court. He'd buy chicken and invited me over. If he was going to buy me chicken, I'm gonna go." (Millie {Gemelke} Janulewicz)

Millie worked at Hinky-Dinky in Norfolk, Nebraska. Millie and a girlfriend decided to move to Omaha. Bob Brueggeman moved her down there. There was a store in Omaha and an opening for a meat wrapper. The store was at 24th and Ames in North Omaha, but Millie ended up at a store in South Omaha, or Leo and Millie would have never met.

Leo and Millie's daughters, Jo, left, and Renae

Millie Janulewicz

Funeral services for Mildred Janulewicz, 84, of Omaha were April 23, 2015, at St. Vincent de Paul Catholic Church in Omaha, with interment in the Calvary Catholic Cemetery in Omaha.

Mildred (Millie) Janulewicz was born July 11, 1930, to Louisa (Koehlmoos) and Ernst Gemelke at Pilger, Nebraska. She was baptized and confirmed at St. John's Lutheran Church of Pilger and attended District #43 country school. She lived on the family farm north of Pilger until the death of her father in 1944 when the family moved into Pilger.

She married Leo Janulewicz at Omaha on October 14, 1961. The couple had two daughters, Renae and Jo.

She died April 18, 2015, at her home.

She is survived by two daughters, Renae Janulewicz, and Jo (Michael) Freel; two granddaughters, Mason and Ryann Freel, all of Omaha; brother-in-law Robert Brueggeman of Norfolk, and sister-in-law Bernitha Gemelke of Beemer.

She was preceded in death by her husband of 50 years, Leo Janulewicz; her parents, Ernst and Louisa Gemelke; and siblings and spouses Herbert and Margaret Gemelke, Gertrude and Floyd Vollmer, Wilhelma and Ivan Kemper, Emil Gemelke, Anita and George Reimnitz and Viola Brueggeman.

Leo A. Janulewicz

Born September 27, 1924 at Litchfield, Nebraska

Died November 16, 2011, at Omaha, Nebraska

Age 87. Preceded in death by parents, two brothers, Raymond and Cash Janulewicz, and sister, Barbara Moraczewski. Survived by loving wife of 50 years, Mildred *Millie*; daughters, Renae Janulewicz, Jolene (Michael) Freel; two granddaughters, Mason and Ryann; siblings, Paul Janulewicz, Wanda (Bob) Klimek and Eloise (Richard) Riley; many nieces, nephews and good friends.

Funeral services Monday, 10:00 a.m. at St. Vincent DePaul Catholic Church with interment in Calvary Catholic Cemetery. Visitation with the family begins Sunday, after 3:00 p.m. at the Pacific Street Chapel with a wake service at 4:00 p.m. Memorials to Tangier Shrine or St. Vincent DePaul Catholic Church.

Farm Scenes

Dad (Emil) talked about a year they had a short corn crop and cut silage, digging a silage pit east of the farmplace. It was so hot the kids slept out on the lawn, and listened to the chickens dropping dead off the roosts. (LaRayne {Gemelke} Topp)

How I wish I'd been more careful and avoided spills…. This is a recipe given to me by Grandma Louisa for Plum and Raisin Jam. (LaRayne {Gemelke} Topp)

Plum & raisin jam

6 C pitted prunes or plums
2C seeded raisins
2 C water
4 C sugar. Put raisin trough food chopper or else chop them with knife. cook plum in water till they began to soften. add sugar and raisins. stiring to prevent scorching. takes about 40 minutes cooking to make the mixture thick enough for jam. Pour in sterilized glasses and cover with parifine. you may put ½ a lemon to this recipe put in with the plums so that it will be cooking the entire time

I hope you will find some nice plums to try the recipie. it needs a lot of stiring

Love Grandma

Grandma (Louisa) raised lots of chickens. She also liked to can. Dad (Emil) said she canned anything she could get in a jar. (LaRayne {Gemelke} Topp)

Mother pickled everything. She canned everything, even canned ripe cucumbers. She raised everything you could think of. She had a knack for canning. (Viola {Gemelke} Brueggeman)

Memories

We raised a couple hundred Leghorns and White Rocks—one for butchering and one for eggs. Remember how many chickens we fried when the threshing crew came? (Anita {Gemelke} Reimnitz)

My favorite time was butchering. Emil would steak a certain piece of meat to eat. One time Shep, the dog, got into the smokehouse and took a bite out of a lot of the sausages. (Millie {Gemelke} Janulewicz)

We didn't get to town very often, but we would go sometimes on Saturday nights. Dad would go into the pool hall, and women and children didn't go in there. But I had to go in and ask Dad for money. I didn't talk to him until he asked me to, so I would stand there. He'd reach in his pocket, and whatever came out, I got. I knew enough not to go back until the money was gone. (Millie {Gemelke} Janulewicz)

Whatever he said, goes. (Anita {Gemelke} Reimnitz, about her dad)

What I remember most about my father: he was a very quiet man. He read mostly German magazines. One was *Die Haus Frau*. He nearly always drank coffee from a saucer. Mother baked a lot of bread and coffee cake and played a lot of cards with us kids. (Emil Gemelke)

I respected my dad. We didn't talk to him. Whatever he said, goes. He was sitting there (in the kitchen) reading the paper. I was running back and forth from the porch to the pantry (hitting the pantry window each time). He didn't take the newspaper down, and he said "You maybe better quit that." The pantry window broke. I tried to run and hide in the bathroom. I got the only spanking I ever got in my life, and I deserved it. (Millie {Gemelke} Janulewicz)

Chores were mostly milking cows and feeding calves. (Emil Gemelke)

After we separated (milk) we'd sing. Somebody stopped by and came up the sidewalk. We were singing like everything and you (said to Anita and Millie), you let me sing with that guy there. Cows give more milk when you sing, "Here comes Dolly, through the window…." When we'd take away the baby calves from their mother, they had nothing to eat. We had to get down, put our hand in the bucket of milk, and straddle that little sucker. He'd drink off our finger. (Viola {Gemelke} Brueggeman)

Viola was the only woman my mom (Bernitha) ever knew who could harness a horse, as the harnesses were so heavy. (LaRayne {Gemelke} Topp)

Viola worked in the field. Some of the more difficult things, Anita said, she left to Viola, while Anita walked behind the drag or cultivated. Viola was the only one who ever started the John Deere tractor, the only one strong enough. "It was embarrassing," she said. "The men couldn't do it. You know what else? I had to feed the pigs." (There were fed slop: scraps from the house. One time the horses got away, running all the way home, and the girls had to walk. While the girls worked in the field, Millie brought a fresh team out to them as needed. In the late afternoon, Louisa and Millie started chores, and Millie got the cows from the pasture. She would milk one or two at a time—of the 30 to 40 head they milked—until the rest of the kids came home to help. My dad (Emil) milked a cow every morning before he was old enough to start school, so this means he milked when he was only five or six years old. (As related in interview with Viola, Anita and Millie, plus memory of Emil, LaRayne {Gemelke} Topp)

After dad died, Emil and the girls farmed. Wilhelma came to the farm; Ivan was in the service. I was 14. I helped Mother. (Millie {Gemelke} Janulewicz)

Dad (Emil) bought a matched set of workhorses at his mom's farm sale. He had to pay a lot to get the bid. The next morning, one of them died. (LaRayne {Gemelke} Topp)

After the chores were done, we would lay out on the lawn. Viola got a bug in her ear doing that. (Anita {Gemelke} Reimnitz)

I will sell the following described personal property of the late Ernest Gemelke at Administratrix Sale at the farm located 3 miles north and 1 west of Pilger, 12 miles south and 3 west of Wayne, 16 miles east of Norfolk on Hiway 275 and 2 north. and 1 mile west and 2 north of the Bordner Filling Station, on—

Thurs., Dec. 20

Sale Starts at 12:00

Ladies Aid to Serve Hot Lunches

6 Head of Horses

Team Grey Mares, 2900, 7 years old
Grey Mare, 1500, 8 years old
Black Mare, 1250, smooth mouth
Gelding, 1250, smooth mouth
Gelding, 1300, 4 years old

36 Head of Cattle

(RED POLLED)

15 Milk Cows, some fresh and others to freshen soon, bred to Registered Red Polled Bull; 9 Yearlings; 9 Bucket Calves; 3 Bull Calves

14 Head Summer Pigs

12 Dozen Austra White Chickens   1931 Model Chevrolet 4-Door Sedan

Farm Machinery, Hay, Etc.

TRACTOR MACHINERY

2-Bottom, 16-in. Tractor Plow
22-in. Threshing Machine
John Deere Corn Sheller, No. 5
Combination Letz Grinder, No. 230

HORSE DRAWN

Deering Grain Binder
John Deere Corn Binder
10-ft. McCormick Deering Disc
24-ft. Drag, 4 section
20-ft. Drag, 4 section
John Deere Planter
6-ft. John Deer Mower
Daine Hay Stacker

Hay Sweep
Car Hay Sweep
Hay Rake
2-row Chace Cultivator
2-bottom 13-in. Plow
16-in. Sulky Riding Plow
16-in. Walking Plow
Single-row Lister
Fanning Mill
Litchfield Manure Spreader
2 Hay Racks with Running Gear
Feed Wagon
3 Box Wagons
John Deere Engate Seeder
Press Drill with Grass Seed
   Attachment

John Deere 1-horse Gas Engine
4-Wheel Trailer
Drive Belt, 75-ft.
2 Sets of Harness
Fly Nets
Saddle
Cream Separator
Tank Heater
Pump Jack with Electric Motor
3 10-gallon Cream Cans
Milk Pails
Brooder Stove
2 Chick Batteries
Some Household Goods
Tools and other articles too
   numerous to mention

● BROOMIS GRASS SEED ● 12 STACKS ALFALFA ● STACK PRAIRIE HAY ● OATS

TERMS:—Cash or make arrangements with clerk before sale. No property to be removed until settlement has been made with clerk.

Louisa Gemelke, Admx.

Adolph Zicht, Auctioneer

Farmers National Bank, Clerk

Memories

Dad (Emil) said that the kids always sang when milking cows. If a neighbor or salesman came, he or she would head to the barn because that's where the singing was. (LaRayne {Gemelke} Topp)

Clothes in my day were full suits on Sunday, but going to town or parties we wore mostly clean overalls and an old suit coat and necktie. (Emil Gemelke)

Dad (Emil) said that when he was a boy his Uncle Gustav lived upstairs. The house, at that time, had an odd-shaped room at the bottom of the stairs. One door led to the upstairs, another to the parlor, one to the kitchen and one outside (or onto a large, attached porch). At Christmastime, Gustav would go upstairs to play his concertina. All of a sudden the kids would notice Santa peeking in the kitchen windows. They were afraid of Santa, perhaps because he watched to see if they behaved or not. They would hide by Grandma Louisa, and she would point to a window, "There's Santa, there." After a while they would think to go up and tell Gustav, never noticing that the music had stopped. He was back in his room by that time. Grandma put the tree up in the parlor, but no one was ever allowed in it. On Christmas Eve Santa brought a Christmas tree and gifts. (LaRayne {Gemelke} Topp)

For Christmas, I got a little cabinet, doll beds and little chairs. They were under the tree on Christmas Eve, all repainted. I only had one doll. Her name was Margie. I was writing a letter to Santa. All of a sudden it was gone. (Millie {Gemelke} Janulewicz)

Think of all the Christmas cookies we would bake, like 500 or so. It was the only time we could have coffee. (Anita {Gemelke} Reimnitz)

Childhood memories were going to school, church and farming. We never had many toys but had a good imagination. We had a curved mirror like steel on the reservoir of the stove. It was always good for a few funny faces. Or the kerosene lamps were always good for a few shadow pictures on the wall. (Emil Gemelke)

Sometimes we would drink brandy or schnapps or home brew. Vi and I would get a snort when the folks went to town. It was in the pantry on the top shelf. (Millie {Gemelke} Janulewicz)

One time I got into the Ex-Lax by mistake. (Viola {Gemelke} Brueggeman)

I remember going to South Dakota. Never could understand why we should go north to South Dakota. (Emil Gemelke)

Koehlmooses came on Sunday afternoons. (Millie {Gemelke} Janulewicz) (Note: Perhaps, this was the Henry Koehlmoos family)

Neighborhood gatherings were mostly the old Sheephead bunch—about six or seven neighborhood families. (Emil Gemelke)

Dad (Emil) said that a croquet court was set up on the farm in the summertime. Neighbors would come over and all would play croquet. No one dared drive across it, he said, or they'd answer to Louisa. (LaRayne {Gemelke} Topp)

When we got into mischief (hardly never!) Mom would send us out for a stick. If we came back with too small of one, she threatened to get one herself. She never used the one we got. When I got pouty I always threatened to run away from home. She would start to pack my lunch and tell me how much she'd miss me. Somehow I never left. (Emil Gemelke)

Dad (Emil) counted the cousins he grew up with from his mom's family, as Herman's with five, Fred's with six, his own (Louisa's) with seven, Minnie's with eight, Henry's with nine, and Dora's with ten. (LaRayne {Gemelke} Topp)

Gemelke family in the absence of Ernst. (Louisa was married at age 23. She and Ernst were married for 33 years and she lived as a widow for 35).

Top photograph, front row, from the left: Viola, Louisa, Millie; and back row: Gertrude, Herb, Wilhelma, Emil and Anita.

Photograph to the right, front row: Louisa; back row, from the left: Emil, Anita, Herb and Viola.

Because Floyd and Gertrude ran a motel in California, they were seldom able to come to family events together or often. Top, from the left: Millie, Anita, George, Margaret, Herb, Wilhelma, Ivan, Viola, Bob, Emil and Bernitiha. Bottom, front row: Emil and Bernitha; back row, from the left: Ivan, Wilhelma, George, Anita, Bob, Viola, Millie, Leo and Floyd.

Siblings with the background of cistern and summer kitchen, from the left: Emil, Viola, Wilhelma, Herb, Anita and Millie. Gertrude, not pictured.

Gemelke reunion at Louisa Gemelke's home in Pilger in the mid-1960s. Front row, from the left: Joyce Reimnitz, James Reimnitz, Coreen Brueggeman, Mark Brueggeman, David Reimnitz; second row, Mary Kemper (Ivan's mother), Louisa holding Barbara Brueggeman, Ella Siemsglusz; back row: Ivan or husband of unidentified woman next to him in back row, Anita, unidentified woman, Viola, Margaret, Millie, Herb, Bernitha, Gertrude and Wilhelma. I believe this was the first time Gertrude and Wilhelma had seen each other for 19 years. A number were present but not on hand for the photograph. (LaRayne {Gemelke} Topp)

Assorted

Rural Telephone Lines by Virgie Frerichs (Neighbor) *Pilger, Nebraska: Centennial Edition, 1887-1987*

Most rural neighborhoods organized and built their own telephone lines. I think ours was built in 1909. The number of subscribers per company varied according to the community but most ranged from a dozen to 20.

Each patron had their own signal ring—example: one short and one long, or two short and one long or two longs and a short, etc. Of course, everyone knew which ring belonged to which family. The phone number indicted whether it was a rural line such as: 43F210-showing it was a farm line and the signal ring was two shorts and one long. If the ring would have been two shorts, a long and a short, the number would have been 43F211. Real simple.

Some people had the reputation for listening in on every ring that went through. Others considered eavesdropping in the same category with window peeping and wouldn't dream of listening. Policy in our family was not to say anything on the phone you wouldn't put in the local paper (not a bad idea).

Each company had an emergency ring. I think ours was four longs. If that one sounded, everyone went to the phone because someone needed help. It was also used to notify everyone of the time and place of the next meeting. You called people on your own line by ringing their ring yourself with the little crank on the side of the phone. When you were calling someone in town or another farm line you rang one long ring for *Central.* "Hello, Central, please give me _____," was a common phrase.

The rural telephones were always the large box type wall phone so they could accommodate the needed dry cell batteries. Because of limited life of batteries, you didn't make unnecessary calls or carry on long conversations. We grew up realizing the phone was respected and appreciated. It hadn't been a common possession for too many years so it was still some sort of miracle.

The cost of having a rural phone was unbelievably cheap. I haven't been able to find records but it seems it ranged from $12 to $20 per normal year. The farmers did all their own service work. There was always an official *lineman* elected each year but if something major happened, everybody helped if at all possible.

The line had to be rebuilt one year and for a couple of years our annual cost ran close to $40. Seemed high at the time! *Progress* caused us to abandon our home-owned line and join the Bell system several years ago. One final meeting was held and the company was dissolved. In exchange, we now have private lines, extra phones and enormous telephone bills.

They were wonderful while they lasted.

Note: When Dad (Emil) and Mom were first married, their bill one year for the year was $9.00. I believe their company was called Pioneer. When I was a kid our ring was two shorts and one long. (LaRayne {Gemelke} Topp)

Alice

When Grandma and Grandpa's family was young, they took in a foster daughter for a short time by the name of Alice Byerly. I remember hearing a story about her. They had a mean bull who would let only Grandpa peacefully in the cattle yard with him. One day, Alice put on Grandpa's overalls to walk through the yard so the bull would think it was Grandpa and not her. However, she gingerly walked around all the cow pies and the bull knew she wasn't Grandpa and took after her. Dad didn't know if Alice felt she had to work too hard, taking care of the children, but one day she ran away. At that time, confirmation students took the train from Pilger to Wisner each week to take Catechism classes from the pastor at the Missouri Synod church there. Alice took the train and never came back home. They hunted and hunted for her, but never knew what happened to her. They never heard from her again. I could find no photographs of her.

For many years Grandma kept scrapbooks. I inherited that pastime myself. I found this clipping in one of her scrapbooks. According to the writer, Grandma never responded although Grandma kept the clipping.

Writer Looks for Mother

No Trace of Her Since Hospital

Dear Mary Lane: Can you help me find my mother? I was born in 92, at Verges Hospital, Norfolk, Nebraska. No one seems to have heard of my mother since she left the hospital.

I have found her brother but he says he hasn't seen my mother since she was 6. Her parents are dead.

My foster mother died when I was about 3 or 4 but she used to chum around with my mother, according to my grandmother. This all took place in Fremont. I think my mother was raised in the Lutheran Home there.

Mother's maiden name was Alice Byerly and she should be around 45 or 50 years old. I have heard she married again and is living in the western part of the state.

I am 24 years old. I know in my heart my mother has thought of me and I want so badly to find her. Thank you for any help you can give me.

Allen.

Will anyone who knows the whereabouts of Allen's mother or any pertinent facts concerning her please write or call my office?

The War Cry, published by the Salvation Army, is often used as a medium for locating missing persons. It might be worth trying if Allen's letter is unsuccessful.

Years later, after Grandma had passed away, the Allen who wrote the letter stopped by Emil and Bernitha's home for information about his mother. Somehow he tracked his mother to the Gemelke family, perhaps through adoption or foster parent records at the children's home. He later wrote that he found Alice in a nursing home in California and she died shortly afterwards. Allen was the only child Alice ever had, he said. He had shown us a photograph of Alice, taken at the Verges Sanatorium in Norfolk. Possibly, she stayed there as an unwed mother before Allen was born. I recall seeing the photograph of Alice as an adult with one or two other women at the Sanatorium, but I haven't been able to locate it. (LaRayne {Gemelke} Topp)

Dear cousin Louisa, I received your letter and was more than glad to hear from you. I will send you this card for your birthday. Wish you a happy birthday and many more happy ones to come. I sure was glad to get the picture of your little girls. It sure is nice. Is Alice still with you? I will close. Best – Love to all from all your cousins, As ever. Anna H.

Perhaps the photograph at the left is Alice with her young charges, Herbert, left and Gertrude. Or perhaps it's two youngsters with a china doll. Or perhaps it's no one we know at all. (LaRayne {Gemelke} Topp)

These two photographs were taken at a Sunday picnic at the Dohren farm, located on the next section east of the Gemelke farms. The corncrib sat south of the Dohren house. Top photo from the left: Unidentified man, Freida and Peter Hallstein, Henry Gemelke, Elsa and Irmagard Dohren, Unidentified girl, Emma Dohren (back), and Sophie Gemelke. Ella Siemsglusz is the woman on the right behind the two little girls and John Dohren is standing in overalls. Below, left: the man holding cards in the forefront is John Dohren, the man in the back is identified as Gus Gemelke, Gerhard Jacobsen is reading the newspaper and the two men on the right are Bill Dohren and Pete Hallstein (as identified by Dohren grandson David Tobias).

Top photograph, front row, from the left: Irmagard and Elsa Dohren; second row: their mother Emma Dohren, Freida Gemelke Hallstein, Ella Gemelke Siemsglusz; back row: Henry Gemelke, Peter Hallstein, Unidentified man. Below: This District #43 parade entry has two names listed on the back: Mildred Gemelke and Lillian Koehlmoos.

This is believed to be a school photograph of Sophie Koehlmoos, back row, left. It is not, however, District #43 or District #18 where Sophie would have attended, and may have been taken at someone's home. It pictures a little girl who appears younger than school age, so perhaps it's a neighborhood party, but the woman in black, back row, appears older and could be a teacher. Ella Gemelke is in the back row, right. It could be a photograph of Sunday School students from First Trinity in Altona, but I was told they didn't have a Sunday School until much later. Ella was confirmed there in 1907 and Sophie in 1910. I was told by Doris Ritze that Ernst attended classes for two years after he came to Nebraska to learn English along with her grandfather. That could have been at Catechism classes at First Trinity (although he was confirmed at a Lutheran Church in Germany), or classes at a country school. A Wilhelm Gemelke is listed as being confirmed at Frist Trinity in 1906. Perhaps that's Ernst Friedrich Wilhelm Gemelke, and Ella also attended. (LaRayne {Gemelke} Topp)

Also buried at this family plot is Richard Gemelke, son of Herbert and Margaret Gemelke. He died at three years of age, when run over with a livestock truck on the family farm.

LOUISA
1888 ⸺ 1979
MOTHER

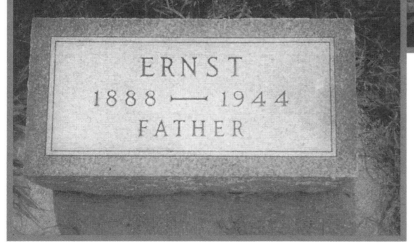

ERNST
1888 ⸺ 1944
FATHER

Final thoughts on Grandma Louisa
by LaRayne (Gemelke) Topp

I was standing next to Mary, my cousin from Minnesota, on the day of my Grandma Louisa's funeral as a car drove up and a man stepped out.

"Is that my Uncle Ivan?" she asked.

I realized it then.

One of the next times I realized it was on the day of my mother's funeral, in the same church from which we'd buried Grandma Louisa. The Ladies Aid members formed a line for us to walk between. They'd done it for Louisa, after all, a charter member of St. John's Ladies Aid, and now for Bernitha. At 95, Mom was the oldest member of Ladies Aid and even the congregation itself. It is a decades-old tradition, and it's as familiar to me as my name.

There were definite advantages, I realized, in growing up next to Grandma.

I am a middle-in-succession cousin. I'm not the oldest; I'm not the youngest. My oldest daughter, Trish, is just a shade or two younger than my Aunt Anita's baby daughter, Sheila. When my Grandma's kids came from states away to visit her, zooming up from Texas, drifting down from Minnesota and South Dakota, or sidling over from California, we were just a coyote's cry from Grandma's house. Top that with being an in-the-middle cousin, and you'll find a person who was fortunate to get to know all of the aunts, uncles and cousins. And Grandma herself. I've been truly blessed by that.

You see, we picked Grandma up for church on Sundays, pulling up close to her cement steps so she could grab onto the railing to get to our car. She taught me Chinese Checkers and furthered my education in Pitch and Sheephead. She commiserated with me about being left-handed. On Saturday nights when Mom and Dad went dancing, I stayed at her house where we watched Perry Mason, or sat on her front porch with its long bank of windows, watching the traffic drive by and listening to her mantle clock chiming the time. When a blizzard shut off her lights in town, Dad brought her out to the farm where Grandma and I watched All-Star Wrestling, rooting for Mr. X who took on all challengers. I had to giggle when Ralph, the grocer, told me how he picked up a six-pack of beer at the tavern for my grandma when he delivered her groceries.

While the older cousins, including my brothers, remember Grandma as a person who could easily walk around the farm, I have only a few vague memories of that: mostly of her walking in her backyard to a small block shed to get a bushel basket to pick apples from her tree. In later years when we visited her, as we left we'd reposition the chairs to the same places we'd found them. That's how she got from room to room, relying on handholds on backs of chairs. Grandma and a neighbor, Martha, called each other every morning to see if they made it safely through the night. That may be the Grandma with which younger cousins were familiar.

I recall Grandma sitting on a red vinyl stepstool as she peeled apples for applesauce. Her basement was poured in two levels, the highest level rimmed with canning jars, full from her efforts. When I married, she gave me some of her canning jars, along with her favorite recipes. She advised me to buy a pressure cooker to keep the kitchen from getting too hot from the boiling water of a cold pack canner. After 45 years, I still use it today.

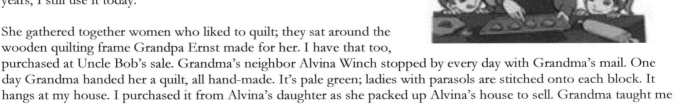

She gathered together women who liked to quilt; they sat around the wooden quilting frame Grandpa Ernst made for her. I have that too, purchased at Uncle Bob's sale. Grandma's neighbor Alvina Winch stopped by every day with Grandma's mail. One day Grandma handed her a quilt, all hand-made. It's pale green; ladies with parasols are stitched onto each block. It hangs at my house. I purchased it from Alvina's daughter as she packed up Alvina's house to sell. Grandma taught me how to crochet rugs from leftover strips of fabric. I'm working on one now.

When Grandma moved to the nursing home, my husband Kevin snuck her food she enjoyed, like rhubarb pie and sausage. She liked to keep busy, stitching around squares cut from bleach bottles that they sewed into purses. As residents received potted plants as gifts and the plants wilted, Grandma used the dirt to fill up Styrofoam cups. Grandma pinched off a leaf from one of her violets and tucked it into the dirt, one leaf for each cup. These cups lined her north window. Eventually these small leaf sprouts grew to bushy plants, dotted with happy, purple blooms. She handed them to visitors or to folks she wanted to thank.

As I sorted through Mom's box of photographs after her death, I realized it again—that I'm the one to write my grandma's and grandpa's history. When Ernst's family came from Hainhaus and Louisa's from Cooper's Grove, Illinois, providence chose for them to meet and settle near Pilger, Nebraska. I remain.

I'm the one who baked rhubarb pies from Grandma's recipe with rhubarb picked from her plants. I grew up on Grandma's farm, ate mulberries from her nursery stock trees, drilled oats, disced fields and walked cockleburs on land she owned.

I can name her siblings. I can tell you what Great-aunt Dora looked like because I went to see her with my grandma.

So, I have filled this book with memories of my Grandma Louisa and her husband Ernst, a man I never met but have loved anyway. All because I realized, if anyone is to write this book, the privilege and the honor is mine.

Final thoughts on Grandpa Ernst
by LaRayne (Gemelke) Topp

Have you ever asked yourself who's the first person you'll want to meet in Heaven? Some say Christ, himself. Well, I think that's a given. Abraham Lincoln? Mother Theresa? Moses? Maya Angelou? For me, it's always been my Grandpa Gemelke.

Believe me, I've tried to get to know him. I played the violin he brought from Germany when he came to the States. I modeled the waiter's coat he wore as he served riders of the train at Bremen station. I studied his photo, and then the faces of Dad's cousin Marvin, my brother Ron and my cousin James, who I'm told might most closely resemble Grandpa. My cousin Karin and I even gathered together the uncles and aunts and asked them all what Grandpa was like. He was a quiet man, we were told. My mom said he was the kindest man ever.

Then in 2006, I was able to go to Germany with my cousin Gloria. I hoped I could learn more about this mystery man from Hanover who went to church in Bissendorf and lived in the little, nearby town of Hainhaus. I can't remember ever being so young that I didn't want to visit Germany, so fascinated I was with this Grandpa I never knew. So it's no surprise, then, that I cried as we landed on German soil, when I viewed the Alps, and when I walked through the Bremen train station.

We rented a car, Gloria and I, with a GPS gremlin riding along who spoke German. Fortunately, so did Gloria. As the voice shouted out, for example, to turn "*Richtig*," Gloria would laugh and say, "I am, I am turning right."

We arrived in Bissendorf one morning, marveled at the scenery, took a slug of photos, ate lunch, and finally asked a few natives, "Where is Hainhaus?" No one had heard of it. "But there is another Bissendorf," they said, an easy 100-kilometer drive north. As we arrived, the sun was settling in the afternoon sky, much like I imagine Grandpa would have done in his rocker after chores were completed to read another issue of *Die Haus Frau*.

We asked a young woman for directions to the church, an ages-old stone building. Inside, a group of singers were practicing. When they discovered we were from America, they sang a few selections in English, just for us. Although I enjoyed their concert, I was impatient, as we had to hurry to get to Hainhaus before dark.

But as we listened, a man drove up and came inside to speak to the director. This man spoke no English, but had come to lead the American women to Hainhaus, the town of his birth. He was the father of the young woman from whom we'd asked directions. It seemed like a God-moment to me. I wondered if we'd have found Hainhaus without him, winding through the countryside. Partway through the 8-kilometer stretch, he stopped, got out of his car, and motioned to us to keep following. We reached Hainhaus at dusk. A giant stone with the name of the hamlet chiseled in its face fronted the acres my Grandpa's family once farmed, now a luxurious golf course.

In 2011, I returned with my new husband Dale, brother Duane and Linda, and Dale's brother and sister-in-law. We drove to the location in daylight this time, with assistance in navigation from a German friend, Klaus-Gerd Meyer.

This time, I brought along a photograph of my grandfather's home and school. As we tried to match the photos with a few of the older buildings still standing in an old-town portion of the grounds, a woman, Elda, stopped to greet us. She introduced us to the landowner, Friedhelm Meyer, who had come pedaling down the road on a rickety bicycle.

"He's a millionaire," she said, as we gazed at his mansion in the background. As we pulled out the photographs of Grandpa's home, Friedhelm became excited. Utilizing Elda as a translator, he described how he had torn down the home and carefully saved the front doorway to incorporate into the golf course's new clubhouse.

"See those trees," he said, pointing to two young saplings on the photo. "They are now these," he explained, showing us trees which towered over the grounds.

We explored the expansive clubhouse and then settled onto a back patio as Friedhelm's guests. He told how the farmers, when he was a boy, raised corn, potatoes and sugar beets on land now overlaid with lush green turf and a score of German golfers.

We asked if he was familiar with the name Gemelke. He was not. I wish we'd have asked about the name Mindemann, as Grandpa Ernst's mother's family, the Mindemanns, had once been the owners of the golf course land on which we now luxuriated. Ernst's father's family, the Gemelkes, had been tenant farmers.

I like to imagine this: When Grandpa came to the States, history came right along with him, ready to repeat itself. Much as his father Henry married the farm owner's daughter Maria from Hainhaus, so did my Grandpa Ernst marry Louisa, the farm owner's daughter from Nebraska.

Some day when I get to Heaven (and I *do* plan to get there), I will finally get to meet my Grandpa Ernst. I figure I'll ask him what it was like to live in two countries, one in which he was born and one that he adopted. I'm storing up questions now, you see, because I'll only have an eternity to get to know him better.

I wonder if it will be long enough.

The photograph below was included in those among many I searched through. The only words written on the back are, "My baptism." So, this is my way of saying if I've incorrectly identified photographs with no names on the back, or have "dis-remembered" information and it's incorrect, I deeply apologize. Also, I used photographs from Mom and Dad's collection primarily or those I could beg or borrow; I was sometimes unable to locate photographs or information that would have been good to include. I traveled as far back in time as I was able, and stopped at my generation going forward. I also included several genealogy logs I inherited, but have not updated them, stopping where they stop. I know there are a multitude of family stories that have not made it into these pages, but I did my best. Perhaps this will prompt you to write down the stories you remember and share them with your family. (LaRayne {Gemelke} Topp)

toppларayne@gmail.com
www.laraynetopp.com
Facebook: Larayne M. Topp, author

Made in the USA
San Bernardino, CA
14 February 2020